THE FALL OF THE MOGHUL EMPIRE OF HINDUSTAN

First published 1887
This edition published by Lector House in 2025

ISBN: 978-93-6138-567-4

Lector House LLP
Registered Office: H. No. 96, Block C, Tomar Colony,
Burari, Delhi – 110084, India
info@lectorhouse.com
www.lectorhouse.com

THE FALL OF THE MOGHUL EMPIRE OF HINDUSTAN

HENRY GEORGE KEENE

2025

LECTOR HOUSE LLP

THE FALL OF THE MOGHUL EMPIRE OF HINDUSTAN

BY

H. G. KEENE, C.I.E.,

AUTHOR OF "THE HISTORY OF HINDUSTAN," ETC., ETC.

A NEW EDITION, WITH CORRECTIONS AND ADDITIONS.

PREFACE.

Two editions of this book having been absorbed, it has been thought that the time was come for its reproduction in a form more adapted to the use of students. Opportunity has been taken to introduce considerable additions and emendations.

The rise and meridian of the Moghul Empire have been related in Elphinstone's "History of India: the Hindu and Mahometan Period;" and a Special Study of the subject will also be found in the "Sketch of the History of Hindustan" published by the present writer in 1885. Neither of those works, however, undertakes to give a detailed account of the great Anarchy that marked the conclusion of the eighteenth century, the dark time that came before the dawn of British power in the land of the Moghul. Nor is there is any other complete English book on the subject.[1]

The present work is, therefore, to be regarded as a monograph on the condition of the capital and neighbouring territories, from the murder of Álamgir II. in 1759 to the occupation of Dehli by Lake in 1803. Some introductory chapters are prefixed, with the view of showing how these events were prepared; and an account of the campaign of 1760-1 has been added, because it does not seem to have been hitherto related on a scale proportioned to its importance. That short but desperate struggle is interesting as the last episode of mediæval war, when battles could be decided by the action of mounted men in armour. It is also the *sine quâ non* of British Empire in India. Had the Mahrattas not been conquered then, it is exceedingly doubtful if the British power in the Bengal Presidency would ever have extended beyond Benares.

The author would wish to conclude this brief explanation by reproducing the remarks which concluded the *Preface* to his second edition.

"There were two dangers," it was there observed; "the first, that of giving too much importance to the period; the second, that of attempting to illustrate it by stories—such as those of Clive and Hastings—which had been told by writers with whom competition was out of the question. Brevity, therefore, is studied; and what may seem baldness will be found to be a conciseness, on which much pains have been bestowed."

.. "The narrative," it was added, "is one of confusion and transition; and chiefly interesting in so far as it throws light on the circumstances which preceded and caused the accession of the East India Company to paramount power in India." The author has only to add an expression of his hope that, in conjunction with Mr.

[1] One or two English writers, however, have dealt with portions of this history; and reference to their works will be found hereafter; most of them are of old date, and scarce.

S. Owen's book,[2] what he has here written may help to remove doubts as to the benefits derived by the people of India from the Revolution under consideration.

Finally, mention should be made of Mr. Elphinstone's posthumous work, "The Rise of British Power in the East."[3] That work does not, indeed, clash with the present book; for it did not enter into the scope of the distinguished author to give the native side of the story, or to study it from the point of view here presented. For the military and political aims and operations of the early British officers in Madras and Bengal, however, Elphinstone will be found a valuable guide. His narrative bears to our subject a relation similar to that of the "Roman de Rou" to the history of the Carling Empire of Northern France.

OXFORD, 1887.

[2] *India on the Eve of the British Conquest,* 2nd Ed. (W. H. Allen, 1887.)
[3] *Edited by Sir E. Colebrooke.* (Murray, 1887.)

CONTENTS.

CHAPTER V.

A.D. 1754-60.

CHAPTER VI.

PART II.

CHAPTER I.

AD. 1760-65.

CHAPTER II.

A.D. 1765-71.

CHAPTER III.

A.D. 1771-76.

CHAPTER IV.

A.D. 1776-85.

CHAPTER V.

A.D. 1786-88.

CHAPTER VI.

A.D. 1788.

PART III.

CHAPTER I.

A.D. 1789-94.

CHAPTER II.

A.D. 1794-1800.

CHAPTER III.

A.D. 1801-3.

CHAPTER IV.

CONCLUSION.

APPENDICES.

PART I.

CHAPTER I.

Preliminary Observations on Hindustan and the City of Dehli.

THE country to which the term Hindustan is strictly and properly applied may be roughly described as a rhomboid, bounded on the north-west by the rivers Indus and Satlej, on the south-west by the Indian Ocean, on the south-east by the Narbadda and the Son, and on the north-east by the Himalaya Mountains and the river Ghagra. In the times of the emperors, it comprised the provinces of Sirhind (or Láhore), Rajputána, Gujrát, Málwa, Áudh (including Rohilkand, strictly Rohelkhand, the country of the Rohelas, or "Rohillas" of the Histories), Agra, Alláhábád, and Dehli: and the political division was into *subahs*, or divisions,[4] *sarkars* or districts; *dasturs*, or sub-divisions; and *parganahs*, or fiscal unions.

The Deccan, Panjáb (Punjab), and Kábul, which also formed parts of the Empire in its widest extension at the end of the seventeenth century, are omitted, as far as possible, from notice, because they did not at the time of our narration form part of the territories of the Empire of Hindustan, though included in the territory ruled by the earlier and greater Emperors.

Bengal, Bihár, and Orissa also formed, at one time, an integral portion of the Empire, but fell away without playing an important part in the history we are considering, excepting for a very brief period.[5] The division into Provinces will be understood by reference to the map. Most of these had assumed a practical independence during the first quarter of the eighteenth century, though acknowledging a weak feudatory subordination to the Crown of Dehli.

The highest point in the plains of Hindustan is probably the plateau on which stands the town of Ájmir, about 230 miles south of Dehli. It is situated on the eastern slope of the Áravalli Mountains, a range of primitive granite, of which Ábu, the chief peak, is estimated to be near 5,000 feet above the level of the sea; the plateau of Ájmir itself is some 3,000 feet lower.

The country at large is, probably, the upheaved basin of an exhausted sea which once rendered the highlands of the Deccan an island like a larger Ceylon.[6] The general quality of the soil is accordingly sandy and light, though not unproductive; yielding, perhaps, on an average about one thousand *lbs. av.* of wheat to the acre. The cereals are grown in the winter, which is at least as cold as in the corresponding parts of Africa. Snow never falls, but thin ice is often formed

[4] A *subah* often contained two or more Provinces, the one being of historical origin, the other an administrative arrangement.

[5] *Vide* Part II. chap. i.

[6] But *see* "Geological Report," by Messrs. Blanford and Medlicott, Calcutta, 1879.

during the night. During the spring heavy dews fall, and strong winds set in from the west. These gradually become heated by the increasing radiation of the earth, as the sun becomes more vertical and the days longer.

Towards the end of May the monsoon blows up from the Indian Ocean and from the Bay of Bengal, when a rainfall averaging about twenty inches takes place and lasts during the ensuing quarter. This usually ceases about the end of September, when the weather is at its most sickly point. Constant exhalations of malaria take place till the return of the cold weather.

After the winter, cucurbitaceous crops are grown, followed by sowings of rice, sugar, and cotton. About the beginning of the rainy season the millets and other coarse grains are put in, and the harvesting takes place in October. The winter crops are reaped in March and April. Thus the agriculturists are never out of employ, unless it be during the extreme heats of May and June, when the soil becomes almost as hard from heat as the earth in England becomes in the opposite extreme of frost.

Of the hot season Mr. Elphinstone gives the following strong but just description:—"The sun is scorching, even the wind is hot, the land is brown and parched, the dust flies in whirlwinds, all brooks become dry, small rivers scarcely keep up a stream, and the largest are reduced to comparative narrow channels in the midst of vast sandy beds." It should, however, be added, that towards the end of this terrible season some relief is afforded to the river supply by the melting of the snow upon the higher Himalayas, which sends down some water into the almost exhausted stream-beds. But even so, the occasional prolongation of the dry weather leads to universal scarcity which amounts to famine for the mass of the population, which affects all classes, and which is sure to be followed by pestilence. Lastly, the malaria noticed above as following the monsoon gives rise to special disorders which become endemic in favouring localities, and travel thence to all parts of the country, borne upon the winds or propagated by pilgrimages and other forms of human intercourse. Such are the awful expedients by which Nature checks the redundancy of a non-emigrating population with simple wants. Hence the construction of drainage and irrigation-works has not merely a direct result in causing temporary prosperity, but an indirect result in a large increase of the responsibilities of the ruling power. Between 1848 and 1854 the population of the part of Hindustan now called the North-West Provinces, where all the above described physical features prevail, increased from a ratio of 280 to the square mile till it reached a ratio of 350. In the subsequent sixteen years there was a further increase. The latest rate appears to be from 378 to 468,[7] and the rate of increase is believed to be about equal to that of the British Islands.

There were at the time of which we are to treat few field-labourers on daily wages, the Metayer system being everywhere prevalent where the soil was not actually owned by joint-stock associations of peasant proprietors, usually of the same tribe.

The wants of the cultivators were provided for by a class of hereditary brokers,

[7] The former for N.W.P.; the latter for Áudh.

who were often also chandlers, and advanced stock, seed, and money upon the security of the unreaped crops.

These, with a number of artisans and handicraftsmen, formed the chief population of the towns; some of the money-dealers were very rich, and 36 per cent. per annum was not perhaps an extreme rate of interest. There were no silver or gold mines, external commerce hardly existed, and the money-price of commodities was low.

The literary and polite language of Hindustan, called *Urdu* or *Rekhta,* was, and still is, so far common to the whole country, that it everywhere consists of a mixture of the same elements, though in varying proportions; and follows the same grammatical rules, though with different accents and idioms. The constituent parts are the Arabised Persian, and the Prákrit (in combination with a ruder basis, possibly of local origin), known as Hindi.[8] Speaking loosely, the Persian speech has contributed nouns substantive of civilization, and adjectives of compliment or of science; while the verbs and ordinary vocables and particles pertaining to common life are derived from the earlier tongues. So, likewise, are the names of animals, excepting those of beasts of chase.

The name *Urdu,* by which this language is usually known, is said to be of Turkish origin, and means literally "camp." But the Moghuls of India first introduced it in the precincts of the Imperial camp; so that as *Urdu-i-muáli* (High or Supreme Camp) came to be a synonym for new Dehli after Shahjahán had made it his permanent capital, so *Urdu-ki-zabán* meant the *lingua franca* spoken at Dehli. It was the common method of communication between different classes, as English may have been in London under Edward III. The classical languages of Arabia and Persia were exclusively devoted to uses of law, learning, and religion; the Hindus cherished their Sanskrit and Hindi for their own purposes of business or worship, while the Emperor and his Moghul courtiers kept up their Turkish speech as a means of free intercourse in private life. The Chaghtai dialect resembled the Turkish still spoken in Kashgar.

Out of such elements was the rich and still growing language of Hindustan formed, and it is yearly becoming more widely spread over the most remote parts of the country, being largely taught in Government schools, and used as a medium of translation from European literature, both by the English and by the natives. For this purpose it is peculiarly suited, from still possessing the power of assimilating foreign roots, instead of simply inserting them cut and dried, as is the case with languages that have reached maturity. Its own words are also liable to a kind of chemical change when encountering foreign matter (e.g., *jau,* barley: when oats were introduced some years ago, they were at once called *jaui*—"little barley").

The peninsula of India is to Asia what Italy is to Europe, and Hindustan may be roughly likened to Italy without the two Sicilies, only on a far larger scale. In this comparison the Himalayas represent the Alps, and the Tartars to the north are the Tedeschi of India; Persia is to her as France, Piedmont is represented by Kábul, and Lombardy by the Panjáb. A recollection of this analogy may not be without

[8] Kindred tongues are still spoken by some of the Sudras of the Deccan; and it is the common element of the various rustic dialects of the Northern Districts of Hindustan.

use in familiarizing the narrative which is to follow.

Such was the country into which successive waves of invaders, some of them, perhaps, akin to the actual ancestors of the Goths, Huns, and Saxons of Europe, poured down from the plains of Central Asia. At the time of which our history treats, the aboriginal Indians had long been pushed out from Hindustan into the mountainous forests that border the Deccan; which country has been largely peopled, in its more accessible regions, by the Sudras, who were probably the first of the Scythian invaders. After them had come the Sanskrit-speaking race, a congener of the ancient Persians, who brought a form of fire-worshipping, perhaps once monotheistic, of which traces are still extant in the Vedas, their early Scriptures. This form of faith becoming weak and eclectic, was succeeded by a reaction, which, under the auspices of Gautama, obtained general currency, until in its turn displaced by the gross mythology of the Puránas, which has since been the popular creed of the Hindus.

This people in modern times has divided into three main denominations: the Saráwagis or Jains (who represent some sect allied to the Buddhists or followers of Gautama); the sect of Shiva, and the sect of Vishnu.

In addition to the Hindus, later waves of immigration have deposited a Musalman population—somewhat increased by the conversions that occurred under Aurangzeb. The Mohamadans are now about one-seventh of the total population of Hindustan; and there is no reason to suppose that this ratio has greatly varied since the fall of the Moghuls.

The Mohamadans in India preserved their religion, though not without some taint from the circumjacent idolatry. Their celebration of the Moharram, with tasteless and extravagant ceremonies, and their forty days' fast in Ramzán, were alike misplaced in a country where, from the movable nature of their dates, they sometimes fell in seasons when the rigour of the climate was such as could never have been contemplated by the Arabian Prophet. They continued the bewildering lunar year of the Hijra, with its thirteenth month every third year; but, to increase the confusion, the Moghul Emperors also reckoned by Turkish cycles, while the Hindus tenaciously maintained in matters of business their national Sambat, or era of Rájá Bikram Ajit.

The Emperor Akbar, in the course of his endeavours to fuse the peoples of India into a whole, endeavoured amongst other things to form a new religion. This, it was his intention, should be at once a vindication of his Tartar and Persian forefathers against Arab proselytism, and a bid for the suffrages of his Hindu subjects. Like most eclectic systems it failed. In and after his time also Christianity in its various forms has been feebly endeavouring to maintain a footing. This is a candid report, from a source that cannot but be trusted, of the result of three centuries of Missionary labour.

> "There is nothing which can at all warrant the opinion that the heart of the people has been largely touched, or that the conscience of the people has been affected seriously. There is no advance in the direction of faith in Christ, like that which Pliny

describes, or Tertullian proclaims as characteristic of former eras. In fact, looking at the work of Missions on the broadest scale, and especially upon that of our own Missions, we must confess that, in many cases, the condition is one rather of stagnation than of advance. There seems to be a want in them of the power to edify, and a consequent paralysis of the power to convert. The converts, too often, make such poor progress in the Christian life, that they fail to act as leaven in the lump of their countrymen. In particular, the Missions do not attract to Christ many men of education; not even among those who have been trained within their own schools. Educated natives, as a general rule, will stand apart from the truth; maintaining, at the best, a state of mental vacuity which hangs suspended, for a time, between an atheism, from which they shrink, and a Christianity, which fails to overcome their fears and constrain their allegiance." —*Extract from Letter of the Anglican Bishops of India, addressed to the English Clergy, in May,* 1874.

The capital cities of Northern India have always been Dehli and Agra; the first-named having been the seat of the earlier Musalman Empires, while the Moghuls, for more than a full century, preferred to hold their Court at Agra. This dynasty, however, re-transferred the metropolis to the older situation; but, instead of attempting to revive any of the pristine localities, fixed their palace and its environs upon a new—and a preferable—piece of ground.

If India be the Italy of Asia, still more properly may it be said that Dehli is its Rome. This ancient site stretches ruined for many miles round the present inhabited area, and its original foundation is lost in a mythical antiquity. A Hindu city called Indráprastha was certainly there on the bank of the Jamna near the site of the present city before the Christian era, and various Mohamadan conquerors occupied sites in the neighbourhood, of which numerous remains are still extant. There was also a city near the present Kutb Minár, built by a Hindu rájah, about 57 B.C. according to General Cunningham. This was the original (or old) Dilli or Dehli, a name of unascertained origin. It appears to have been deserted during the invasion of Mahmud of Ghazni, but afterwards rebuilt about 1060 A.D.[9] The last built of all the ancient towns was the Din Panáh of Humáyun, nearly on the site of the old Hindu town; but it had gone greatly to decay during the long absence of his son and grandson at Agra and elsewhere.

At length New Dehli—the present city—was founded by Shahjahán, the great-grandson of Humáyun, and received the name, by which it is still known to Mohamudans, of Shahjahánabad. The city is seven miles round, with seven gates, the palace or citadel one-tenth of the area. Both are a sort of irregular semicircle on the right bank of the Jamna, which river forms their eastern arc. The plain is about 800 feet above the level of the sea, and is bordered at some distance by a low range of hills, and receiving the drainage of the Mewát Highlands. The greatest heat is in June, when the mean temperature in the shade is 92° F.; but it falls as low as 53° in January. The situation—as will be seen by the map—is extremely well chosen

[9] *Vide* "Handbook to Dehli." By the Author.

as the administrative centre of Hindustan; it must always be a place of commercial importance, and the climate has no peculiar defect. The only local disorder is a very malignant sore, which may perhaps be due to the brackishness of the water. This would account for the numerous and expensive canals and aqueducts which have been constructed at different periods to bring water from remote and pure sources. Here Shahjahán founded, in 1645 A.D., a splendid fortified palace, which continued to be occupied by his descendants down to the Great Revolt of 1857.

The entrance to the palace was, and still is, defended by a lofty barbican, passing which the visitor finds himself in an immense arcaded vestibule, wide and lofty, formerly appropriated to the men and officers of the guard, but in later days tenanted by small shopkeepers. This opened into a courtyard, at the back of which was a gate surmounted by a gallery, where one used to hear the barbarous performances of the royal band. Passing under this, the visitor entered the 'Am-Khás[10] or courtyard, much fallen from its state, when the rare animals and the splendid military pageants of the earlier Emperors used to throng its area. Fronting you was the Diwán-i-Ám (since converted into a canteen), and at the back (towards the east or river) the Diwán-i-Khás, since adequately restored. This latter pavilion is in echelon with the former, and was made to communicate on both sides with the private apartments.

On the east of the palace, and connected with it by a bridge crossing an arm of the river, is the ancient Páthan fort of Salimgarh, a rough and dismal structure, which the later Emperors used as a state prison.[11] It is a remarkable contrast to the rest of the fortress, which is surrounded by crenellated walls of high finish. These walls being built of the red sandstone of the neighbourhood, and seventy feet in height, give to the exterior of the buildings a solemn air of passive and silent strength, so that, even after so many years of havoc, the outward appearance of the Imperial residence continues to testify of its former grandeur. How its internal and actual grandeur perished will be seen in the following pages. The Court was often held at Agra, where the remains of a similar palace are still to be seen. No detailed account of this has been met with at all rivalling the contemporary descriptions of the Red Palace of Dehli. But an attempt has been made to represent its high and palmy state in the *General Introduction* to the *History of Hindustan* by the present writer.

Of the character of the races who people the wide Empire of which Dehli was the metropolis, very varying estimates have been formed, in the most extreme opposites of which there is still some germ of truth. It cannot be denied that, in some of what are termed the unprogressive virtues, they exceeded, as their sons still exceed, most of the nations of Europe; being usually temperate, self-controlled, patient, dignified in misfortune, and affectionate and liberal to kinsfolk and dependents. Few things perhaps show better the good behaviour—one may almost say the good breeding—of the ordinary native than the sight of a crowd

[10] *Quasi*, "Intermediate area."

[11] This building is assigned to Salim, son of Sher Sháh, the Afghán interrex of Humáyun, A.D. 1546. Others suppose it to be of the time of Jahángir. In any case it is much older than the rest of the modern City and Palace.

of villagers going to or returning from a fair in Upper India. The stalwart young farmers are accompanied by their wives; each woman in her coloured wimple, with her shapely arms covered nearly to the elbow with cheap glass armlets. Every one is smiling, showing rows of well-kept teeth, talking kindly and gently; here a little boy leads a pony on which his white-bearded grandfather is smilingly seated; there a baby perches, with eyes of solemn satisfaction, on its father's shoulder. Scenes of the immemorial East are reproduced before our modern eyes; now the "flight into Egypt," now St. John and his lamb. In hundreds and in thousands, the orderly crowds stream on. Not a bough is broken off a way-side tree, not a rude remark addressed to the passenger as he threads his horse's way carefully through the everywhere yielding ranks. So they go in the morning and so return at night.

But, on the other hand, it is not to be rashly assumed that, as India is the Italy, so are the Indian races the Italians of Asia. All Asiatics are unscrupulous and unforgiving. The natives of Hindustan are peculiarly so; but they are also unsympathetic and unobservant in a manner that is altogether their own. From the languor induced by the climate, and from the selfishness engendered by centuries of misgovernment, they have derived a weakness of will, an absence of resolute energy, and an occasional audacity of meanness, almost unintelligible in a people so free from the fear of death. Many persons have thought that moral weakness of this kind must be attributable to the system of caste by which men, placed by birth in certain grooves, are forbidden to even think of stepping out of them. But this is not the whole explanation. Nor, indeed, are the most candid foreign critics convinced that the system is one of unmixed evil. The subjoined moderate and sensible estimate of the effects of caste, upon the character and habits of the people is from the Bishops' letter quoted above. "In India, Caste has been the bond of Society, defining the relations between man and man, and though essentially at variance with all that is best and noblest in human nature, has held vast communities together, and established a system of order and discipline under which Government has been administered, trade has prospered, the poor have been maintained, and some domestic virtues have flourished."

Macaulay has not overstated Indian weaknesses in his Essay on Warren Hastings, where he has occasion to describe the character of Nand Komár, who, as a Bengali man-of-the-pen, appears to have been a marked type of all that is most unpleasing in the Hindoo character. The Bengalis, however, have many amiable characteristics to show on the other side of the shield, to which it did not suit the eloquent Essayist to draw attention. And in going farther North many other traits, of a far nobler kind, will be found more and more abundant. Of the Musalmans, it only remains to add that, although mostly descended from hardier immigrants, they have imbibed the Hindu character to an extent that goes far to corroborate the doctrine which traces the morals of men to the physical circumstances that surround them. The subject will be found more fully treated in the concluding chapter.

CHAPTER II.

A.D. 1707-19.

Greatness of Timur's Descendants—Causes of the Empire's Decline—Character of Aurangzeb—Progress of Disruption under his Successors—Muhamadan and Hindu enemies—The Stage emptied.

For nearly two centuries the throne of the Chaghtais continued to be filled by a succession of exceptionally able Princes. The brave and simple-hearted Bábar, the wandering Humáyun, the glorious Akbar, the easy but uncertain-tempered Jahángir, the magnificent Shahjahán, all these rulers combined some of the best elements of Turkish character—and their administration was better than that of any other Oriental country of their date. Of Shahjahán's government and its patronage of the arts—both decorative and useful—we have trustworthy contemporary descriptions. His especial taste was for architecture; and the Mosque and Palace of Dehli, which he personally designed, even after the havoc of two centuries, still remain the climax of the Indo-Saracenic order, and admitted rivals to the choicest works of Cordova and Granada.

The abilities of his son and successor Álamgir, known to Europeans by his private name, Aurangzeb, rendered him the most famous member of his famous house. Intrepid and enterprising as he was in war, his political sagacity and statecraft were equally unparalleled in Eastern annals. He abolished capital punishment, understood and encouraged agriculture, founded numberless colleges and schools, systematically constructed roads and bridges, kept continuous diaries of all public events from his earliest boyhood, administered justice publicly in person, and never condoned the slightest malversation of a provincial governor, however distant his province. Such were these emperors; great, if not exactly what we should call good, to a degree rare indeed amongst hereditary rulers.

The fact of this uncommon succession of high qualities in a race born to the purple may be ascribed to two main considerations. In the first place, the habit of contracting marriages with Hindu princesses, which the policy and the latitudinarianism of the emperors established, was a constant source of fresh blood, whereby the increase of family predisposition was checked. Few if any races of men are free from some morbid taint: scrofula, phthisis, weak nerves, or a disordered brain, are all likely to be propagated if a person predisposed to any such ailment marries a woman of his own stock. From this danger the Moghul princes were long kept free. Khuram, the second son of Jahángir, who succeeded his father under the title of Sháh Jahán, had a Hindu mother, and two Hindu grandmothers. All his sons, however, were by a Persian consort—the lady of the Táj.

Secondly, the invariable fratricidal war which followed the demise of the Crown gave rise to a natural selection (to borrow a term from modern physical science), which eventually confirmed the strongest in possession of the prize. However humanity may revolt from the scenes of crime which such a system must perforce entail, yet it cannot be doubted that the qualities necessary to ensure success in a struggle of giants would certainly both declare and develop themselves in the person of the victor by the time that struggle was concluded.

It is, however, probable that both these causes aided ultimately in the dissolution of the monarchy.

The connections which resulted from the earlier emperors' Hindu marriages led, as the Hindus became disaffected after the intolerant rule of Aurangzeb, to an assertion of partisanship which gradually swelled into independence; while the wars between the rival sons of each departing emperor gave more and more occasion for the Hindu chiefs to take sides in arms.

Then it was that each competitor, seeking to detach the greatest number of influential feudatories from the side of his rivals, and to propitiate such feudatories in his own favour, cast to each of these the prize that each most valued. And, since this was invariably the uncontrolled dominion of the territories confided to their charge, it was in this manner that the reckless disputants partitioned the territories that their forefathers had accumulated with such a vast expenditure of human happiness and human virtue. For, even from those who had received their titledeeds at the hands of claimants to the throne ultimately vanquished, the concession could rarely be wrested by the exhausted conqueror. Or, when it was, there was always at hand a partisan to be provided for, who took the gift on the same terms as those upon which it had been held by his predecessor.

Aurangzeb, when he had imprisoned his father and conquered and slain his brothers, was, on his accession, A.D. 1658, the most powerful of all the Emperors of Hindustan, and, at the same time, the ablest administrator that the Empire had ever known. In his reign the house of Timur attained its zenith. The wild Páthans of Kábul were temporarily tamed; the Sháh of Persia sought his friendship; the ancient Musalman powers of Golconda and Bijapur were subverted, and their territories rendered subordinate to the sway of the Empire; the hitherto indomitable Rájputs were subdued and made subject to taxation; and, if the strength of the Mahrattas lay gathered upon the Western Gháts like a cloud risen from the sea, yet it was not to be anticipated that a band of such marauders could long resist the might of the great Moghul.

Yet that might and that greatness were reduced to a mere show before his long reign terminated; and the Moghul Empire resembled—to use a familiar image—one of those Etruscan corpses which, though crowned and armed, are destined to crumble at the breath of heaven or at the touch of human hands. And still more did it resemble some splendid palace, whose gilded cupolas and towering minarets are built of materials collected from every quarter of the world, only to collapse in undistinguishable ruin when the *Ficus religiosa* has lodged its destructive roots in the foundation on which they rest. Thus does this great ruler furnish another instance of the familiar but everneeded lesson, that countries may be over-governed. Had he been less anxious to stamp his own image and superscription upon the palaces of princes and the temples of priests; upon the moneys of every market, and upon every human heart and conscience; he might have governed with as much success as his free-thinking and pleasure-seeking predecessors. But he was the Louis Quatorze of the East; with less of pomp than his European contemporary, but not less of the lust of conquest, of centralization, and of religious conformity. Though each monarch identified the State with himself, yet it may be doubted if either, on his deathbed, knew that his monarchy was dying also. But so it was that to each succeeded that gradual but complete cataclysm which seems the inevitable consequence of the system which each pursued.

One point peculiar to the Indian emperor is that the persecuting spirit of his reign was entirely due to his own character. The jovial and clement Chaghtai Turks, from whom he was descended, were never bigoted Mohamadans. Indeed it may be fairly doubted whether Akbar and his son Jahángir were, to any considerable extent, believers in the system of the Arabian prophet. Far different, however, was the creed of Aurangzeb, and ruthlessly did he seek to force it upon his Hindu subjects. Thus there were now added to the usual dangers of a large empire the two peculiar perils of a jealous centralization of power, and a deep-seated disaffection of the vast majority of the subjects. Nor was this all. There had never been any fixed settlement of the succession; and not even the sagacity of this politic emperor was superior to the temptation of arbitrarily transferring the dignity of heir-apparent from one son to another during his long reign. True, this was no vice confined exclusively to Aurangzeb. His predecessors had done the like; but then their systems had been otherwise genial and fortunate. His successors, too, were destined to pursue the same infatuated course; and it was a defeated intrigue of this sort which probably first brought the puppet emperor of our own time into that fatal contact with the power of England which sent him to die in a remote and dishonoured exile.

When, therefore, the sceptre had fallen from the dead man's hands, there were numerous evil influences ready to attend its assumption by any hands that were less experienced and strong. The prize was no less than the possession of the whole peninsula, estimated to have yielded a yearly revenue of the nominal value of thirty-four millions of pounds sterling, and guarded by a veteran army of five hundred thousand men.

The will of the late emperor had left the disposal of his inheritance entirely unsettled. "Whoever of my fortunate sons shall chance to rule my empire," is the only reference to the subject that occurs in this brief and extraordinary document.

His eldest surviving son consequently found two competitors in the field, in the persons of his brothers. These, however, he defeated in succession, and assumed the monarchy under the title of Bahádur Sháh. A wise and valiant prince, he did not reign long enough to show how far he could have succeeded in controlling or retarding the evils above referred to; but his brief occupation of the monarchy is marked by the appearance of all those powers and dynasties which afterwards participated, all in its dismemberment, and most in its spoil. Various enemies, both Hindu and Musalman, appeared, and the Empire of the Chaghtai Turks was sapped and battered by attempts which, though mostly founded on the most selfish motives, involved a more or less patriotic feeling. Sikhs, Mahrattas, and Rájputs, all aimed at independence; while the indigenous Mohamadans, instead of joining the Turks in showing a common front to the common enemy, weakened the defence irrecoverably by opposition and rivalry.

In the attempt to put down the Sikhs, Bahádur died at Láhor, just five years after the death of his father. The usual struggle ensued. Three of the princes were defeated and slain in detail; and the partisans of the eldest son, Mirza Moizudin, conferred upon him the succession (by the title of JÁHÁNDÁR SHÁH), after a wholesale slaughter of such of his kindred as fell within their grasp. After a few months, the aid of the governors of Bihár and Alláhábád, Saiyids of the tribe of Bárha, enabled the last remaining claimant to overthrow and murder the incapable Emperor. The conqueror succeeded his uncle under the title of FAROKHSIAR.

The next step of the Saiyids, men of remarkable courage and ability was to attack the Rájputs; and to extort from their chief, the Mahárájáh Ajit Sing, the usual tribute, and the hand of his daughter for the Emperor, who, like some of his predecessors, was anxious to marry a Hindu princess. But the levity and irresolution of the Emperor soon led to his being, in his turn, dethroned and slaughtered. The race was now quite worn out.

A brief interregnum ensued, during which the all-powerful Saiyids sought to administer the powers of sovereignty behind the screen of any royal scion they could find of the requisite nonentity. But there was a Nothing still more absolute than any they could find; and after two of these shadow-kings had passed in about seven months, one after the other, into the grave, the usurpers were at length constrained to make a choice of a more efficient puppet. This was the son of Bahádur Sháh's youngest son, who had perished in the wars which followed that emperor's demise. His private name was Sultán Roshan Akhtar ("Prince Fair Star"), but he assumed with the Imperial dignity the title of MOHAMMAD SHAH, and is memorable as the last Indian emperor that ever sat upon the peacock throne of Sháh Jahán.

The events mentioned in the preceding brief summary, though they do not comprehend the whole disintegration of the Empire, are plainly indicative of what is to follow. In the final chapters of the First Part we shall behold somewhat more in detail the rapidly accelerating event. During the long reign of Mohammad foreign violence will be seen accomplishing what native vice and native weakness have commenced; and the successors to his dismantled throne will be seen passing like other decorations in a passive manner from one mayor of the palace to another, or making fitful efforts to be free, which only rivet their chains and hasten their destruction. One by one the provinces fall away from this distempered centre. At length we shall find the throne literally without an occupant, and the curtain will seem to descend while preparations are being made for the last act of this Imperial tragedy.

CHAPTER III.

A.D. 1719-48

Muhammad Sháh—Chin Kulich Khán, his retirement from Dehli—Movements of the Mahrattas—Invasion of Nádir Sháh—Ahmad Khán repulsed by the Moghuls.

Guided by his mother, a person of sense and spirit, the young Emperor began his reign by forming a party of Moghul friends, who were hostile to the Saiyids on every conceivable account. The former were Sunnis, the latter Shias; and perhaps the animosities of sects are stronger than those of entirely different creeds. Moreover, the courtiers were proud of a foreign descent; and, while they despised the ministers as natives of India, they possessed in their mother tongue—Turkish—a means of communicating with the Emperor (a man of their own race) from which the ministers were excluded. The Saiyids were soon overthrown, their ruin being equally desired by Chin Kulich, the head of the Turkish party, and Säádat Ali, the newly-arrived adventurer from Persia. These noblemen now formed the rival parties of Turán and Irán; and became distinguished, the one as founder of the principality of Áudh, abolished in 1856, the other as that of the dynasty of Haidarábád, which still subsists. Both, however, were for the time checked by the ambition and energy of the Mahrattas. Chin Kulich was especially brought to his knees in Bhopál, where the Mahrattas wrung from him the cession of Málwa, and a promise of tribute to be paid by the Imperial Government to these rebellious brigands.

This was a galling situation for an ancient nobleman, trained in the traditions of the mighty Aurangzeb. The old man was now between two fires. If he went on to his own capital, Haidarábád, he would be exposed to wear out the remainder of his days in the same beating of the air that had exhausted his master. If he returned to the capital of the Empire, he saw an interminable prospect of contempt and defeat at the hands of the Captain-General Khán Daurán, the chief of the courtiers who had been wont to break their jests upon the old-fashioned manners of the veteran.

Thus straitened, the Nizám, for by that title Chin Kulich was now beginning to be known, took counsel with Säádat, the Persian, who was still at Dehli. Nádir Sháh, the then ruler of Persia, had been for some time urging on the Court of Dehli remonstrances arising out of boundary quarrels and similar grievances.[12] The two nobles, who may be described as opposition leaders, are believed to have in 1738

[12] So the *Siyar-ul-Mutákharin* and Áli Házin.

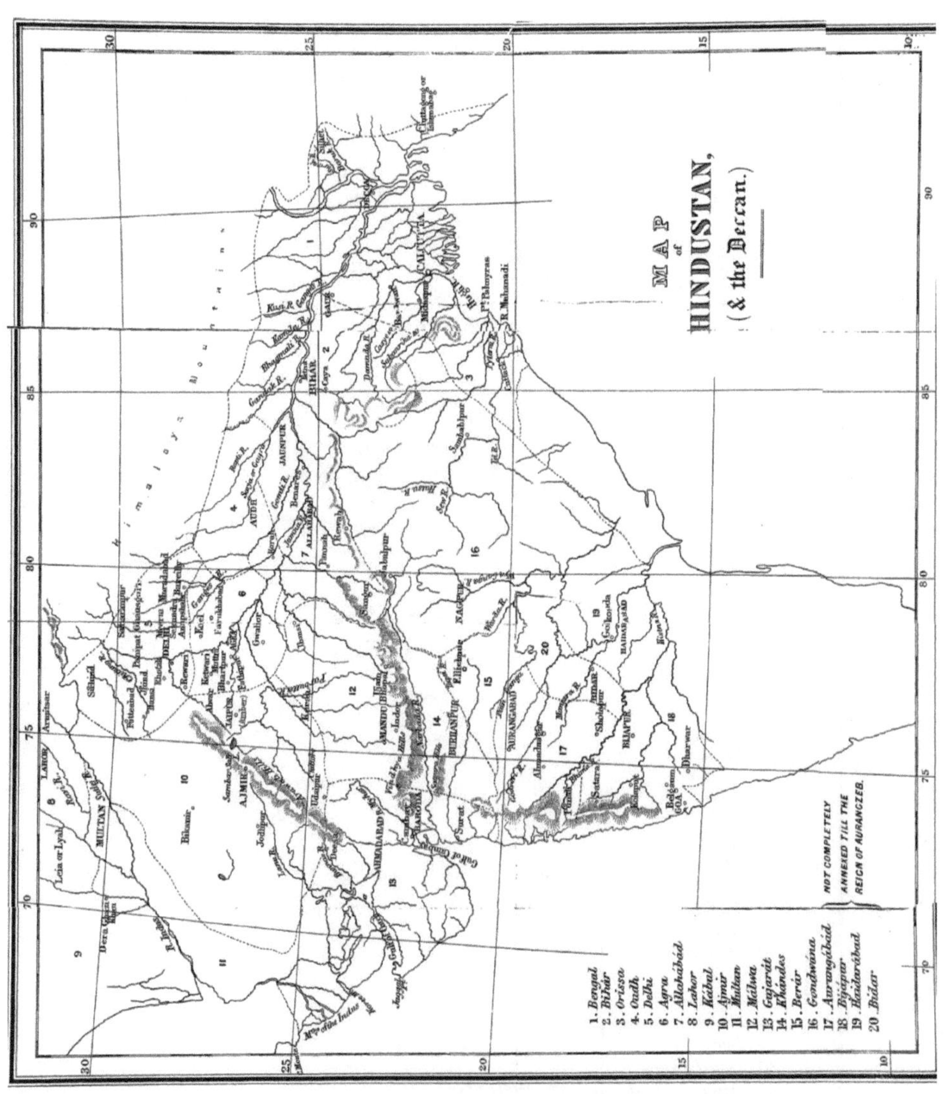

Map of Hindustan, (& the Deccan.)

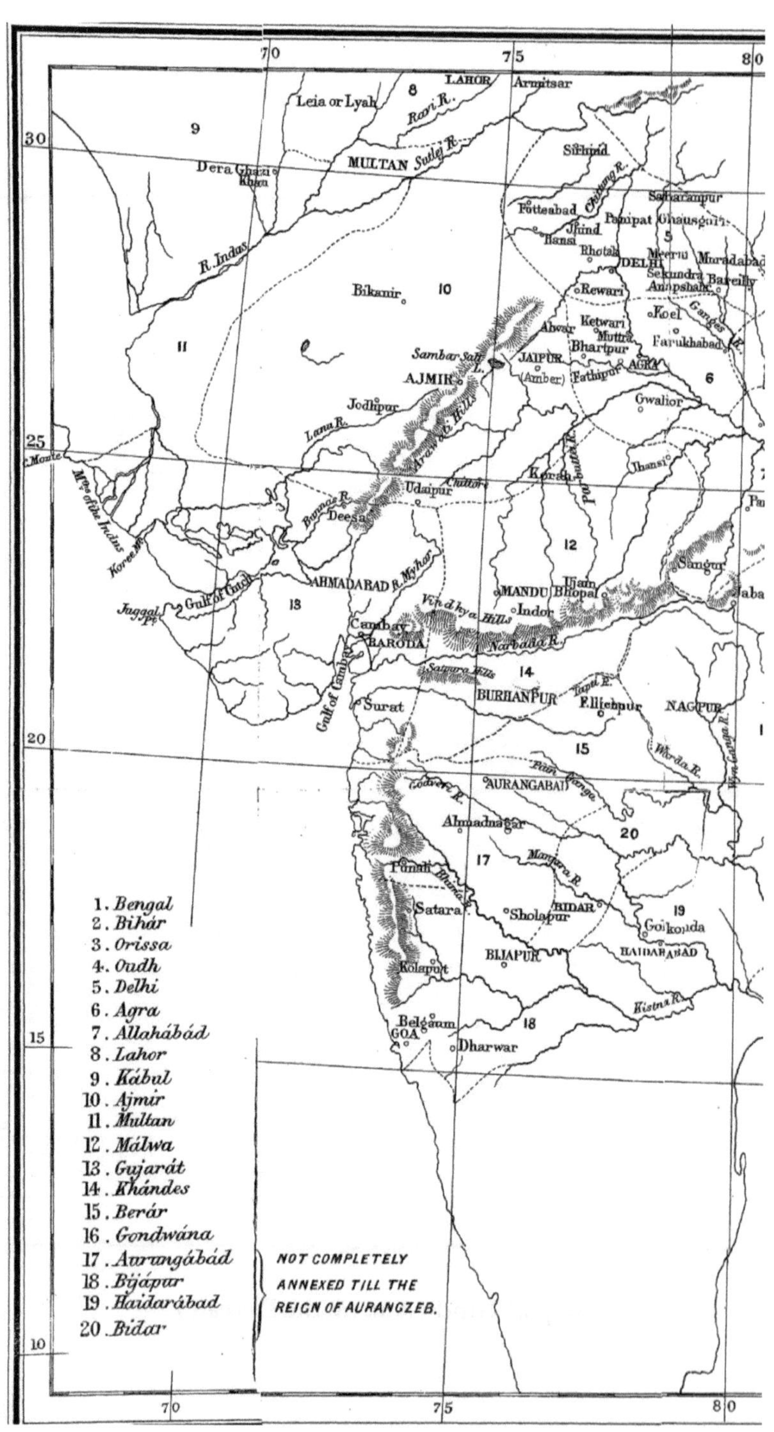

Map of Hindustan, (& the Deccan.) [Enlarged - Left]

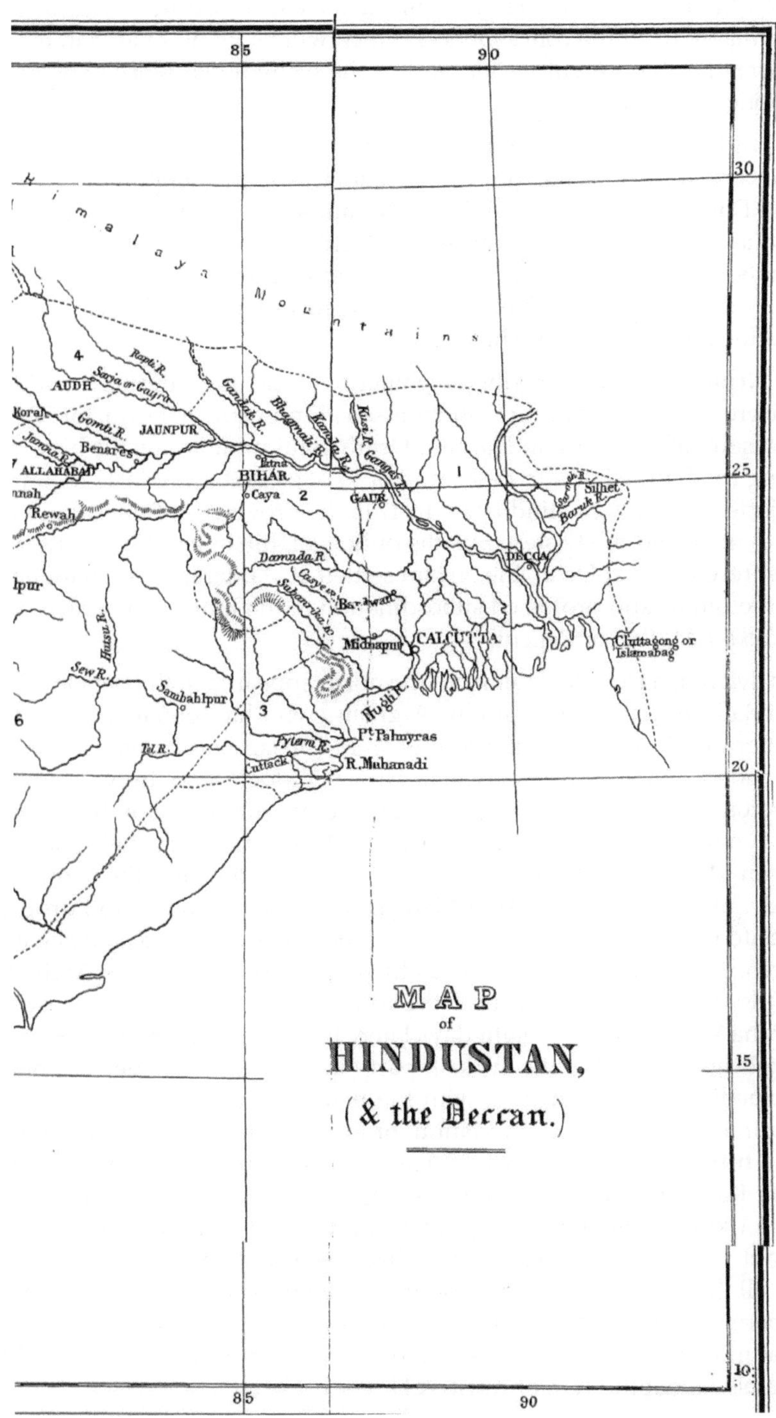

Map of Hindustan, (& the Deccan.) [Enlarged - Right]

addressed the Persian monarch in a joint letter which had the result of bringing him to India, with all the consequences which will be found related in the *History of Hindustan* by the present writer, and in the well-known work of Mountstuart Elphinstone.

It would be out of place in this introduction to dwell in detail upon the brief and insincere defence of the Empire by Säädat 'Ali, in attempting to save whom the Khán Daurán lost his life, while the Nizám attempted vain negotiations. The Persians, as is well-known, advanced on Dehli, massacred some 100,000 of the inhabitants, held the survivors to ransom, and ultimately retired to their own country, with plunder that has been estimated at eighty millions sterling, and included the famous Peacock Throne.

The Nizám was undoubtedly the gainer by these tragic events. In addition to being Viceroy of the Deccan, he found himself all-powerful at Dehli, for Säädat 'Ali had died soon after the Khán Daurán. Death continuing to favour him, his only remaining rival, the Mahratta Peshwa, Báji Rao, passed away in 1740, on the eve of a projected invasion of Hindustan. In 1745 the Province of Rohelkhand became independent, as did the Eastern Subahs of Bengal, Bihár, and Orissa. Leaving his son to represent him at Dehli, the Nizám settled at Haidarábád as an independent ruler, although he still professed subordination to the Empire, of which he called himself *Vakil-i-Mutlak*, or Regent.

Shortly after, a fresh invader from the north appeared in the person of Ahmad Khán Abdáli, leader of the Daurání Afgháns, who had obtained possession of the frontier provinces during the confusion in Persian politics that succeeded the assassination of Nádir. But a new generation of Moghul nobles was now rising, whose valour formed a short bright Indian summer in the fall of the Empire; and the invasion was rolled back by the spirit and intelligence of the heir-apparent, the Vazir's son Mir Mannu, his brother-in-law Ghází-ud-din, and the nephew of the deceased Governor of Áudh, Abul-Mansur Khán, better known to Europeans by his title Safdar Jang. The decisive action was fought near Sirhind, and began on the 3rd March, 1748. This is memorable as the last occasion on which Afgháns were ever repulsed by people of India until the latter came to have European leaders. The death of the Vazir took place eight days later. This Vazir (Kamr-ul-din Khán), who had long been the head of the Turkish party in the State, was the nominal leader of the expedition, in conjunction with the heir-apparent, though the chief glory was acquired by his gallant son Mannu, or Moin-ul-din. The Vazir did not live to share the triumph of his son, who defeated the enemy, and forced him to retire. The Vazir Kamr-ul-din died on the 11th, just before the retreat of the Afgháns. A round shot killed him as he was praying in his tent; and the news of the death of this old and constant servant, who had been Mohammad's personal friend through all the pleasures and cares of his momentous reign, proved too much for the Emperor's exhausted constitution. He was seized by a strong convulsion as he sate administering justice in his despoiled palace at Dehli, and expired almost immediately, about the 16th of April, A.D. 1748.

CHAPTER IV.

A.D. 1748-54.

Ahmad Sháh—The Rohillas—Ghózi-ud-din the younger—Perplexities of the Emperor—Álamgir II. placed on the throne.

SELDOM has a reign begun under fairer auspices than did that of Ahmad Sháh. The Emperor was in the flower of his age; his immediate associates were men distinguished for their courage and skill; the Nizám was a bar to the Mahrattas in the Deccan, and the tide of northern invasion had ebbed out of sight.

There is, however, a fatal element of uncertainty in all systems of government which depend for their success merely upon personal qualities. The first sign of this precarious tenure of greatness was afforded by the death of the aged Nizám Chin Kulich, Viceroy of the Deccan, which took place immediately after that of the late Emperor.

The eldest son of the old Nizám contended with the nephew of the deceased Säädat—whose name was Mansur, but who is better known by his title of Safdar Jang—for the Premiership, or office of Vazir, and his next brother Násir Jang held the Lieutenancy of the Deccan. The command in Rájpután, just then much disturbed, devolved at first on a Persian nobleman who had been his *Bakhshi*, or Paymaster of the Forces, and also *Amir-ul-Umra*, or Premier Peer. His disaster and disgrace were not far off, as will be seen presently. The office of Plenipotentiary was for the time in abeyance. The Vazirship, which had been held by the deceased Kamr-ul-din was about the same time conferred upon Safdar Jang, who also succeeded his uncle as Viceroy or Nawáb of Áudh. Hence the title, afterwards so famous, of Nawáb-Vazir.

Having made these dispositions, the Emperor followed the hereditary bent of his natural disposition, and left the provinces to fare as best they might, while he enjoyed the pleasures to which his opportunities invited him. The business of state fell very much into the hands of a eunuch named Jáwid Khán, who had long been the favourite of the Emperor's mother, a Hindu *danseuse* named Udham Bai, who is known in history as the Kudsiya Begam. The remains of her villa are to be seen in a garden still bearing her name, on the Jamna side a little beyond the Kashmir Gate of New Dehli. For a time these two had all at their command; and the lady at least appears to have made a beneficent use of her term of prosperity. Meanwhile, the two great dependencies of the Empire, Rohilkand[13] and the Panjáb, become

[13] Called above, more correctly, "Rohelkhand." The present name will be used as more familiar to English readers.

the theatre of bloody contests.

The Rohillas routed the Imperial army commanded by the Vazir in person, and though Safdar Jung wiped off this stain, it was only by undergoing the still deeper disgrace of encouraging the Hindu powers to prey upon the growing weakness of the Empire.

Aided by the Mahrattas under Holkar and by the Játs under Suraj Mal, the Vazir defeated the Rohillas at the fords of the Ganges; and pushed them up into the malarious country at the foot of the Kumaon mountains, where famine and fever would soon have completed their subjugation, but for the sudden reappearance in the north-west of their Afghán kindred under Ahmad Khán the Abdáli.

The Mahrattas were allowed to indemnify themselves for these services by seizing on part of the Rohilla country, and drawing *chauth* from the rest; in consideration of which they promised their assistance to cope with the invading Afgháns; but on arriving at Dehli they learned that the Emperor, in the Vazir's absence, had surrendered to Ahmad the provinces of Láhor and Multán, and thus terminated the war.

An expedition was about this time sent to Ájmir, under the command of Säädat Khán, the *Amir-ul-Umra,* the noble of the Shiah or "Iránian" party already mentioned as commanding in Rájpután, and who was also the Imperialist Viceroy of Agra. He wasted his time and strength, however, in an attack upon the Játs, through whose country the way went. When at last he neared Ájmir he allowed himself to be entangled in the local intrigues which it was the object of his expedition to suppress. He returned after about fifteen months of fruitless campaigning, and was dismissed from his office by the all-powerful Jáwid, Gházi-ud-din succeeded as *Amir-ul-Umra.*

Almost every section of the *History of Ahmad Sháh* abstracted by Professor Dowson (VIII.) ends with some sinister allusion to this favourite eunuch and his influence. The Emperor had nothing to say as to what went on, as his mother and Jáwid were the real rulers. The Emperor considered it to be most suitable to him to spend his time in pleasure; and he made his *Zanána* extend a mile. For weeks he would remain without seeing the face of a male creature. There was probably no sincere friend to raise a warning; and the doom deepened and the hand wrote upon the wall unheeded. The country was overrun with wickedness and wasted with misery. The disgrace of the unsuccessful Säädat returning from Ájmir, was enhanced by his vainly attempting to strike a blow at the Empress and her favourite. They called in the Turkish element against him, and contrived to alienate his countryman, Safdar Jang, who departed towards his Viceroyship of Áudh; leaving the wretched remains of an Empire to ferment and crumble in its own way.

The cabinet of the Empress was now, in regard to Gházi-ud-din and the Mahrattas, in the position of a necromancer who has to furnish his familiars with employment on pain of their destroying him. But an escape seemed to be afforded them by the projects of Gházi-ud-din, who agreed to draw off the dangerous auxiliaries to aid him in wresting the lieutenancy of the Deccan from his third brother Salabat Jang who had possessed himself of the administration on the death of Násir Jang, the second son and first successor of Chin Kulich, the old Nizám. He was to be represented at Dehli by a nephew.

Gladly did the Persian party behold their rival thus depart; little dreaming of the dangerous abilities of the boy he had left behind. This youth, best known by the family affix of Gházi-ud-din (2nd), but whose name was Shahábuddin, and who is known in native histories by his official title of Aamád-ul-Mulk, was son of Firoz Jang, the old Nizám's fourth son. He at once assumed the head of the army, and may be properly described, henceforth, as "Captain-General." He was but sixteen when the news of his uncle's sudden death at Aurangábád was brought to Dehli. Safdar Jang, returning from Lucknow, removed the Emperor's chief favourite, Jáwid, by assassination (28th August, 1752) and doubtless thought himself at length arrived at the goal of his ambition. But the young Gházi, secretly instigated by the weak and anxious monarch, renewed against the Persian the same war of Turán and Irán, of Sunni and Shia, which in the last reign had been waged between the uncle of the one and the grandfather of the other. The only difference was that both parties being now fully warned, the mask of friendship that had been maintained during the old struggle was now completely dropped; and the streets of the metropolis became the scene of daily fights between the two factions. Many splendid remains of the old cities[14] are believed to have been destroyed during these struggles. The Játs from Bhurtpore came up under Suraj Mal, their celebrated leader, and plundered the environs right and left. The Vazir's people, the Persian party, breached a bastion of the city wall, and their victory seemed near at hand. But Mir Mannu, the famous Viceroy of the Punjab—who was Gházi's near kinsman—sent a body of veterans to aid the Moghul cause; the account is confused, but this seems to have turned the tide. The Moghuls, or Turks, for the time won; and Gházi assumed the command of the army. The Vazirship was conferred on Intizám-ud-daulah the Khán Khánán (a son of the deceased Kamr-ul-din,[15] and young Gházi's cousin), while Safdar Jang falling into open rebellion, called the Játs under Surajmal to his assistance. The Moghuls were thus led to have recourse to the Mahrattas; and Holkar was even engaged as a nominal partizan of the Empire, against his co-religionists the Játs, and his former patron the Viceroy of Áudh. The latter, who was always more remarkable for sagacity than for personal courage, soon retired to his own country, and the hands of the conqueror Gházi fell heavily upon the unfortunate Játs.

The Khán Khánán and the Emperor now began to think that things had gone far enough; and the former, who was acquainted with his kinsman's unscrupulous mind and ruthless passions, persistently withheld from him a siege-train which was required for the reduction of Bhartpur, the Ját capital. The Emperor was thus in a situation from which the utmost judgment in the selection of a line of conduct was necessary for success, indeed for safety. The gallant Mir Mannu, son of his father's old friend and servant Kamar-uddin, was absent in the Panjáb, engaged on the arduous duty of keeping the Afgháns in check. But his brother-in-law, the Khán Khánán, was ready with alternative projects, of which each was courageous and

[14] *Vide sup.*, p. 5, 6.

[15] *Vide sup.*, p. 16.

sensible. To call back Safdar Jung, and openly acknowledge the cause of the Játs, would probably cost only one campaign, well conceived and vigorously executed. On the other hand, to support the Captain-General Ghâzi honestly and without reserve, would have secured immediate repose, whilst it crushed a formidable Hindu power.

The irresolute voluptuary before whom these plans were laid could decide manfully upon neither. He marched from Dehli with the avowed intention of supporting the Captain-General, to whom he addressed messages of encouragement. He at the same time wrote to Surajmal, to whom he promised that he would fall upon the rear of the army (his own!), upon the Játs making a sally from the fortress in which they were besieged.

Safdar Jang not being applied to, remained sullenly aloof: the Emperor's letter to the Játs fell into the hands of Gházi-ud-din, the Captain-General, who returned it to him with violent menaces. The alarmed monarch began to fall back upon his capital, pursued at a distance by his rebellious general. Holkar meanwhile executed a sudden and independent attack upon the Imperial camp, which he took and plundered at Sikundrábád, near Bolandshahr. The ladies of the Emperor's family were robbed of everything, and sent to Dehli in country carts. The Emperor and his minister lost all heart, and fled precipitately into Dehli, where they had but just time to take refuge in the palace, when they found themselves rigorously invested.

Knowing the man with whom they had to deal, their last hope was obviously in a spirited resistance, combined with an earnest appeal to the Áudh Viceroy and to the ruler of the Játs. And it is on record in a trustworthy native history that such was the tenor of the Vazir's advice to the Emperor. But the latter, perhaps too sensible of the difficulties of this course from the known hostility of Safdar Jang, and the great influence of Gházi-ud-din over the Moghul soldiery, rejected the bold counsel. Upon this the Vazir retired to his own residence, which he fortified, and the remaining adherents of the Emperor opened the gates and made terms with the Captain-General. The latter then invested himself with the official robes of the Vazirate (5th June, 1754) and convened the Moghul Darbár, from which, with his usual address, he contrived to obtain as a vote of the cabinet what was doubtless the suggestion of his own unprincipled ambition. "This Emperor," said the assembled nobles, "has shown his unfitness for rule. He is unable to cope with the Mahrattas: he is false and fickle towards his friends. Let him be deposed, and a worthier son of Timur raised to the throne." This resolution was immediately acted upon; the unfortunate monarch was blinded and consigned to the State prison of Salim Garh, adjoining the palace; and a son of Jáhándár Sháh, the competitor of Farokhsiar, proclaimed Emperor under the sounding title of Álamgir II., July, 1754 A.D. The new Emperor (whose title was due to the fact that his predecessor—the great Aurangzeb—had been the first to bear it) was in the fifty-fourth year of his age. He was a quiet old devotee, whose only pleasures were reading religious books and attending divine service. His predecessor was not further molested, and lived on in his captivity to his death in 1775, from natural causes, at the age of fifty. Gházi-ud-din was at the same time acknowledged as Vazir in the room of the Khán Khánán. That officer was murdered about five years later, according to Beale

(*Orl. Bl. Dicty in voc.*) So also the *Siyar-ul-mutikharin*.

One name, afterwards to become very famous, is heard of for the first time during these transactions; and, since the history of the Empire consists now of little more than a series of biographies, the present seems the proper place to consider the outset of his career. Najib Khán was an Afghán soldier of fortune, who had attained the hand of the daughter of Dundi Khán, one of the chieftains of the Rohilkand Páthans. Rewarded by this ruler with the charge of a district, now Bijnaur, in the north-west corner of Rohilkand, he had joined the cause of Safdar Jang, when that minister occupied the country; but on the latter's disgrace had borne a part in the campaigns of Ghází-ud-din. When the Vazir first conceived the project of attacking the government, he sent Najib in the command of a Moghul detachment to occupy the country about Sahéránpur, then known as the Báwani Mahál, which had formed the jagir of the Ex-Vazir Khán Khánán. This territory thus became in its turn separated from the Empire, and continued for two generations in the family of Najib. Though possessing the unscrupulous nature of his class, he was not without the virtues that are found in its best specimens. He was active, painstaking, and faithful to engagements; when he had surmounted his early difficulties he proved a good administrator. He ruled the dwindled Empire for nine years, and died a peaceful death, leaving his charge in an improved and strengthened condition, ready for its lawful monarch. He was highly esteemed by the British in India.—(*v. inf.*, 52.)

The dominions of Akbar and Aurangzeb had now indeed fallen into a pitiable state. Although the whole of the peninsula still nominally owned the sway of the Moghul, no provinces remained in the occupation of the Government besides part of the upper Doáb, and a few districts south of the Satlaj. Gujarat was overrun by the Mahrattas; Bengal, Bihár, and Orissa were occupied by the successor of Aliverdi Khán, Áudh and Alláhábád by Safdar Jang, the central Doáb by the Afghán tribe of Bangash, the province now called Rohilkand by the Rohillas. The Panjáb had been virtually abandoned; the rest of India had been recovered by the Hindus, with the exception of such portions of the Deccan as still formed the arena for the family wars of the sons of the old Nizám. Small encroachments continued to be made by the English traders.

CHAPTER V.

A.D. 1754-60.

Progress of Gházi ud-din—Ahmad Khán enters Dehli—Escape of the Prince Ali Gauhar—Murder of the Emperor—Ahmad the Abdáli advances on Dehli—End of Gh//ázi's career.

No sooner was the revolution accomplished than the young kingmaker took effective measures to secure his position. He first seized and imprisoned his relation the Khán Khánán, whose office he had usurped, as above stated. The opportune death of Safdar Jang (17th October, 1754) removed another danger, while the intrepidity and merciless severity with which (assisted by Najib Khán) he quelled a military mutiny provoked by his own arbitrary conduct, served at once as a punishment to the miserable offenders and a warning to all who might be meditating future attacks.

Of such there were not a few, and those too in high places. The imbecile Emperor became the willing centre of a cabal bent upon the destruction of the daring young minister; and, though the precautions of the latter prevented things from going that length, yet the constant plotting that went on served to neutralize all his efforts at administration, and to increase in his mind that sense of misanthropic solitude which is probably the starting-point of the greatest crimes.

As soon as he judged that he could prudently leave the Court, the Minister organized an expedition to the Panjáb, where the gallant Mir Mannu had been lately killed by falling from his horse. Such had been the respect excited in men's minds towards this excellent public servant, that the provinces of Láhor and Multán, when ceded to the Afgháns in the late reign, had been ultimately left in his charge by the new rulers. Ahmad the Abdáli even carried on this policy after the Mir's death, and confirmed the Government in the person of his infant son. The actual administrators during the minority were to be the widow of Mannu and a statesman of great local experience, whose name was Adina Beg. This man was a Hindu by origin, a self-made man, bold and intelligent.

It was upon this opportunity that the Vazir resolved to strike. Hastily raising such a force as the poor remnant of the imperial treasury could furnish, he marched on Láhor, taking with him the heir apparent, Mirza Ali Gauhar. Seizing the town by a *coup de main*, he possessed himself of the Lady Regent and her daughter, and returned to Dehli, asserting that he had extorted a treaty from the Afghán monarch, and appointed Adina Beg sole Commissioner of the provinces.

However this may have been, the Court was not satisfied; and the less so that the success of the Minister only served to render him more violent and cruel than ever. Nor is it to be supposed that Ahmad the Abdáli would overlook, for any period longer than his own convenience might require, any unauthorized interference with arrangements made by himself for territory that he might justly regard as his own. Accordingly the Afghán chief soon lent a ready ear to the representations of the Emperor's party, and swiftly presented himself at the head of an army within twenty miles of Dehli. Accompanied by Najib Khán, (who was in secret correspondence with the invader,) the Minister marched out to give battle; and so complete was the isolation into which his conduct had thrown him, that he learned for the first time what was the true state of affairs when he saw the chief part of the army follow Najib into the ranks of the enemy, where they were received as expected guests.

In this strait the Minister's personal qualities saved him. Having in the meantime made Mannu's daughter his wife, he had the address to obtain the intercession of his mother-in-law; and not only obtained the pardon of the invader, but in no long time so completely ingratiated himself with that simple soldier as to be in higher power than even before the invasion.

Ahmad Khán now took upon himself the functions of government, and deputed the Minister to collect tribute in the Doáb, while Sardár Jahán Khán, one of his principal lieutenants, proceeded to levy contributions from the Játs, and Ahmad himself undertook the spoliation of the capital.

From the first expedition Gházi returned with considerable booty. The attack upon the Játs was not so successful; throwing themselves into the numerous strongholds with which their country was dotted, they defied the Afghán armies and cut off their foraging parties in sudden sallies. Agra too made an obstinate defence under a Moghul governor; but the invaders indemnified themselves both in blood and plunder at the expense of the unfortunate inhabitants of the neighbouring city of Mathra, whom they surprised at a religious festival, and massacred without distinction of age or sex.

As for the citizens of Dehli, their sufferings were grievous, even compared with those inflicted twenty years before by the Persians of Nádir Sháh, in proportion as the conquerors were less civilized, and the means of satisfying them less plentiful. All conceivable forms of misery prevailed during the two months which followed the entry of the Abdáli, 11th September, 1757, exactly one hundred years before the last capture of the same city by the avenging force of the British Government during the Great Mutiny.

Having concluded these operations, the invader retired into cantonments at Anupshahar, on the Ganges, and there proceeded to parcel out the Empire among such of the Indian chiefs as he delighted to honour. He then appointed Najib to the office of *Amir-ul-umra*, an office which involved the personal charge of the Palace and its inmates; and departed to his own country, from which he had lately received some unsatisfactory intelligence. The Emperor endeavoured to engage his influence to bring about a marriage which he desired to contract with a daughter of the penultimate Emperor, Muhammad Sháh: but the Abdáli, on his attention being drawn to the young lady, resolved upon espousing her himself. He at the same time married his son Timur Sháh to the daughter of the heir apparent, and, having left that son in charge of the Panjáb, retired with the bulk of his army to Kandahár.

Relieved for the present from his anxieties, the Minister gave sway to that morbid cruelty which detracted from the general sagacity of his character. He protected himself against his numerous enemies by subsidizing a vast body-guard of Mahratta mercenaries, to pay whom he was led to the most merciless exactions from the immediate subjects of the Empire. He easily expelled Najib (who since his elevation must be distinguished by his honorific name of Najib ud daula, "Hero of the State"): he destroyed or kept in close confinement the nobles who favoured the Emperor, and even sought to lay hands upon the heir apparent, Ali Gohar.

This prince was now in his seven-and-thirtieth year, and exhibited all those generous qualities which we find in the men of his race as long as they are not enervated by the voluptuous repose of the Palace. He had been for some time residing in a kind of open arrest in the house of Ali Mardán Khán, a fortified building on the banks of the river. Here he learned that the Minister contemplated transferring him to the close captivity of Salim Garh, the state prison which stood within the precincts of the Palace. Upon this he consulted with his companions, Rájah Ramnáth and a Musalman gentleman, Saiyid Ali, who with four private troopers agreed to join in the hazardous enterprise of forcing their way through the bands which by this time invested the premises. Early the following morning they descended to the courtyard and mounted their horses in silence.

There was no time to spare. Already the bolder of the assailants had climbed upon the neighbouring roofs, from which they began to fire upon the little garrison, while their main forces guarded the gateway. But it so happened that there was a breach in the wall upon the river side, at the rear of the premises. By this the Prince and his friends galloped out, and without a moment's hesitation plunged their horses into the broad Jamna. One alone, Saiyid Ali, stayed behind, and single-handed held the pursuers at bay until the prince had made good his escape. The loyal follower paid for his loyalty with his life. The fugitives found their way to Sikandra, which was the centre of Najib's new fief; and the Prince, after staying some time under the protection of the *Amir-ul-Umra*, ultimately reached Lucknow, where, after a vain attempt to procure the co-operation of the new Viceroy in an attack upon the British, he was eventually obliged to seek the protection of that alien power.

Ahmad the Abdáli being informed of these things by letters from Dehli, prepared a fresh incursion; the rather that Adina Beg, with the help of the Mahrattas had at the same time chased his son, Timur Sháh, from Láhor; while with another force they had expelled Najib from his new territory, and forced him to seek safety in his forts in the Báwani Mahál. The new Viceroy of Áudh raised the Rohillas and his own immediate followers in the Abdáli's name; the Mahrattas were driven out of Rohilkand; and the Afgháns, crossing the Jamna in Najib's territory to the north of Dehli, arrived once more at Anupshahar about September, 1759, whence they were enabled to hold uninterrupted communication with Áudh.

The ruthless Gházi was now almost at the end of his resources. He therefore resolved to play his last card, and either win all by the terror of his monstrous crime, or lose all, and retire from the game.

The harmless Emperor, amongst his numerous foibles, cherished the pardonable weakness of a respect for the religious mendicants, who form one of the chronic plagues of Asiatic society. Taking advantage of this, a Kashmirian in the interest of the Minister took occasion to mention to Álamgir that a hermit of peculiar sanctity had recently taken up his abode in the ruined fort of Firozábád, some two miles south of the city, and (in those days) upon the right bank of the Jamna, which river has now receded to a considerable distance. The helpless devotee resolved to consult with this holy man, and repaired to the ruins in his palanquin. Arrived at the door of the room, which was in the N.E. corner of the palace of Firoz Sháh, he was relieved of his arms by the Kashmirian, who admitted him, and closed the entrance. A cry for aid being presently heard was gallantly responded to by Mirza Bábar, the emperor's son-in-law, who attacked and wounded the sentry, but was overpowered and sent to Salim Garh in the Emperor's litter. The latter meanwhile was seized by a savage Uzbek, named Bálábásh, who had been stationed within, and who sawed off the defenceless monarch's head with a knife. Then stripping off the rich robe he cast the headless trunk out of the window, where it lay for some hours upon the sands until the Kashmirian ordered its removal. The date of this tragic event is between the 10th and 30th of November, 1759 (the latter being the day given by Dowson, vol. viii. p. 243). The late Minister, Intizám-ud-Daula, had been murdered by order of his successor three days earlier. A grandson of Kam Bakhsh (the unfortunate son of Aurangzeb) was then taken out of the Salim Garh and proclaimed Emperor by the sonorous title of "Sháh Jahán II." But he is not recognised on the list of emperors, and his reign—such as it was—lasted but a moment. Gházi- (or Shaháb) ud-din attempted to reproduce the policy of the Sáyyids by governing behind this puppet; but the son of the murdered emperor proclaimed himself in Bihár (*v. inf.*), and Ahmad the Abdáli moved against Gházi, as we shall see in the next chapter. Discretion was the only part of valour left, and the young and unscrupulous politician fled to Bhartpur, where he found a temporary asylum with Suraj Mal.

As this restless criminal here closes his public life, it may be once for all mentioned that he reluctantly and slowly retired to Farukhabad, where he remained till Sháh Alám came there in 1771 (*inf.* pp. 57-58); that being driven from thence at the Restoration he once more became a wanderer, and spent the next twenty years of his life in disguise and total obscurity; till being accidentally discovered by the British police at Surat, about 1791, he was, by the Governor-General's orders, allowed to depart with a small sum of money to Mecca, the refuge of many a Mohamadan malcontent. Returning thence he visited Kábul, where he joined one of the Dehli princes in an attempted invasion of India. The prince went mad at Multán, and Gházi, leaving him there, went on to Bandelkhand, where he received a grant of land on which he chiefly passed the remainder of his days. He died in 1800, and was buried at Pakpatan in the Panjáb (*v. Journal of the As. Soc. of Bengal,*

No. CCXXVI. 1879, pp. 129, ff.)

The vengeance of the Abdáli, therefore, fell upon the unoffending inhabitants of the capital—once more they were scourged with fire and sword. Leaving a garrison in the palace, the Abdáli then quitted the almost depopulated city, and fell back on his old quarters at Anupshahar, where he entered into negotiations with the Rohillas, and with the Nawáb of Áudh, of which the result was a general combination of the Musalmans of Hindustan with a view of striking a decisive blow in defence of Islám. But these events will form the subject of a separate chapter.

CHAPTER VI.

The Campaign of Pánipat.

The Mahratta confederacy was in 1759 irresistible from the borders of Berár to the banks of the Ganges. On one side they were checked by the Nizám and Haidar, on the other by Shujäá-ud-daula, the young ruler of Áudh. Between these limits they were practically paramount. To the westward a third Mohamadan power, the newly-formed Daurâni empire, was no doubt a standing menace; but it is very possible that, with Ahmad Sháh, as with the other Moslem chiefs, arrangements of a pacific nature might have been made. All turned upon the character and conduct of one man. That man was Sadásheo Rao, the cousin and minister of the Mahratta leader, the Peshwa, into whose hands had fallen the sway of Mahratta power. For their titular head, the descendant of Siváji the original founder, was a puppet, almost a prisoner, such as we, not many years ago, considered the Mikado of Japan.

The state of the country is thus described by a contemporary historian, quoted by Tod:—"The people of Hindustan at this period thought only of personal safety and gratification. Misery was disregarded by those who escaped it; and man, centred solely in self, felt not for his kind. This selfishness, destructive of public, as of private, virtue, became universal in Hindustan after the invasion of Nádir Sháh; nor have the people become more virtuous since, and consequently are neither happy nor more independent."

Ahmad Khán (known as "the Abdáli"), whom we are now to recognise as Ahmad Sháh, the Daurâni emperor, returned to Hindustan (as stated in the last chapter) late in the summer, and marched to Dehli, when he heard of the murder of Álamgir II. The execrable Shahábuddin (or Ghâzi-ud-din the younger) fled at his approach, taking refuge with the Játs. Mahratta troops, who had occupied some places of strength in the Panjáb, were defeated and driven in. The capital was again occupied and plundered, after which the Sháh retired to the territory of his ally Najib, and summoned to his standard the chiefs of the Rohillas. On the other hand the Mahrattas, inviting to their aid the leaders of the Rájputs and Játs, moved up from the South. They possessed themselves of the capital in December 1759.

The main force of the Mahrattas that left the Deccan consisted of 20,000 chosen horse, under the immediate command of the minister, Sadásheo, whom for convenience we may in future call by his title of "the Bhao." He also took with him a powerful disciplined corps of 10,000 men, infantry and artillery, under a Mohamadan soldier of fortune, named Ibráhim Khán. This general had learned French discipline as *commandant de la qarde* to Bussy, and bore the title, or nickname, of "gardi," a souvenir of his professional origin.

The Bhao's progress was joined by Mahratta forces under Holkar, Sindhia, the Gaikwár, Gobind Pant, and others. Many of the Rájput States contributed, and Suraj Mal brought a contingent of 20,000 hardy Játs. Hinduism was uniting for a grand effort; Islám was rallied into cohesion by the necessity of resistance. Each party was earnestly longing for the alliance of the Shias under Shujäá, Viceroy of Áudh, whose antecedents led men on both sides to look upon them as neutral.

The Bhao had much prestige. Hitherto always victorious, his personal reputation inspired great respect. His camp, enriched with the plunder of Hindustan, was on a scale of unwonted splendour. "The lofty and spacious tents," says Grant-Duff, "lined with silks and broadcloths, were surmounted by large gilded ornaments, conspicuous at a distance. . . . Vast numbers of elephants, flags of all descriptions, the finest horses, magnificently caparisoned . . . . seemed to be collected from every quarter . . . . it was an imitation of the more becoming and tasteful array of the Moghuls in the zenith of their glory." Nor was this the only innovation. Hitherto the Mahrattas had been light horsemen, each man carrying his food, forage, bedding, head and heel ropes, as part of his accoutrements; marching fifty miles after a defeat, and then halting in complete readiness to "fight another day." Now, for the first time, they were to be supported by a regular park of artillery, and a regular force of drilled infantry. But all these seeming advantages only precipitated and rendered more complete and terrible their ultimate overthrow.

Holkar and Suraj Mal, true to the instincts of their old predatory experience, urged upon the Bhao, that regular warfare was not the game that they knew. They counselled, therefore, that the families and tents, and all heavy equipments, should be left in some strong place of safety, such as the almost impregnable forts of Jhánsi and Gwalior, while their clouds of horse harassed the enemy and wasted the country before and round him. But the Bhao rejected these prudent counsels with contempt. He had seen the effect of discipline and guns in Southern war; and, not without a shrewd foresight of what was afterwards to be accomplished by a man then in his train, resolved to try the effect of scientific soldiership, as he understood it. The determination proved his ruin; not because the instrument he chose was not the best, but because it was not complete, and because he did not know how to handle it. When Mádhoji Sindhia, after a lapse of twenty years, mastered all Asiatic opposition by the employment of the same instrument, he had a European general, the Count de Boigne, who was one of the great captains of his age; and he allowed him to use his own strategy and tactics. Then, the regular battalions and batteries, becoming the nucleus of the army, were moved with resolution and aggressive purpose, while the cavalry only acted for purposes of escort, reconnoissance, and pursuit. In the fatal campaign before us, we shall find the disciplined troops doing all that could fairly be expected of them under Asiatic leaders, but failing for want of numbers, and of generalship.

On arriving at Dehli, the Bhao surrounded the citadel in which was situated the palace of the emperors. It was tenanted by a weak Musalman force, which had been hastily thrown in under the command of a nephew of Sháh Wali Khán, the Dauráni Vazir. After a brief bombardment, this garrison capitulated, and the Bhao took possession and plundered the last remaining effects of the emperors, including the silver ceiling of the *diwán khas*, which was thrown into the melting-pot and furnished seventeen lakhs of rupees (£170,000).

Ahmad, in the meantime, was cantoned at Anupshahr, on the frontier of the Rohilla country, where he was compelled to remain while his negotiations with Shujäá were pending. So came on the summer of 1760, and the rainy season was at hand, during which, in an unbridged country, military operations could not be carried on. All the more needful that the time of enforced leisure should be given to preparation. Najib, the head of the Rohillas, was very urgent with the Sháh that Shujäá should be persuaded to take part against the Mahrattas. He pointed out that, such as the Moghul empire might be, Shujäá was its Vazir. As Ahmad Sháh had hitherto been foiled by the late Nawáb Safdar Jang, it was for his majesty to judge how useful might be the friendship of a potentate whose predecessor's hostility had been so formidable. "But," added the prudent Rohilla, "it must be remembered that the recollection of the past will make the Vazir timorous and suspicious. The negotiation will be as delicate as important. It should not be entrusted to ordinary agency, or to the impersonal channel of epistolary correspondence."

The Sháh approved of these reasonings, and it was resolved that Najib himself should visit the Vazir, and lay before him the cause which he so well understood, and in which his own interest was so deep. The envoy proceeded towards Áudh, and found the Vazir encamped upon the Ganges at Mahdi Ghát. He lost no time in opening the matter; and, with the good sense that always characterized him, Najib touched at once the potent spring of self. Shia or Sunni, all Moslems were alike the object of Mahratta enmity. He, Najib, knew full well what to expect, should the Hindu league prevail. But would the Vazir fare better? "Though, after all, the will of God will be done, it behoves us not the less to help destiny to be beneficent by our own best endeavours. Think carefully, consult Her Highness, your mother: I am not fond of trouble, and should not have come all this distance to see your Excellency were I not deeply interested." Such, as we learn from an adherent of Shujäá's, was the substance of the advice given him by the Rohilla chieftain.

The nature of these negotiations is not left to conjecture. The narrative of what occurred is supplied by Kási Ráj Pandit, a Hindu writer in the service of the Nawáb Vazir, and an eye-witness of the whole campaign. He was present in both camps, having been employed in the negotiations which took place between the Mahrattas and Mohamadans; and his account of the battle (of which a translation appeared in the *Asiatic Researches* for 1791, reprinted in London in 1799) is at once the most authentic that has come down to our times, and the best description of war ever recorded by a Hindu.[16]

Shujäá-ud-daulah, after anxious deliberation, resolved to adopt the advice of his Rohilla visitor. And, having so resolved, he adhered honestly to his resolution. He sent his family to Lucknow, and accompanied Najib to Anupshahr, where he was warmly received by the Daurání Sháh, and his minister Sháh Wali Khán.

Shortly after, the united forces of the Moslems moved down to Sháhdara, the hunting-ground of the emperors, near Dehli, from which, indeed, it was only

[16] There is another account by an eye-witness (Mohamad Jáfar Khán Shámlu (Dowson, viii.), but it is almost inconceivably inaccurate.

separated by the river Jamna. But, the monsoon having set in, the encounter of the hostile armies was for the present impossible. The interval was occupied in negotiation. The Bhao first attempted the virtue of Shujäá, whom he tempted with large offers to desert the Sunni cause. Shujäá amused him with messages in which our Pandit acted as go-between; but all was conducted with the knowledge of Najib, who was fully consulted by the Nawáb Vazir throughout. The Sháh's minister, also, was aware of the transaction, and apparently disposed to grant terms to the Hindus. Advantage was taken of the opportunity, and of the old alliance between Shujäá and the Játs, to shake the confidence of Suraj Mal, and persuade him to abandon the league, which he very willingly did when his advice was so haughtily rejected. It was the opinion of our Pandit, that a partition of the country might even now have been effected had either party been earnest in desiring peace. He did not evidently know what were the Bhao's real feelings, but probably judged him by the rest of his conduct, which was that of a bold, ambitious statesman. From what he saw in the other camp, he may well have concluded that Najib had some far-seeing scheme on foot, which kept him from sincerely forwarding the proposed treaty. Certainly that astute Rohilla was ultimately the greatest gainer from the anxieties and sufferings of the campaign. But the first act of hostility came from the Bhao, who moved up stream to turn the invader's flank.

About eighty miles north of Dehli, on the meadowlands lying between the Western Jamna Canal and the river (from whose right bank it is about two miles distant), stands the small town of Kunjpura. In the invasion of Nádir Sháh, it had been occupied by a force of Persian sharpshooters, who had inflicted much loss on the Moghul army from its cover. Induced, perhaps, by the remembrance of those days, Ahmad had made the mistake of placing in it a garrison of his own people, from which he was now separated by the broad stream of the Jamna, brimming with autumnal floods. Here the Bhao struck his first blow, taking the whole Afghán garrison prisoners after an obstinate defence, and giving up the place to plunder, while the main Afghán army sat idle on the other side.

At length arrived the *Dasahra,* the anniversary of the attack of Lanka by the demigod Rám, a proverbial and almost sacred day of omen for the commencement of Hindu military expeditions. Ahmad adopted the auspices of his enemy and reviewed his troops the day before the festival. The state of his forces is positively given by the Pandit, as consisting of 28,000 Afgháns, powerful men, mounted on hardy Turkoman horses, forty pieces of cannon, besides light guns mounted on camels; with some 28,000 horse, 38,000 foot, and about forty guns, under the Hindustáni Musalmans. The Mahrattas had more cavalry, fewer foot, and an artillery of 200 guns; in addition to which they were aided, if aid it could be called in regular warfare, by clouds of predatory horsemen, making up their whole force to over 200,000, mostly, as it turned out, food for the sabre and the gun.

On the 17th of October, 1760, the Afghán host and its allies broke up from Sháhdara; and between the 23rd and 25th effected a crossing at Bághpat, a small town about twenty-four miles up the river. The position of the hostile armies was thus reversed; that of the northern invaders being nearer Dehli, with the whole of Hindustan at their backs, while the Southern defenders of their country were in the attitude of men marching down from the north-west with nothing behind them but the dry and war-wasted plains of Sirhind. In the afternoon of the 26th, Ahmad's advanced guard reached Sambalka, about half-way between Sonpat and Pánipat, where they encountered the vanguard of the Mahrattas. A sharp conflict ensued, in which the Afgháns lost a thousand men, killed and wounded, but drove back the Mahrattas on their main body, which kept on retreating slowly for several days, contesting every inch of the ground until they reached Pánipat. Here the camp was finally pitched in and about the town, and the position was at once covered by digging a trench sixty feet wide and twelve deep, with a rampart on which the guns were mounted. The Sháh took up ground four miles to the south, protecting his position by *abattis* of felled timber, according to his usual practice, but pitching in front a small unprotected tent from which to make his own observations.

The small reverse of the Mahrattas at Sambalka was soon followed by others, and hopes of a pacific solution became more and more faint. Gobind Pant Bundela, foraging near Meerut with 10,000 light cavalry, was surprised and slain by Atái Khán at the head of a similar party of Afgháns. The terror caused by this affair paralysed the Bhao's commissariat, while it greatly facilitated the foraging of the Sháh. Shortly after, a party of 2,000 Mahratta horsemen, each carrying a bag of specie from Dehli, fell upon the Afghán pickets, which they mistook for their own in the dark of night. On their answering in their own language to the sentry's challenge, they were surrounded and cut up by the enemy, and something like £200,000 in silver was lost to the Bhao. Ibráhim and his disciplined mercenaries now became very clamorous for their arrears of pay, on which Holkar proposed that the cavalry should make an immediate attack without them. The Bhao ironically acquiesced, and turned the tables upon Holkar, who probably meant nothing less than to lead so hare-brained a movement.

During the next two months constant skirmishes and duels took place between parties and individual champions upon either side. In one of these Najib lost 3,000 of his Rohillas, and was very near perishing himself; and the chiefs of the Indian Musalmans became at last very urgent with the Sháh to put an end to their suspense by bringing on a decisive action. But the Sháh, with the patience of a great leader, as steadily repressed their ardour, knowing very well that (to use the words of a modern leader on a similar occasion) the enemy were all the while "stewing in their own gravy." For this is one of the sure marks of a conqueror, that he makes of his own troubles a measure of his antagonist's misfortunes; so that they become a ground, not of losing heart, but of gaining courage.

Meanwhile the vigilance of his patrol, for which service he had 5,000 of his best cavalry employed through the long winter nights, created almost a blockade of the Mahrattas. On one occasion 20,000 of their camp-followers, who had gone to collect provisions, were massacred in a wood near the camps by this vigilant force.

The Bhao's spirit sank under these repeated blows and warnings, and he sent to the Nawáb Vazir, Shujäá-ud-daulah, to offer to accept any conditions that might still be obtainable. All the other chiefs were willing, and the Sháh referred them to the Rohillas. But Najib proved implacable. The Pandit went to the Rohilla leader, and urged on him every possible consideration that might persuade him to agree. But his clear good sense perceived the nature of the crisis. "I would do much," he said, "to gratify the Nawáb and show my respect for his Excellency. But oaths are not chains; they are only words, things that will never bind the enemy when once he has escaped from the dangers which compel him to undertake them. By one effort we can get this thorn out of our sides."

Proceeding to the Sháh's tent he obtained instant admission, though it was now midnight. Here he repeated his arguments; adding that whatever his Majesty's decision might be was personally immaterial to himself. "For I," he concluded, "am but a soldier of fortune, and can make terms for myself with either party." The blunt counsel pleased the Sháh. "You are right, Najib," said Ahmad, "and the Nawáb is misled by the impulses of youth. I disbelieve in the Mahratta penitence, and I am not going to throw you over whom I have all along regarded as the manager of this affair. Though in my position I must hear every one, yet I promise never to act against your advice."

While these things were passing in the Moslem camp, the Mahrattas, having exhausted their last resource by the plunder of the town of Pánipat, sent all their chiefs on the same evening to meet in the great durbar-tent. It was now the 6th of January, and we may fancy the shivering, starving Southerners crouched on the ground and discussing their griefs by the wild torchlight. They represented that they had not tasted food for two days, and were ready to die fighting, but not to die of hunger. *Pán*[17] was distributed, and all swore to go out an hour before daybreak and drive away the invaders or perish in the attempt.

As a supreme effort, the Bhao, whose outward bearing at durbar had been gallant and dignified, had despatched a short note to our Pandit, who gives the exact text. "The cup is full to the brim, and cannot hold another drop. If anything can be done, do it. If not, let me know plainly and at once; for afterwards there will be no time for writing, or for speech." The Pandit was with Shujäá, by the time this note arrived—the hour was 3 A.M.—and he handed it to his master, who began to examine the messenger. While he was so doing, his spies ran in with the intelligence that the Mahrattas had left their lines. Shujäá, at once hastened to the Sháh's tent.

Ahmad had lain down to rest, but his horse was held ready saddled at the entry. He rose from his couch and asked, "What news?" The Nawáb told him what he had heard. The Sháh immediately mounted and sent for the Pandit. While the latter was corroborating the tidings brought by his master, Ahmad, sitting on his horse, was smoking a Persian pipe and peering into the darkness. All at once the Mahratta cannon opened fire, on which the Sháh, handing his pipe to an orderly, said calmly to the Nawáb, "Your follower's news was very true I see." Then summoning his prime minister, Sháh Wali, and Sháh Pasand the chief of his staff, he made his dispositions for a general engagement when the light of day came.

Yes, the news was true. Soon after the despatch of the Bhao's note, the Mahratta

[17] The *pán,* or pepper leaf, wrapped round an aromatic preparation of betel nut and shell-lime, is a favourite condiment, and is bestowed by a great man on the breaking-up of an assemblage. In the present case it had also a sacramental character.

troops broke their fast with the last remaining grain in camp, and prepared for a mortal combat; coming forth from their lines with turbans dishevelled and turmeric-smeared faces, like devotees of death. They marched in an oblique line, with their left in front, preceded by their guns, small and great. The Bhao, with the Peshwa's son and the household troops, was in the centre. The left wing consisted of the *gárdis* under Ibráhim Khán; Holkar and Sindhia were on the extreme right.

On the other side the Afgháns formed a somewhat similar line, their left being formed by Najib's Rohillas, and their right by two brigades of Persian troops. Their left centre was led by the two vazirs, Shujäá-ud-daulah and Sháh Wali. The right centre consisted of Rohillas, under the well-known Háfiz Rahmat and other chiefs of the Indian Páthans. Day broke, but the Afghán artillery for the most part kept silence, while that of the enemy, losing range in its constant advance, threw away its ammunition over the heads of the enemy and dropped its shot a mile to their rear. Sháh Pasand Khán covered the left wing with a choice body of mailed Afghán horsemen, and in this order the army moved forward, leaving the Sháh at his usual post in the little tent, which was now in rear of the line, from whence he could watch and direct the battle.

On the other side no great precautions seem to have been taken, except indeed by the *gárdis* and their vigilant leader, who advanced in silence and without firing a shot, with two battalions of infantry bent back to their left flank, to cover their advance from the attack of the Persian cavalry forming the extreme right of the enemy's line. The valiant veteran soon showed the worth of French discipline, and another division such as his would have probably gained the day. Well mounted and armed, and carrying in his own hand the colours of his own personal command, he led his men against the Rohilkhand columns with fixed bayonets, and to so much effect that nearly 8,000 were put *hors de combat*. For three hours the *gárdis* remained in unchallenged possession of that part of the field. Shujäá-ud-daulah, with his small but compact force, remained stationary, neither fighting nor flying, and the Mahrattas forebore to attack him. The corps between this and the Páthans was that of the Dauráni Vazir, and it suffered severely from the shock of an attack delivered upon them by the Bhao himself at the head of the household troops. The Pandit, being sent through the dust to inform Shujäá of what was going on, found Sháh Wali vainly trying to rally the courage of his followers, of whom many were in full retreat. "Whither would you run, friends," cried the Vazir, "your country is far from here."

Meanwhile, on the left of the Mohamadan line, the prudent Najib had masked his advance by a series of breastworks, under cover of which he had gradually approached the hostile force. "I have the highest stake to-day," he said, "and cannot afford to make any mistakes." The part of the enemy's force immediately opposed to him was commanded by the then head of the Sindhia house, who was Najib's personal enemy. Till noon Najib remained on the defensive, keeping off all close attacks upon his earthworks by continuous discharges of rockets. But so far the fortune of the day was evidently inclined towards the Mahrattas. The Mohamadans' left still held their own under the two Vazirs and Najib; but the centre was cut in two, and the right was almost destroyed. Victory seemed to await the Mahrattas.

Of the circumstances which turned the tide and gave the crisis to the Moslems, but one account necessarily exists. Hitherto we have had the guidance of Grant-Duff for the Mahratta side of the affair, but now the whole movement was to be from the other side, and we cannot do better than trust the Pandit. Dow, the only other contemporary author of importance—if we except Gholám Hosain, who wrote at a very remote place—is most irremediably inaccurate and vague about all these transactions. The Pandit, then, informs us that, during those earlier hours of the conflict, the Sháh had watched the fortunes of the battle from his tent, guarded by the still unbroken forces on his left. But now, hearing that his right was reeling and his centre was defeated, he felt that the moment was come for a final effort. In front of him the Hindu cries of *Har! Har! Jai Máhadeo!* were maintaining an equal and dreadful concert with those of *Alláh! Alláh! Din! Din!* from his own side. The battle wavered to and fro like that of Flodden as described by Scott. The Sháh saw the critical moment in the very act of passing. He therefore sent 500 of his own body-guard with orders to drive all able-bodied men out of camp, and send them to the front at any cost. 1,500 more he sent to encounter those who were flying, and slay without pity any who would not return to the fight. These, with 4,000 of his reserve troops, went to support the broken ranks of the Rohilla Páthans on the right. The remainder of the reserve, 10,000 strong, were sent to the aid of Sháh Wali, still labouring unequally against the Bhao in the centre of the field. The Sháh's orders were clear. These mailed warriors were to charge with the Vazir in close order, and at full gallop. As often as they charged the enemy in front, the chief of the staff and Najib were directed to fall upon either flank.[18] These orders were immediately carried out.

The forward movement of the Moslems began at 1 P.M. The fight was close and obstinate, men fighting with swords, spears, axes, and even with daggers. Between 2 and 3 P.M. the Peshwa's son was wounded, and, having fallen from his horse, was placed upon an elephant. The last thing seen of the Bhao was his dismounting from another elephant, and getting on his Arab charger. Soon after the young chief was slain. The next moment Holkar and the Gaikwár left the field. In that instant resistance ceased, and the Mahrattas all at once became helpless victims of butchery. Thousands were cut down; other thousands were drowned

---

[18] It is a curious coincidence, and one which well illustrates the similar character of war in West and East, that the critical movement of the Sháh's victory at Pánipat should so closely resemble that by which the Duke of Marlborough had won the battle of Blenheim, more than half a century before, viz., breaking the hostile line of battle by a violent assault of a large body of reserve cavalry at the end of a long engagement.

The fact is, no doubt, to be accounted for by the character of Ahmad, who was a man combining qualities not often found in the same person. Being a self-made man, and brought up in a good school, he had learned to be cautious and prudent without sacrifice of his native originality and of the initiative spirit, which, in common circumstances, often goes no further than eccentricity. It is extremely unlikely that he had ever heard of the very name of the English general whose tactics he unconsciously reproduced. An episode in history, like this campaign of Pánipat, possesses therefore an interest, as a study of human nature, in addition to what is due to its importance in the movement of events.

in escaping, or were slaughtered by the country people whom they had so long pillaged. The Sháh and his principal commanders then retired to camp, leaving the pursuit to be completed by subordinate officers. Forty thousand prisoners are said to have been slain. Among the prisoners was Ibráhim, the valiant and skilful leader of the *gárdis*. Though severely wounded, he was taken care of in Shujäá's tents, where his wounds received surgical attention. Shujäá also endeavoured to extend protection to the head of the house of Sindhia. A subordinate member of the clan, the afterwards celebrated Mádhoji—who was to become in his turn master of the whole country—fled from the field; and the late Colonel Skinner used to describe how this chief—in whose service he at one time was—would relate the mental agonies he endured on his light Deccanee mare from the lobbing paces and roaring breath of a big Northern horse, on which he was pursued for many miles by an Afghán, greedy of blood and booty.

Jánkoji, the then head of the family, was killed next day, a victim to the enmity of Najib, whose policy included relentlessness. Ibráhim Gárdi was taken from Shujäá by a mixture of force and fraud. He was put into the charge of the Afghán Vazir, and died in that charge a week after. A headless body, supposed to be that of the Bhao, was found some twenty or thirty miles off. The body, with that of the Peshwa's son, received the usual honours of Hindu cremation at the prayer of the Nawáb Shujäá. Several pretenders to the name of this Oriental Sebastian afterwards appeared from time to time; the last was in captivity in 1782, when Warren Hastings procured his liberation.

After these things the allies moved to Dehli; but the Daurání troops became mutinous and quarrelsome; and they parted on ill terms. Shujäá marched back to Mahdi Ghát, whence he had come six months before, with the titular appointment of Vazir of the Empire. The Sháh, having written to the fugitive Sháh Alám, to salute him as emperor, got what money he could out of the exhausted treasury and departed to his own country. Najib Khán remained at Dehli under the title of Najib-ud-daulah, with a son of the absent emperor as ostensible regent. Having made these dispositions, Ahmad the Abdáli returned to his own country, and only once again interposed[19] actively in the affairs of the Indian peninsula.

Such was the famous Campaign of Pánipat, the first disaster, on a great scale, of the power of the Mahratta confederacy, and the besom which swept the land of Hindustan for the advent of the British.

It appears that, at this period, the Sháhzáda had applied to Colonel Clive for an Asylum in Calcutta, while the Colonel was at the same time in receipt of a letter from the minister at Dehli—the unscrupulous Gházi-ud-din—calling on him to arrest the prince as a rebel and forward him to Court in custody. Clive contented himself by sending him a small present in money. About the same time, however, Clive wrote to Lord Chatham (then Prime Minister, and Mr. Pitt), recommending the issue of orders sanctioning his demanding the Viceroyship of the Eastern Subahs on behalf of the King of England; an application which he guaranteed the Emperor's granting on being assured of the punctual payment of fifty lakhs a year, the estimated fifth of the revenues. "This," he says, "has of late been very ill-paid,

[19] *Vide inf.*, p. 51.

owing to the distractions in the heart of the Moghul Empire, which have prevented the Court from attending to their concerns in those distant provinces."[20] Although nothing came of these proceedings, they are here noted as the presage of future events.

[20] Gleig's "Life of Clive," p. 123.

PART II.

CHAPTER I.

AD. 1760-65.

The English—Shujäá-ud-daulah—Sháhzáda enters Bihár; his character—Rámnaráyan defeated—M. Law—Battle of Gáya—March towards Hindustan—Massacre of Patna—Flight of Kásim and Sumroo—Battle of Buxar—Treaty with British—Text of Treaty—Establishment at Alláhábád—Emperor's establishment—Authorities cited—Broome's Bengal Army—Legal position.

THE events related in the foregoing introductory chapters had led to a complete obscuration of the Timuride family and power. Whether or no that dynasty was to resume its sway once more depended entirely on the turn that events were to take at this crisis; and chiefly on what might happen in the eastern provinces of Bihár and Bengal, where a new power was rapidly making itself felt. To that quarter, therefore, general attention was henceforth drawn; and the new power—the English—began to be, by common consent, treated as arbiter of the future. The Nawáb of Áudh was also an important element in the problem, as it then appeared; and the return of the ruler of Kábul to the plains where he had so lately struck a blow that seemed decisive, was a matter of almost daily expectation.

1759.—When in 1759 the heir to what was left of the empire of Hindostan had gallantly cut his way through the myrmidons sent against him by the ruthless Minister, he crossed the Jamna and took refuge with Najib-ud-daulah, the Afghán, who was then at Saháránpur in the Fifty-Two Parganas.[21] But finding that noble unable to afford him material support, and still fearing the machinations of his enemy, he gradually retired to Lucknow, intending perhaps to wait there until the return of the Abdáli leader might afford him an opportunity of turning upon the Mohamadan and Hindu rebels.

The present viceroy of Áudh was Shujäá-ud-daulah, the son of the famous Safdar Jang, whom he equalled in ability, and far exceeded in soldierly qualities. On his first succession to his father's now almost independent fief he was young, and content with the unbounded indulgence of those bodily faculties with which he was largely endowed. He is described as extremely handsome, and above the average stature; with an acute mind, somewhat too volatile; and more prone by nature to the exercises of the field than to the deliberations of the cabinet. But neither was the son of Safdar Jang likely to be brought up wholly without lessons in that base and tortuous selfishness which, in the East even more than elsewhere, usually

[21] *Vide* Sup., p. 21.

passes for statecraft; nor were those lessons likely to be read in ears unprepared to understand them. Shujäá's conduct in the late Rohilla war had been far from frank; and he was particularly unwilling to throw himself irredeemably into the cause of a ruined sovereign's fugitive heir. Foiled in his application to the Viceroy of Áudh, the Sháhzáda (Prince) then turned to a member of the same family who held the Fort and District of Alláhábád, and was named Mohammad Kuli Khán. To this officer he exhibited an imperial patent in his own name for the lieutenancy of Bahar, Bengal, and Orissa, which were then the theatre of wars between the British traders of Calcutta and the family of the usurping Viceroy of those Subahs, Aliverdi Khán. The Prince proposed to Mohammad Kuli that they should raise the Imperial standard and reduce both competitors to their proper level. The governor, a man of ambition and spirit, was warmly encouraged to this scheme by his relation, the Viceroy of Áudh (for reasons of his own, which we shall speedily discover, Shujäá highly approved of the arrangement); and a powerful official, named Kámgár Khán, promised assistance in Bihár. Thus supported, the Prince crossed the frontier stream (Karamnassa) in November, 1759, just at the time that his unfortunate father lost his life in the manner related above. (Part I. chapter v.)

1760.—In the distracted state of the country it was more than a month before the news of this tragedy arrived in camp, which was then pitched at a village called Kanauti, in Bihár. The Prince immediately assumed the succession, and, as a high aim leads to high shooting, his title was to be nothing short of "sovereign of the known world," or SHÁH ALÁM. He is recorded to have ordered that his reign should be reckoned from the day of his father's "martyrdom"; and there are *firmáns* of his patent-office still forthcoming in confirmation of the record. He was at once recognised as emperor by all parties; and, for his part, he wisely confirmed Shujäá-ud-daulah as Vazir; while he intrusted the command of the army in Hindustan, in the room of the assassin Gházi, to Najib-ud-daulah, the Abdáli's nominee.

Having made these arrangements he proceeded to collect revenue and establish himself in Bihár. He was at this time a tall, portly man, forty years old, or thereabout, with the constitutional character of his race, and some peculiarities of his own. Like his ancestors, he was brave, patient, dignified, and merciful; but all contemporary accounts support the view suggested by his whole history, and debit him with defects which more than balanced these great virtues. His courage was rather of the nature of fortitude than of that enterprising boldness which was absolutely necessary in his situation. His clemency did great harm when it led him to forgive and ignore all that was done to him, and to lend his ear and his hand to any person of stronger will who was nearest to him at the moment. His patience was of a kind which ere long degenerated into a simple compromise with fortune, in which he surrendered lofty hopes for the future in exchange for immediate gratifications of sense. In a word, writers unacquainted with English history have combined to produce a picture which bears a strong likeness, both in features and position, to that of Charles the Second of Britain, after the death of his father.

The Eastern Subahs were at this time held by Clive's nominee, Mir Jáfár Khán, known in English histories as Meer Jaffier, and the Deputy in Bihár was a Hindu man of business, named Rájá Rámnaráyan. This official, having sent to

Murshidábád and Calcutta for assistance, attempted to resist the proceedings of his sovereign; but the Imperial army defeated him with considerable loss, and the Hindu official, wounded in body and alarmed in mind, retired into the shelter of Patna, which the Moghuls did not, at that time, think fit to attack.

Meantime, the army of the Nawáb having been joined by a small British contingent, marched to meet the Emperor, who was worsted in an engagement that occurred on the 15th of February, 1760. On this the Emperor adopted the bold plan of a flank march, by which he should cut between the Bengal troops and their capital, Murshidábád, and possess himself of that town in the absence of its defenders. But before he could reach Murshidábád, he was again overtaken and repulsed by the activity of the English (7th April), and, being by this time joined by a small body of French under a distinguished officer, he resolved to remain in Bihár and set about the siege of Patna.

These French were a party of about one hundred officers and men who had refused to join in the capitulation of Chandarnagar three years before, and had since been wandering about the country persecuted by their relentless victor Clive. Their leader was the Chevalier Law, a relation of the celebrated speculator of the Regency; and he now hastened to lay at the feet of the Royal adventurer the skill and enterprise of his followers and himself. His ambition was high and bold, perhaps more so than his previous display of abilities might well warrant.[22] But he soon saw enough of the weakness of the Emperor, of the treachery and low motives of the Moghul nobles, to contract the hopes his self-confidence had fostered. To the historian Gholám Hossain Khán he said:—

> "As far as I can see, there is nothing that you could call government between Patna and Dehli. If men in the position of Shujäá-ud-daulah would loyally join me, I could not only beat off the English, but would undertake the administration of the Empire."[23]

The very first step in this ambitious programme was never to be taken. Whilst the Emperor with his new adherents—(and a hundred Frenchmen under even such a leader as Law were as strong as a reinforcement of many thousand native troops under a faithless Moghul)—whilst these strangely matched associates were beleaguering Patna, Captain Knox, at the head of a small body of infantry, of which only 200 men were European, ran across the 300 miles between Murshidábád and Patna in the space of thirteen days, and fell upon the Imperial army, whom he utterly routed and drove southward upon Gáya. The Imperial army was now commanded by Kámgár Khán; for Mohammad Kuli had returned to Alláhábád, and been murdered by his unscrupulous cousin Shujäá, who seized upon the province and fort. The Emperor, as is evident from his retreating southward, still hoped to raise the country in his favour, and his hopes were so far justified that he was joined by another Moghul officer, named Khádim Hossain. Thus reinforced, he again advanced on Patna opposed by Knox, who in his turn had been joined

[22] The misadventures of this brave but unlucky soldier have been related by Col. Malleson.

[23] *Siar-ul-Mutákharin.*

by a Hindu Rájá named Shatáb Rai. Another defeat was the result, and the baffled sovereign at length evacuated the country, and fled northward, pursued by the whole united forces of the British and the Bengal Nawáb. The son[24] of the latter, however, being killed in a thunderstorm in July, the allied armies retired to cantonments at Patna, and the pertinacious Imperialists once more posted themselves between that place and the capital, at their old station of Gáya.

1761.—Early next year, therefore, the Anglo-Bengali troops once more took the field, and encountering the Imperialists at Suán, near the city of Bihár, gave them a fresh overthrow, in which Law was taken prisoner, fighting to the last, and refusing to surrender his sword, which he was accordingly permitted to retain.

Next morning the British commander paid his respects to the Emperor, who was now quite weary of the hopeless struggle he had been maintaining for nearly two years, and who willingly departed towards Hindustan. He had by this time heard of the battle of Pánipat, and of the plans formed by the Abdáli for the restoration of the empire; and there is reason to believe that, but for the jealousy of Mir Kásim, whom a late revolution (brought about by the English) had placed in the room of Mir Jáfár, the Emperor would have been at once reinstated at Dehli under British protection. Before he went he created Mir Kásim Subahdar; and the fiscal administration also vested in him, the English having so determined. The Emperor was to have an annual tribute of £240,000.

1762.—As affairs turned out there was much to be done and suffered by the British before they had another opportunity of interfering in the affairs of Hindustan; and a strange series of vicissitudes impended upon the Emperor before he was to meet them in the palace of his fathers. On his way to the northwest he fell into the hands of the ambitious Nawáb Vazir of Áudh, who had received the Abdáli's orders to render the Emperor all assistance, and who carried out the letter of these instructions by retaining him for some two years in an honourable confinement, surrounded by the empty signs of sovereignty, sometimes at Benares, sometimes at Alláhábád, and sometimes at Lucknow.

1763.—In the meanwhile the unscrupulous heroes who were founding the British Government of India had thought proper to quarrel with their new instrument Mir Kásim, whom they had so lately raised to the *Masnad* of Bengal. This change in their councils had been caused by an insubordinate letter addressed to the Court of Directors by Clive's party, which had led to their dismissal from employ. The opposition then raised to power consisted of all the more corrupt members of the service; and the immediate cause of their rupture with Mir Kásim was about the monopoly they desired to have of the local trade for their own private advantage. They were represented at that Nawáb's Court by Mr. Ellis, the most violent of their body; and the consequence of his proceedings was, in no long time, seen in the murder of the Resident and all his followers, in October, 1763. The scene of this atrocity (which remained without a parallel for nearly a century) was at Patna, which was then threatened and soon after stormed by the British; and the actual instrument was a Franco-German, Walter Reinhardt by name, of whom, as we are to hear much more hereafter, it is as well here to take note.

[24] Mir Sádik Ali Khán, known to the English as "Meerun."

This European executioner of Asiatic barbarity is generally believed to have been a native of Treves, in the Duchy of Luxemburg, who came to India as a sailor in the French navy. From this service he is said to have deserted to the British, and joined the first European battalion raised in Bengal. Thence deserting he once more entered the French service; was sent with a party who vainly attempted to relieve Chandarnagar, and was one of the small party who followed Law when that officer took command of those who refused to share in the surrender of the place to the British. After the capture of his ill-starred chief, Reinhardt (whom we shall in future designate by his Indian *sobriquet* of "Sumroo," or Sombre) took service under Gregory, or Gurjin Khán, Mir Kásim's Armenian General.

Broome, however, adopts a somewhat different version. According to this usually careful and accurate historian, Reinhardt was a Salzburg man who originally came to India in the British service, and deserted to the French at Madras, whence he was sent by Lally to strengthen the garrison of the Bengal settlement. The details are not very material: Sumroo had certainly learned war both in English and French schools.

After the massacre of the British, Kásim and his bloodhound escaped from Patna (which the British stormed and took on the 6th of November), and found a temporary asylum in the dominions of Shojaa-ud-daulah. That nobleman solemnly engaged to support his former antagonist, and sent him for the present against some enemies of his own in Bundelkand, himself marching to Benares with his Imperial captive, as related in the preceding page.

1764.—In February, 1764, the avenging columns of the British appeared upon the frontier, but the Sepoys broke into mutiny, which lasted some time, and was with difficulty and but imperfectly quelled by Colonel Carnac. Profiting by the delay and confusion thus caused, the allies crossed into Bihár, and made a furious, though ultimately unsuccessful attack upon the British lines under the walls of Patna on the 3rd of May. Shujäá-ud-daulah, the Nawáb of Áudh, temporarily retiring, the Emperor resumed negotiations with the British commander; but before these could be concluded, the latter was superseded by Major (afterwards Sir Hector) Monro. This officer's arrival changed the face of affairs. Blowing from guns twenty-four of the most discontented of the sepoys, the Major led the now submissive army westward to Buxar (Baksár), near the confluence of the Karamnassa with the Ganges, where the two Nawábs (for Kásim and the Áudh Viceroy had now united their forces) encountered him to be totally routed on the 23rd October, 1764.[25]

The Emperor, who had taken no part in the action, came into the camp on the evening of the following day. By the negotiations which ultimately ensued, the British at last obtained a legal position as administrators of the three Subahs, with the further grant of the Benares and Gh// zipur sarkars as fiefs of the Empire. The remainder of the Subah of Alláhábád was secured to the Emperor with a pecuniary

[25] For a full account of these transactions see Mill; "Lord Clive's Life," by Rev. R. Gleig; Broome's "History of the Bengal Army;" and Macaulay's Essays, Art. "Clive." Also Elphinstone's posthumous work, "The Rise of British Power in the East." Murray. 1887.

stipend[26] which raised his income to the nominal amount of a million a year of our money.

But the execution of these measures required considerable delay, and some further exercise of that pertinacious vigour which peculiarly distinguished the British in the eighteenth century.

Shujää-ud-daulah fled first to Faizábád in his own territories; but, hearing that Alláhábád had fallen, and that the English were marching on Lucknow, he had recourse to the Páthans of Rohilkand, whose hospitality he afterwards repaid with characteristic ingratitude. Not only did the chiefs of the Rohillas harbour the Nawáb Vazir's family at Bareilly, but they also lent him the aid of 3,000 of their troops. Further supported by the restless Mahrattas of Malhár Ráo Holkar, a chief who always maintained relations with the Musulmans, Shujää returned to the conflict.

1765.—It may be easily imagined that what he failed to do with the aid of Mir Kásim and his own territory, he did not effect with his present friends as an exile; and Kásim having fled, and Sumroo having entered the service of the Játs of Bhartpur, the Vazir consented to negotiate with the English; the latter, under strong pressure from Clive, who had lately returned to India, showing themselves perfectly placable, now that it had become impossible for them to insist upon the terms, so distasteful to an Eastern chief, which required the surrender of his infamous guests. General Carnac, who had resumed the command, gave the Nawáb and his allies a final defeat near Cawnpore, and drove the Mahrattas across the Jamna. The treaty confirming the terms broached after the battle of Buxar was now concluded, and Áudh, together with part of the Doáb, made over to the Nawáb Vazir Shujää-ud-daulah, who, being thus reinstated as a feudatory of the British Diwáns, returned to his own country, leaving Sháh 'Alám at Alláhábád as a British pensioner.

The terms accorded to the Emperor will be seen from the counterpart issued by him, part of which is subjoined:—

> "+ + + Whereas, in consideration of the attachment and services of the high and mighty, the noblest of nobles, the chief of illustrious warriors, our faithful servants and loyal well-wishers, worthy of royal favour, the English Company, we have granted to them the Diwáni of the Soobahs of Bengal, Bahar, and Orissa, from the beginning of the spring harvest of the Bengal year 1171, as a free gift and fief (*Al tumgha*), without the association of any other person, and with an exemption from the payment of the tribute of the Diwán which used to be paid to this court; it is therefore requisite that the said Company engage to be security for the sum of twenty-six lakhs of rupees a year for our revenue (which sum has been imposed upon the Nawáb), and regularly remit the same.

[26] "Yearly offering" is the translation of the Persian words employed.

"Given on the 8th Safar, in the sixth year of our reign."[27]

The Nawáb was to continue Subahdar, the Company was to be his colleague for purposes of civil and fiscal administration, they were to support the Nawáb's (*Nizámat*) expenses, and to pay the tribute (*Nazarána*) in his name.

The Emperor's establishment during the next few years is thus described by a British officer who enjoyed his intimacy:—"He keeps the poor resemblance of a Court at Alláhábád, where a few ruined omrahs, in hopes of better days to their prince, having expended their fortunes in his service, still exist, the ragged pensioners of his poverty, and burden his gratitude with their presence. The districts in the king's possession are valued at thirty lakhs, which is one-half more than they are able to bear.[28] Instead of gaining by this bad policy, that prince, unfortunate in many respects, has the mortification to see his poor subjects oppressed by those who farm the revenue, while he himself is obliged to compound with the farmers for half the stipulated sum. This, with the treaty payment from the revenues of Bengal, is all Sháh Álum possesses to support the dignity of the Imperial house of Timor." [Dow. ii. 356, A.D. 1767.]

The following further particulars respecting Sháh 'Alám's Court at this period are furnished by Gholám Hossain,[29] and should be noted here as relating to personages of some of whom we shall hear more anon.

Mirza Najaf Khán, the Imperial General, was a Persian noble of high, even of royal, extraction, and destined to play a conspicuous part in the events related in a large portion of the remainder of this history. It will suffice, for the present, to state that, having been a close follower of Mohammad Kuli, he joined the British after that Chief's murder (Vide Sup., p. 40) and was by them recommended to the Emperor for employment. He received a stipend of one lakh a year, and was nominated Governor of Kora, where he occupied himself in the suppression of banditti, and in the establishment of the Imperial authority. Under the modest state of steward of the household, Manir-ud-daulah was the Emperor's most trusted councillor and medium of communication with the English. Rájá Rám Náth, whom we saw accompanying the prince in his escape from Dehli, continued about him; but the chief favourite was an illiterate ruffian called by the title Hissám-ud-daulah, who stooped to any baseness whereby he could please the self-indulgent monarch by pandering to his lowest pursuits. The duties of the office of Vazir were delegated by Shujäá to his son Säädat Ali, who afterwards succeeded him as Nawáb of Áudh.

[27] My purpose being to give the narrative from the native point of view, I have not thought it needful to reproduce the British counterpart of this covenant. The date is August 12th, 1765, and the text will be found in Aitchison's "Treaties and Sunnuds." It will be observed that the Persian instrument is in the form and style of a grant from a Sovereign.

[28] This is, perhaps, as much as the same tracts pay at the present time, with the vast extent of cultivation, and the enormous fall that must have taken place since those days in the value of money. Thirty lakhs in those days would, perhaps, be less easily paid than a hundred now: but a close comparison cannot be instituted, because neither have we the means of exactly knowing what were the limits of the assigned districts, nor what were the prices current at the time. I believe, however, that money in Hindustan during the last century was worth at least ten times what it is now worth in England.

[29] *Vide* Appendix A, p. 156.

Fallen as the Emperor truly was, and sincerely as we may sympathize with his desire to raise the fortunes of his life, it might have been well for him to have remained content with the humble but guaranteed position of a protected Titular, rather than listen to the interested advice of those who ministered, for their own purposes, to his natural discontent.

In this chapter I have been partly referring to Mill. Not only is that indefatigable historian on his strongest ground when describing battles and negotiations of the British from civil and military despatches recorded at the India House, but in treating of the movements of the native powers he has had access to a translation of the very best native work upon the subject—the *Siar-ul-mutákharin*—which was written by Ghulam Hossain Khán, a Musalman gentleman of Patna, himself an eye-witness of many of the scenes described.[30] His account of the capture of Law, for example, given at length in a foot-note to Mill's short account of the action of Gáya after which the affair occurred, is full of truthfulness and local colour.

Since, however, the events were already amply detailed, and the best authorities exhausted in a standard work accessible to most English readers; and since, moreover, they did not occur in Hindustan, and only indirectly pertained to the history of that country, I have not thought it necessary to relate them more minutely than was required to elucidate the circumstances which led to the Emperor Sháh Alám becoming, for the first time, a pensioner on British bounty, or a dependant on British policy.

Those who require a complete account of the military part of the affair will find it admirably given in Broome's *Bengal Army*, a work of which it is to be regretted that the first volume alone has hitherto been made public. Of the value of this book it would be difficult to speak too highly. Coming from the pen of an accomplished professional man, it sets forth, in a manner no civilian could hope to rival, the early exploits of that army of which the author was a member. It may be well to note, in concluding this chapter, what appears to have been at this time the legal relation of the British settlers in Bengal towards the Government of the Empire. In 1678 the Company's Agents had obtained a patent conferring upon them the power of trading in Bengal. In 1696 they purchased from the Nawáb the land surrounding their factory, and proceeded to protect it by rude fortifications. A number of natives soon began to settle here under the protection of the British; and when the Nawáb, on this account, was desirous of sending a judicial officer to reside among them, the factors staved off the measure by means of a donation in money. The grant of land and permission of a formal kind for the fortifications followed in 1716 on Mr. Hamilton's cure of the Emperor Farokhsiar. During all this period tribute continued to be paid (nominally at least) to the Emperor; but in 1759, by espousing, as stated in the beginning of this chapter, the cause of Mir Jáfár, the British committed acts of open rebellion against the Sovereign. By the treaty of Benares, however, they returned to their nominal allegiance, and became once more subjects, tenants and even subordinate officials of the Great Moghul (*Vide* Judgment of Lord Brougham in the case of the *Mayor of Lyons* v. *East India Company*). Elphinstone (*Rise of Brit. Power*, 438*ff*) finds this "treaty difficult to explain." But the

[30] *Vide* Appendix A.

fact is that all the contemporaneous powers concerned looked upon the Empire as the legitimate source of authority; and not only then but for many years after. The British had no legal status until they received the Emperor's grant; and to think of the arrangement as "a treaty" may be a source of misapprehension.

CHAPTER II.

A.D. 1765-71.

Najib-ud-daulah and Jawan Bakht—The Játs—Bhartpur State—Suraj Mal—Najib attacks Játs—Negotiations—Death of Suraj Mal—Játs attack Jaipur—Return of the Mahrattas—They attack Bhartpur—Rohillas yield—Death of Najib—State of Rohilkand—Zábitá Khán—Mahrattas invite Emperor to return to Dehli.

At the conclusion of Part I. we saw that the Abdáli ruler of Kábul had returned to his own land, soon after the battle of Pánipat, in 1761, having recognized the legitimate claims of the exiled heir to the throne (1764), and placed that prince's eldest son, Mirza Jawan Bakht, in the nominal charge of affairs, under the protection of Najib-ud-daulah, the Rohilla (Indian Affghan). A better choice could not have been made in either case. The young regent was prudent and virtuous, as was usual with the men of his august house during their earlier years, and the premier noble[31] was a man of rare intelligence and integrity. Being on good terms with his old patrons, Dundi Khán Rohilla, and the Nawáb of Áudh, Shujäá-ud-daulah, and maintaining a constant understanding with Malhár Ráo Holkar, whom we have seen deserting the cause of his countrymen, and thus exempted from their general ruin at Pánipat, Najib-ud-daulah swayed the affairs of the dwindled empire with deserved credit and success. The Mahratta collectors were expelled from the districts of the Doáb, while Agra admitted a Ját garrison; nor did the discomfited freebooters of the southern confederacy make any farther appearance in Hindustan for eight years, if we except the share borne by Malhár Ráo, acting on his own account in the disastrous campaign against the British in 1765.[32]

The area on which these exertions were made was at first but small, and the lands directly swayed by Najib-ud-daulah were bounded, within 100 miles south of the capital, by the possessions of the Játs, who, however, were at the time friendly.

Of the rise of this singular people few authentic records appear to exist. It is, however, probable that they represent a later wave of that race, whether true Sudras, or a later wave of immigrants from Central Asia, which is found farther south as Mahratta; and perhaps they had, in remote times, a Scythian origin like the earlier and nobler Rájputs. They affect Rájput ways, although the Rájputs would disdain their kinship; and they give to their chiefs the Rájput title of "Thákur," a

[31] So I translate the title *Amir-ul-Omra.*

[32] *Vide* last Chapter.

name common to the Deity and to great earthly lords, and now often used to still lower persons. So much has this practice indeed extended, that some tribes use the term generically, and speak of themselves as of the "Thákur" race. These, however, are chiefly pure Rájputs. It is stated, by an excellent authority, that even now the Játs "can scarcely be called pure Hindus, for they have many observances, both domestic and religious, not consonant with Hindu precepts. There is a disposition also to reject the fables of the Puranic Mythology, and to acknowledge the unity of the Godhead." (Elliot's Glossary, *in voce "Jat."*) Wherever they are found, they are stout yeomen; able to cultivate their fields, or to protect them, and with strong administrative habits of a somewhat republican cast. Within half a century, they have four times tried conclusions with the might of Britain. The Játs of Bhartpur fought Lord Lake with success, and Lord Combermere with credit; and their "Sikh" brethren in the Panjáb shook the whole fabric of British India on the Satlaj, in 1845, and three years later on the field of Chilliánwála. The Sikh kingdom has been broken up, but the Ját principality of Bhartpur still exists, though with contracted limits, and in a state of complete dependence on the British Government. There is also a thriving little principality—that of Dholpur—between Agra and Gwalior, under a descendant of the Ját Rána of Gohad, so often met with in the history of the times we are now reviewing (*v. inf.*, pp. 72-73.) It is interesting to note further, that some ethnologists have regarded this fine people as of kin to the ancient Getæ, and to the Goths of Europe, by whom not only Jutland, but parts of the south-east of England and Spain were overrun, and to some extent peopled. It is, therefore, possible that the yeomen of Kent and Hampshire have blood relations in the natives of Bhartpur and the Panjáb.

The area of the Bhartpur State is at present 2,000 square miles, and consists of a basin some 700 feet above sea level, crossed by a belt of red sandstone rocks. It is hot and dry; but in the skilful hands that till it, not unfertile; and the population has been estimated at near three-quarters of a million.

At the time at which our history has arrived, the territory swayed by the chiefs of the Játs was much more extensive, and had undergone the fate of many another military republic, by falling into the hands of the most prudent and daring of a number of competent leaders. It has already been shown (in Part I.) how Suraj Mal, as Rájá of the Bhartpur Játs, joined the Mahrattas in their resistance to the great Musalman combination of 1760. Had his prudent counsels been followed, it is possible that this resistance would have been more successful, and the whole history of Hindustan far otherwise than what it has since been. But the haughty leader of the Hindus, Sheodásheo Rao Bhao, regarded Suraj Mal as a petty landed chief not accustomed to affairs on a grand scale, and so went headlong on his fate.[33]

Escaping, like his friend Holkar, from the disaster of Pánipat—though in a less discreditable way, for he did not profess to take the field and then fly in the midst of battle, as the other did—Suraj Mal took an early opportunity of displacing the Mahratta Governor of the important fort of Agra, and at the same time, occupied some strong places in the Mewát country. The sagacious speculator, about the same

[33] *Vide* Sup., p. 28.

time, dropped the falling cause of Gházi-ud-din, whose method of statesmanship was too vigorous for his taste, and who, as has been above shown, retired soon after from a situation which he had aided to render impracticable.[34] But a criminal of greater promise, about the same time, joined Suraj Mal. This was none other than the notorious Sumroo, who had wisely left his late protector the Nawáb of Áudh, at the head of a battalion of Sepoys, a detail of artillery, and some three hundred European ruffians of all countries.

Thus supported, the bucolic sagacity of the Ját Rájá began for the first time to fail him, and he made demands which seemed to threaten the small remains of the Moghul Empire. Najib-ud-daulah took his measures with characteristic promptitude and prudence. Summoning the neighbouring Musalman chiefs to the aid of Islám and of the empire, he took the field at the head of a small but well-disciplined Moghul army, and soon found the opportunity to strike a decisive blow.

In this campaign the premier was so fortunate as to obtain solid assistance from the Biloch chiefs of Farokhnagar and Bahadurgarh, who were in those days powerful upon both banks of the Jamna up to as far north as Saháránpur on the eastern, and Hánsi on the western side. The actual commencement of hostilities between Suraj Mal and the Moghuls arose from a demand made by the former for the Faujdárship (military prefecture) of the small district of Farokhnagar. Unwilling to break abruptly with the Ját chief, Najib had sent an envoy to him, in the first instance, pointing out that the office he solicited involved a transfer of the territory, and referring him to the Biloch occupant for his consent. The account of the negotiation is so characteristic of the man and the time, that I have thought it worth preserving. The Moghul envoy introduced himself—in conformity with Eastern custom—by means of a gift, which, in this instance, consisted of a handsome piece of flowered chintz, with which the rural potentate was so pleased that he ordered its immediate conversion into a suit of clothes. Since this was the only subject on which the Ját chief would for the present converse, the Moghul proposed to take his leave, trusting that he might reintroduce the subject of the negotiations at a more favourable moment. "Do nothing rashly, Thákur Sáhib," said the departing envoy; "I will see you again to-morrow." "See me no more," replied the inflated boor, "if these negotiations are all that you have to talk of." The disgusted envoy took him at his word, and returned to Najib with a report of the interview. "Is it so?" said the premier. "Then we must fight the unbeliever; and if it be the pleasure of the Most High God, we will assuredly smite him."

But before the main body of the Moghuls had got clear of the capital, Suraj Mal had arrived near Sháhdara on the Hindan, within six miles of Dehli; and, had he retained the caution of his earlier years, he might have at once shut up the Imperialists in their walled city. But the place being an old hunting-ground of the Emperor's the Thákur's motive in coming had been chiefly the bravado of saying that he had hunted in a royal park, and he was therefore only attended by his personal staff. While he was reconnoitring in this reckless fashion, he was suddenly recognised by a flying squadron of Moghul horse, who surprised the Játs, and

[34] *Vide* Sup., pp. 25-26.

killed the whole party, bringing the body of the chief to Najib. The minister could not at first believe in this unhoped-for success, nor was he convinced until the envoy who had recently returned from the Ját camp identified the body by means of his own piece of chintz, which formed its raiment. Meanwhile the Ját army was marching up in fancied security from Sikandrabad, under Jowáhir Singh, the son of their chief, when they were suddenly charged by the Moghul advanced guard, with the head[35] of Suraj Mal borne on a horseman's lance as their standard.[36] In the panic which ensued upon this ghastly spectacle, the Játs were thoroughly routed and driven back into their own country. This event occurred towards the end of the year.

Foiled in their unaided attempt, they next made a still more signal mistake in allying themselves with Malhár Ráo Holkar, who, as we have seen, was secretly allied to the Musalmans. At first they were very successful, and besieged the premier for three months in Dehli; but Holkar suddenly deserted them, as was only to have been expected had they known what we know now; and they were fain to make the best terms that they could, and return to their own country, with more respectful views towards the empire and its protector.

But the young Thákur's thirst of conquest was by no means appeased, and he proceeded in 1765 to attack Mádhu Sing, the Rájput ruler of Jaipur, son of the Kachwáha Rájá Jai Singh,[37] who had lately founded a fine city there in lieu of the ancestral site, Amber. Descended from Kusha, the eldest son of the Hindu demigod Rámá, this tribe appears to have been once extensive and powerful, traces of them being still found in regions as far distant from each other as Gwalior and the Northern Doáb. (*Vide* Elliot, *in voc.*)

In this attempt Jowáhir appears to have been but feebly sustained by Sumroo, who immediately deserted to the victors,[38] after his employer had been routed at the famous Lake of Pokar, near Ájmir. Jowáhir retreated first upon Alwar, thence he returned to Bhartpur, and soon after took up his abode at Agra, where he not long afterwards was murdered, it is said at the instigation of the Jaipur Rájá. A period of very great confusion ensued in the Ját State; nor was it till two more of the sons of Suraj Mal had perished—one certainly by violence—that the supremacy of the remaining son, Ranjit Singh, was secured. In his time the Ját power was at its height; he swayed a country thick with strongholds, from Alwar on the N.W. to Agra on the S.W., with a revenue of two millions sterling, and an army of 60,000 men.[39]

Meantime the Mahrattas, sickened by their late encounter with Carnac (p. 43), and occupied with their own domestic disputes in the Deccan, paid little or

[35] Some accounts say the hand and arm.

[36] It is curious that a similar effect was produced upon a party of Ját insurgents by a British officer in 1857.—*Vide* descriptions of Sáh Mal's rising in the Meerut District, by Mr. Dunlop, C.B., "Services of the Khakee Resala," &c. London: R. Bentley.

[37] Jai Singh was an eminent astronomer, and constructed the celebrated "Jantar-Mantar" Observatory for the Emperor Mohammad Shah about A.D. 1730.—*Vide* Keene's "Handbook for Dehli."

[38] *Vide* Skinner's "Memoirs," i. 283.

[39] Dow, vol. ii. Dow wrote in 1767, and described the then state of Hindustan.

no attention to the affairs of Hindustan; and the overtures made to them by the Emperor in 1766, from Alláhábád, were for the time disregarded, though it is probable that they caused no little uneasiness in the British Presidency, where it was not desired that the Emperor should be restored by such agency.

At this period Najib, as minister in charge of the metropolis and its immediate dependencies, though skilfully contending against many obstacles, yet had not succeeded in consolidating the empire so much as to render restoration a very desirable object to an Emperor living in ease and security. Scarcely had the premier been freed from the menace of the Eastern Játs by his own prowess and by their subsequent troubles, than their kindred of the Panjáb began to threaten Dehli from the west. Fortunately for the minister, his old patron, the Abdáli, was able to come to his assistance; and in April, 1767, having defeated the Sikhs in several actions, Ahmad once more appeared in the neighbourhood of Pánipat, at the head of 50,000 Afghán horse.

He seems to have been well satisfied with the result of the arrangements that he had made after crushing the Mahrattas in the same place six years before; only that he wrote a sharp reprimand to Shujäá-ud-daulah for his conduct towards the Emperor. But this, however well deserved, would not produce much effect on that graceless politician, when once the Afghán had returned to his own country. This he soon after did, and appeared no more on the troubled scene of Hindustan.[40]

Profiting by the disappearance of their enemy, the Mahrattas, having arranged their intestine disputes, crossed the Chambal (a river flowing eastward into the Jamna from the Ájmir plateau), and fell upon the Jaipur country towards the end of 1768. Hence they passed into Bhartpur, where they exacted tribute, and whence they threatened Dehli in 1769. Among their leaders were two of whom much will be seen hereafter. One was Mádhoji Sindhia—"Patel"[41]—the other was Takuji Holkar. The first of these was the natural son of Ránoji Sindhia, and inherited, with his father's power, the animosity which that chief had always felt against Najib and the Rohillas. The other was a leader in the army of Malhár Ráo Holkar (who had lately died), and, like his master, was friendly to the Páthans. Thus, with the hereditary rivalry of their respective clans, these foremost men of the Mahratta army combined a traditional difference of policy, which was destined to paralyze the Mahratta proceedings, not only in this, but in many subsequent campaigns.

1770.—Aided by Holkar, the Dehli Government entered into an accommodation with the invaders, in which the Játs were sacrificed, and the Rohillas were shortly after induced by Najib-ud-daulah to enter into negotiations. These led to the surrender to the Mahrattas of the Central Doáb, between the provinces held by the Emperor to the eastward, and the more immediate territories administered in his name from Dehli. These latter tracts were spared in pursuance of the negotiations with the Emperor which were still pending.

[40] Dow, writing at this time, thought he meant to assume the empire.

[41] *Patel* is described by Captain Grant-Duff to mean the head man of a Mahratta village. There is nothing like this office in England, but perhaps the old Saxon "Headborough," or the mediæval "Beadle," gives the nearest notion of this humble corregidor. In Sindhia's case the affectation of the rural dignity was a stroke of policy, though not a very deep one.

Soon after these transactions the prudent and virtuous minister died, and was succeeded in his post by his son, Zábitá Khán. It is not necessary to enlarge upon the upright and faithful character of Najib-ud-daulah, which has been sufficiently obvious in the course of our narrative, as have also his skill and courage. It would have been well for the empire had his posterity inherited the former qualities. Had Zábitá, for instance, followed in his father's steps, and had the Emperor at the same time been a man of more decision, it was perhaps even then possible for a restoration to have taken place, in which, backed by the power of Rohilkand, and on friendly terms with the British, the Court of Dehli might have played off Holkar against Sindhia, and shaken off all the irksome consequences of a Mahratta Protectorate.

The preceding record shows how superior Najib-ud-daulah's character and genius were to those of the native Hindustáni nobles. It may be interesting to see how he impressed a European contemporary, who had excellent opportunities of judging:—

> "He is the only example in Hindustan of, at once, a great and a good character. He raised himself from the command of fifty horse to his present grandeur entirely by his superior valour, integrity, and strength of mind. Experience and abilities have supplied the want of letters and education, and the native nobleness and goodness of his heart have amply made amends for the defect of his birth and family. He is now about sixty years of age, borne down by fatigue and sickness."—(Mr. Verelst, to the Court of Directors, March 28th, 1768, ap. Mill.)

Since this prominent mention has been made of the Rohillas, and since they are now for a short time to play a yet more conspicuous part in the fortunes of the falling empire, it will be well to give a brief description of their situation at the time.

It has been seen how Ali Mohammad rose in the reign of Mohammad Sháh, and had been removed from Rohilkand by the aid of Safdar Jang, the Viceroy of Áudh. On the latter falling into disgrace, Ali Mohammad returned to his native province about A.D. 1746.[42] In the next two or three years he continued successfully to administer the affairs of the fair and fertile tract, but, unfortunately for his family, died before his heirs were capable of acting for themselves. Two relations of the deceased chief acted as regents—Dundi Khán, the early patron of Najib, and Rahmat Khán, known in India by the title of Háfiz, or "Protector." Safdar Jang continued to pursue them with relentless purpose; and although the important aid of Ahmad, their foreign fellow-clansman, and the necessity of combining against the Mahrattas, prevented the Áudh Viceroy's hostility from taking any very active form, yet there can be no doubt but that he bequeathed it to his successor, Shujäá, along with many other unscrupulous designs. The Rohilla Páthans, for their part, were as a race determined fighters, but generally false, fickle, and dissolute.

In 1753 the elder son of Ali Mohammad had made an attempt to remove the

[42] *Vide* Part I. chap. ii.

Protector and his colleague from their post. It was not successful, and its only result was to sow dissensions among the Rohillas, which caused their final ruin. In 1761, however, they bore a part in the temporary overthrow of the Mahrattas at Pánipat; and during the next seven years the Rohilla power had passed the frontier of the Ganges, and overflowed the Central Doáb; while the Najibábád family (who had a less close connection with local politics, but were powerful kinsmen and allies) had possession of the Upper Doáb, up to the Siwálik Hills, above Saháránpur. Nevertheless, this seeming good fortune was neither permanent nor real.

In 1769, as we have just seen, Najib, though well disposed, was unable to prevent the Central Doáb from passing under the Mahratta sway, and he died soon after its occupation occurred. Dundi Khán also passed away about the same time; and the Protector Rahmat was left alone in the decline of his ever-darkening days, to maintain, as best he might, an usurped authority menaced by a multitude of foes.

Zábitá Khán, the son and successor of the late minister, and himself an Afghán or Páthan by race, did nevertheless for a time contribute to the resources of the Protector, his co-religionist and *quasi* countryman.

He may, therefore, be reckoned amongst the Rohillas at this period; and, as far as extent of territory went, he might have been an ally of some importance. But territory in imbecile hands and with foes like the Mahrattas was anything but a source of strength. While these indefatigable freebooters spread themselves over the whole Upper and Central Doáb, and occupied all Rohilkand—excepting the small territory of Farakhábád, to the south of the latter and north of the former—Zábitá Khán, instead of endeavouring to prepare for the storm, occupied himself in irritating the Emperor, by withholding the tribute due at Alláhábád, and by violating the sanctity of the Imperial zenana at Dehli by intrigues with the Begams.

Thus passed the winter of 1770-71, at the end of which the Mahrattas swarmed into the Doáb, and occupied the metropolis; only respecting the palace, where the Prince Regent and the Imperial family continued to reside. Zábitá, having organized no plan, could offer no resistance, and escaped towards his northward possessions.

By the connivance of his hereditary ally, Takuji Holkar (as Grant Duff supposes), he left the field open for the Deccani marauders to treat directly with Sháh Alám for his restoration to the throne of his father.

Note.—The authority chiefly followed in the portion of this chapter that relates to Rohilla affairs, has been Hamilton's "History of the Rohillas," a valuable collection of contemporaneous memoirs, although not always quite impartial. Captain Grant Duff's research and fairness are beyond all praise, wherever transactions of the Mahrattas are concerned. The sketch of Ját politics is derived from the *Siar-ul-Mutákharin* and the *Tárikh-i-Mozafari*; but it is as well to state, once for all, that the native chroniclers seldom present anything like complete materials for history. A credulous and uncritical record of gossip combined with a very scanty analysis of character and motive, characterizes their works, which are rather a set of highly-coloured pictures without proportion or perspective, than those orderly annals from which history elsewhere has chiefly been compiled.

CHAPTER III.

A.D. 1771-76.

Agency of Restoration—Mádhoji Sindhia—Zábitá attacked—Mirza Najaf Khán—Flight of Zábitá—Treaty with Rohillas—Zábitá regains office—Mahrattas attack Dehli—Desperation of Mirza Najaf—Mahrattas attack Rohilkand—Opposed by British—Advance of Áudh Troops—Re-employment of Mirza—Abdul Ahid Khán—Suspicious conduct of Háfiz Rahmat and Rohillas—Tribute withheld by Háfiz Rahmat—Battle of Kattra—Death of Shujäá-ud-daulah—Campaign against Játs—Najaf Kuli Khán—Successes of the Imperial Army—Zábitá and Sikhs—Death of Mir Kásim.

It would be interesting to know the exact terms upon which the Mahrattas engaged to restore the Emperor to his throne in the palace of Shahjahán. But, since they have even escaped the research of Captain Grant Duff, who had access to the archives of Punah, it is hopeless for any one else to think of recovering them. The emissary employed appears to have been the person of indifferent character who, like the Brounker and Chiffinch of the English restoration of 1660, had been usually employed in less dignified agencies. Unacquainted with this man's name, we must be content to take note of him by his title of Hissám, or Háshim Ud Daula.[43] The Mahrattas were, amongst other rewards, to receive a present fee of ten lakhs of rupees (nominally expressible at £100,000 sterling, but in those days representing as much, perhaps, as ten times that amount of our present money), nor would they stir in the matter until they received the sum in hard cash. It is also probable that the cession of the provinces of Alláhábád and Korah formed part of the recompense they hoped to receive hereafter.

Though the Emperor, if he guaranteed this latter gift, was parting from a substance in order to obtain a shadow, yet the very receipt of that substance by the others depended upon circumstances over which they had (as the phrase is) no control. Early in the year 1771 the Emperor had sent to the authorities in Calcutta, to consult them on his proposed movements; and they had strongly expressed their disapprobation. But Shujäá-ud-daulah, for reasons of his own, earnestly, though secretly, encouraged the enterprise. The Emperor set out in the month of May, at the head of a small but well-appointed army, amongst whom was a body of sepoys drilled after the European fashion, and commanded by a Frenchman named Médoc, an illiterate man, but a good soldier. The command-in-chief

[43] *Vide* Sup., p. 44.

was held by Mirza Najaf Khán. A British detachment, under Major-General Sir Robert Barker, attended him to the Korah frontier,[44] where the General repeated, for the last time, the unwelcome dissuasions of his Government. The Emperor unheedingly moved on, as a ship drives on towards a lee shore; and the British power closed behind his wake, so that no trace of him or his Government ever reappeared in the provinces that he had so inconsiderately left.

From this date two great parties in the Empire are clearly defined; the Musalmans, anxious to retain (and quarrel over) the leavings of the great Afghán leader, Ahmad Abdáli; and the Mahrattas, anxious to revenge and repair the losses of Pánipat. The Áudh Viceroy acts henceforth for his own hand—ready to benefit by the weakness of whichever party may be worsted; and the British, with more both of vigour and of moderation, follow a like course of conduct.

Arrived at Farrukhábád, the Imperial adventurer confirmed the succession of that petty state to the Bangash chief, whose father was lately dead, and received at the investiture a fine (*peshkash*) of five lakhs of rupees.[45] He then cantoned his army in the neighbourhood, and awaited the cessation of the periodical rains. The Mahratta army, some 30,000 strong, was still encamped at Dehli, but Mádhoji Sindhia, the Patel,[46] waited upon the Emperor in his cantonments, and there concluded whatever was wanting of the negotiations. The Emperor then proceeded, and entered his capital on Christmas Day.

At that time of year Dehli enjoys a climate of great loveliness; and it may be supposed that the unhappy citizens, for their parts, would put on their most cheerful looks and the best remnants of their often plundered finery, to greet the return of their lawful monarch. The spirit of loyalty to persons and to families is very strong in the East, and we can imagine that, as the long procession marched from Sháhdara and crossed the shrunk and sandy Jamna, Sháh Alám, from the back of his chosen elephant, looked down upon a scene of hope and gaiety enough to make him for the moment forget both the cares of the past and the anxieties of the future, and feel himself at last every inch a king.

1772.—Whatever may have been his mood, his new allies did not leave him to enjoy it long. Within three weeks of his return to the palace of his forefathers, he was induced to take the field; and he set out northward at the head of 90,000 men, the greater number of whom were Mahratta horsemen. It has already been shown that Zábitá Khán had escaped to his own estates a year before. The Báwani Mahál (comprising fifty-two pergunnahs, now included in the districts of Saháránpur and Muzaffarnaggar) contained three strongholds: Pathargarh on the left, Sukhartál on the right of the Ganges, and Ghausgarh, near Muzaffarnagar. The first two had been built by the late minister, Najib-ud-daulah, to protect the ford which led to his fief in the north-western corner of Rohilkand, for the Ganges is almost always fordable here, except in the high floods. The last was the work of Zábitá Khán himself, and its site is still marked by a mosque of large size and fine proportions.

[44] Somewhere about Cawnpore.

[45] For an exhaustive account of this family, see *Journal of the Asiatic Society of Bengal*, No. 222-6 (contributed by Mr. W. Irvine, B.C.S.).

[46] *Vide sup.*, p. 50*n*.

Upon these points the first attacks of the Imperialists were directed. Ghausgarh was hurriedly evacuated at their approach to be completely plundered; and Zábitá was soon driven to take refuge in his eastern fort of Pathargarh, nearest to any aid that the Rohilkand Páthans might be able and willing to afford. The open country, and minor strongholds and towns were left to the mercy of the invaders.

Although this campaign was dictated by a Mahratta policy, yet the small Moghul nucleus bore a certain part, being ably commanded by the Persian, Mirza Najaf Khán, who has been already mentioned as Governor of Korah, and of whom we shall hear frequently during the account of the next ten years.

This nobleman, who bore the title "Mirza" in token of belonging to the late royal family of Persia, evinced the same superiority over the natives of India which usually characterized the original immigrants. He had married his sister to a brother of the former Viceroy, Safdar Jang, and attached himself to the late unfortunate Governor of Alláhábád, Mohammad Kuli Khán, a son of his brother-in-law (though whether his own nephew or by another mother does not appear). On the murder of the Governor by his unscrupulous cousin Shujäá, Najaf Khán succeeded to his place in the favour of the Emperor, and commanded, as we have seen, the force which accompanied the Emperor on his restoration.[47]

To the combined armies Zábitá opposed a spirited resistance; but the aid of the Rohilla Afgháns (or Páthans, as they are called in India) was delayed by the menacing attitude of Shujäá; and the Mahratta and Moghul armies having crossed the Ganges by a mixture of boldness and stratagem, Zábitá Khán fled to the Ját country, leaving his family and the greater part of the treasures amassed by his father to fall into the hands of the enemy.

This occasion is especially memorable, because among the children of Zábitá was his eldest son, a beautiful youth, named Gholám Kádir Khán, whom the Emperor is said, by tradition, to have transmuted into a *haram* page, and who lived to exact a fearful vengeance for any ill-treatment that he may have received.

At the approach of the monsoon the Emperor, dissatisfied at not receiving the whole of the share of the spoils promised him by his covetous allies, returned to the metropolis. The Mahrattas (who even during his presence in the camp had paid him but scanty respect) now threw off the last shreds of disguise, and appropriated all the profits of the campaign. They at the same time restored to Zábitá Khán—whom they hoped hereafter to make into a serviceable tool—the members of his family taken at Pathargarh; receiving in exchange a ransom of a lakh and a half of rupees, which was advanced to them on Zábitá's account, by the Viceroy Shujäá-ud-daulah.

The rainy season of 1772 was spent by the Emperor at Dehli; by the Mahrattas at Agra and in the neighbourhood. They would willingly have proceeded to complete the reduction of all Rohilkand, but that Mirza Najaf flatly refused to join or sanction such a course; seeing clearly that it must involve a collision with Shujäá-ud-daulah, who was supported by the British alliance, and of whose traditional policy the annexation of the province formed an essential part. The Rohillas, on

[47] *Vide sup.*, p. 39 and 53.

their part, occupied themselves in negotiations with the Áudh Viceroy, in the hope of reconstructing the Mohamadan League, which had once been so successful.

The result of which was a treaty, drawn up under the good offices of the British general, Sir R. Barker, by which the protector, Háfiz Rahmat Khán, bound himself to join Shujää in any steps he might take for the assistance of Zábitá Khán, and pay him forty lakhs of rupees, in four annual instalments upon condition of the Mahrattas being expelled from Rohilkand. This treaty, which proved the ruin of the Rohillas, was executed on the 11th of July, 1772.[48]

The next step in the destruction of these brave but impolitic Páthans was the outbreak of several violent quarrels, in which brother fought against brother and father against son. Zábitá Khán, meanwhile, being secretly urged by the faithless Shujää, had made terms for himself with the Mahrattas, who engaged to procure not only his pardon but his investiture with the office of Premier Noble, formerly held by his father, Najib-ud-daulah. Their barefaced boldness in restoring Zábitá Khán's family and appropriating the ransom paid to the Emperor's account for them has been already mentioned.

With the view of paving the way for the removal from power of Mirza Najaf, they next addressed themselves to creating disturbances in the country around Dehli. For they knew that this would at once alarm the Emperor and involve the Mirza in difficulty and danger; and they foresaw in the result of such intrigues an easy method of ruining one whom they justly regarded as an obstacle to the recall to office of their *protégé* Zábitá. They accordingly instigated Ranjit Singh, the ruler of the Bhartpur Játs, to prefer a claim to the fief of Balamgarh, held by a petty chieftain of his own nation. This chief solicited aid from the Emperor against his powerful rival; and in the end of the year 1772 Mirza Najaf Khán, who henceforth figures in the native histories by his newly-acquired title of Zulfikár-ud-daulah, sent a force under a Biloch leader to the aid of the Balamgarh man. The Mahrattas, on the other hand, sent a force from Agra, which joining with the Bhartpur Játs, forced the Imperialists to retreat towards the capital; but the Patel, disapproving of the Rohilla element contributed to this confederacy by the presence of Zábitá Khán, retired towards Jaipur, where he occupied himself in plundering the Rájputs. Takuji Holkar and the other Mahratta chiefs, feeling strong enough to dispense with his aid, and anxious, for reasons of their own, to fulfil their promise to Zábitá, advanced towards Dehli, but were met at a place called Baddarpur, ten miles south of the city, by a force under the minister himself. In the action which ensued, the Moghul force which, though well disciplined and well led by Mirza Najaf, seconded by M. Médoc and some efficient native officers, was numerically weak, fell back upon Humáyun's tomb, within four miles of the palace of New Dehli. Here ensued a series of skirmishes, which lasted four days; till the Mirza having had a nephew slain, retreated to the new town by way of Daryaoganj,

[48] It is curious that Professor H. H. Wilson, the continuer, and ordinarily the corrector of Mill, should cite a Persian life of Rahmat Khán to show that this arrangement has been misunderstood, that its real purport was that the forty lakhs were to be given to the Mahrattas to buy them off, but that Shujää was only the surety. If the Viceroy's character and subsequent conduct did not refute this, yet the text of the treaty would do so.—*Vide* Note at end of Chapter.

followed by a strong detachment of the enemy. He still obstinately defended the palace and its environs; but Hissám-ud-daulah (whose backstair influence has been already mentioned) went in person to the Mahratta camp the following day, and informed them, as from his master, that the brave minister would be sacrificed by his weak and ungrateful master. Holkar and his train of black and unkempt pygmies swarmed insolently into the palace, where they dictated their own terms. The Mahrattas, who were anxious to return to the Deccan, were not disposed to make difficulties; their main terms were—the restoration to the office of premier noble of Zábitá Khán, and the cession of those provinces in the Lower Doáb which had been under the direct sway of the Emperor, while he enjoyed British protection.[49] These terms being granted, they picked a quarrel with Mirza Najaf Khán, about a payment which he was alleged to have guaranteed them during the Sukhartál campaign, and obtained an order from the Emperor banishing him the court. These events occurred at the end of December, just a twelvemonth after the unfortunate monarch's restoration.

1773.—Finding Zábitá Khán in office, and the pandar Hisám in high favour, the heroic ex-minister, having still with him a strong and faithful escort of Moghul horse, together with the remains of the trained infantry, and having sent to Sahháránpur for his adopted son, Afrásyáb Khán, who had some squadrons with him for the protection of that district, threw himself into a fortified house outside the Kábul Gate of the city. The forces of the new Minister surrounded him, while the Mahrattas looked on with curiosity, which seems to have been tempered by admiration for his heroism; and the next day he formed one of those desperate resolutions which have so often been known to influence the course of Asiatic politics. Putting on all his armour,[50] and wearing over it a sort of shroud of green, in the fashion used for the grave-clothes of a descendant of the Prophet, Najaf Khán rode out at the head of his personal guards. As the small band approached the Mahratta camp, shouting their religious war-cries of "*Alláh Ho Akbar,*" and "*Ya Hossain,*" they were met by a peaceful deputation of the unbelievers who courteously saluted them, and conducted them to camp in friendly guise.

It can only be supposed that the news of the Peshwa's death, which had recently arrived from Punah, and the unsettled state of the Rohilla quarrel, combined to render the Mahrattas indisposed to push matters to extremity against a man of Najaf Khán's character and influence, and thus gave rise to this extraordinary scene. The result was that the ex-minister's excitement was calmed, and he agreed to Join the Mahrattas in an attack on Rohilkand. One cannot but remark the tortuous policy of these restless rievers. First they move the Emperor upon the Rohillas; then they move the Rohilla, Zábitá Khán, upon the Emperor; and then, having united these enemies, they make use of a fresh instrument to renew the original attack. With this new ally they marched upon Rohilkand by way of Rámghát, below Anupshahar, where the Ganges is fordable during the winter months; and at the same time parties of their troops devastated the Doáb.

[49] *Vide sup.*, p. 44.

[50] The armour of a Moghul noble consisted of a skull-cap and panoply of chain-mail, so exquisitely wrought of pure steel rings that the whole scarcely weighed ten pounds; over this he wore a morion, and four plates of steel, called *Char ayna.*

Meanwhile the British, finding that the Emperor was unable to protect the provinces about Alláhábád, which they had put into his charge, made them over to the Viceroy of Áudh, to whose management they had been attached previous to the negotiations that followed the battle of Buxar, and between whose dominions and those of the British they formed the connecting link. They had been abandoned by the Emperor when he proceeded to Dehli, contrary to the remonstrance of the Bengal Council, and though his own lieutenant had reported, and with perfect accuracy, that he could not regard the order to give them up to the Mahrattas as a free act of his master's. It would, indeed, have been an easy step towards the ruin of the British to have allowed the Mahrattas to take possession of this tract, and so form a permanent lodgement upon the borders of the possessions in Bihár and the Eastern Subahs which the British held by the indefeasible and twofold tenure of conquest, and of an Imperial grant. And it so happened that the necessary transfer could not be carried out without an armed demonstration for the expulsion or coercion of the usurping Mahrattas. The expenses of this expedition were naturally met by the Viceroy. Judged even by modern standards, this cannot but be regarded as a perfectly legitimate act of self-defence. It is, however, thus characterized by Macaulay:[51] "The provinces which had been *torn from the Mogul* were made over to the government of Áudh for about half a million sterling.'' The British having joined their forces to those of the Vazir-Viceroy Shujäá, accordingly marched to meet the invaders. Háfiz Rahmat, whom we have lately seen treating with those powers, now became anxious about the money-payments for which he had engaged, in the usual reckless Oriental way, and entered into negotiations with the Mahrattas.[52] In this scheme, the sudden arrival of the British and Áudh armies surprised him, and he was forced to abandon it for the present and join the allies in an advance against the Mahrattas, who precipitately retired on Etáwa, and thence to their own country in May, 1773.

It has been already seen that Mirza Najaf Khán was a family connection of Shujäá-ud-daulah, and an old friend of the British general; and, on the retreat of his Mahratta supporters, he came over to the allied camp, where he met the reception due to his merits.

The allied armies moved on to Anupshahar, accompanied by the ex-minister, who was attended by his faithful Moghuls. This town, which had, as we have seen, been a cantonment of Ahmad the Abdáli, was particularly well situated for the advanced post of a power like the British, seeking to hold the balance among the native states of Hindustan. To the north were the fords of Sukhartál, by which the Najibábád Rohillas passed from one part of their dominions to another; to the south was the ford of Rámghát, leading from Aligarh to Bareilly. It remained a British cantonment from this time[53] until some time subsequent to the occupation

[51] "Critical and Historical Essays," Art. "Warren Hastings."

[52] Hamilton's "History of the Rohilla Afgháns." It was never quite conclusively determined whether the Viceroy was to receive this money as payment for the service of expelling the Mahrattas, or whether he was security for the payment of that amount, to be made to them as inducement to retire. But see the extract *inf.*, p. 67.

[53] With one or two short interruptions, such as during the brief ascendancy of Francis's opposition in the Calcutta Council.

of the country in general, in 1806; after which the town of Meerut was found more central, and Anupshahar ceased to be a station for troops. It is a thriving commercial entrepôt in our days, though much menaced by the Ganges, on whose right bank it stands. The only memorial of the long-continued presence of a British force is now to be found in two cemeteries, containing numbers of tombs from which the inscriptions have disappeared.

At this station Najaf Khán took leave of his patrons, having received from Shujäá-ud-daulah the portfolio (or, to use the Eastern phrase, the pencase), of Deputy Vazir, and from the British General a warm letter of recommendation to the Emperor. It was especially magnanimous on the part of the Vazir to let bygones be bygones, since they included the murder, by himself, of his new Deputy's kinsman and former patron Mohammad Kuli Khán, the former Governor of Alláhábád; and it was not an impolitic, though probably unintentional, stroke on the part of Sir R. Barker to lend his assistance towards introducing into the direction of the Imperial councils a chief who was as strongly opposed to the Rohillas as to the Mahrattas.

Armed with these credentials, and accompanied by a small but compact and faithful force, the Mirza proceeded to Court to assume his post. The newly-created premier noble, Zábitá Khán, took refuge with the Játs; but Hisám-ud-daulah, who had been for some time in charge of the local revenue (*Diwán-i-Khálsa*) was dismissed, put under arrest, and made to surrender some of his ill-gotten wealth. An inadequate idea may be formed of the want of supervision which characterized Sháh Alám's reign, by observing that this man, who had not been more than two years in charge of the collections of a small and impoverished district, disgorged, in all, no less than fifteen lakhs of rupees.[54] He was succeeded in his appointment by Abdul Ahid Khán (who bears henceforth the title of Majad-ud-daulah), while Manzur Ali Khán, another nominee of the minister's, became Vazir, or Controller of the Household. Of these two officers it is only necessary here to observe, that after events showed the former—who was a Musalman native of Kashmir—as a character marked by the faithlessness and want of manly spirit for which the people of that country are proverbial in India. The latter was to turn out either a very blundering politician, or a very black-hearted traitor.[55]

Title and lucrative office were now conferred upon the Kashmirian, Abdul Ahid, whose pliant manners soon enabled him to secure a complete influence over his indolent master. Najaf Khán seems to have been equally deceived at the time; but after-events showed the difference between the undeceiving of a worn-out voluptuary, and that of a nature unsuspicious from its own goodness.

Such were the first fruits of Najaf's alliance with the Viceroy of Áudh; the price was to be paid in the bestowal of the Imperial sanction upon the final destruction of the Rohilla Páthans. It has been already seen how this province, which ran up between the personal domains of the crown and the fief of the Viceroy of Áudh,

[54] Probably as much as two years' land-tax on the same district now, although the value of money is, of course, very much fallen since those days. Perhaps it would not be an exaggerated estimate if the sum in the text were taken to represent, in purchasing power, about half a million of our present money (sterling).

[55] *Vide inf.*, pp. 68-69, and Chap. vi. *passim*.

had been seized, first by Ali Mohammad, and latterly by his son's guardian, the Protector Rahmat Khán. But ever since Ali Mohammad's wars with the late Vazir, Safdar Jang, the rulers of Áudh had probably coveted the province, and the retreat of the Mahrattas and their occupation in domestic pursuits in the Deccan afforded just the occasion for which Shujää-ud-daulah was waiting. Much eloquent indignation has been vented by Macaulay and Mill on the subject of the accession to this campaign of the British Governor, Mr. Hastings. As I am not writing a history of British administration, I shall only observe that the Emperor, whose servants the British professed themselves, had conferred the authority usurped by Rahmat Khán upon the Vazir, with whom they had been for some years in alliance. As allies of both parties they were clearly at liberty to throw in their help against the common enemies of both, especially when these chanced to be their own enemies also. The Mahrattas were the foes of all rulers on that side of India; and the Rohillas were either in collusion with the Mahrattas or unable to oppose them. It was essential, if not to the safety of the possessions of the Vazir-Viceroy, at least to British interests in Bengal, that a band of faithless usurpers should not be allowed to hold a country which they could not, or would not, prevent from affording a high road for the Mahrattas at all seasons of the year. That view, perhaps, commended itself to the House of Lords when they finally acquitted Mr. Hastings, after a protracted trial, in which some of the ablest of the Whig orators had been engaged against the accused. It is easy for historians, writing long after the passions, the temptations, the necessities of the moment have ceased to press, to criticize the acts of the past by the "dry light" of pure reason and abstract morality. But the claims of necessity should not be ignored in delivering what is intended to form a sort of judicial award.

It is perhaps a mark of the good sense and justice of the English nation that, when they had considered the matter calmly, they should have come to the conclusion that to condemn Hastings would be to condemn their own existence in India. Such a conclusion would logically require their retirement from the country–a step they did not feel at all called upon to take. This appears the moral of the acquittal. Even Macaulay, who objects to the decision of the Peers acquitting Hastings as inadmissible at the bar of history, nevertheless confesses that it was generally approved by the nation. At all events, this particular affair was dropped out of the charges even before the impeachment began.

But, however important to the existence of the British in India might be the possession of this frontier territory by the strongest ally they could secure, the conduct of the Emperor (or rather of Mirza Najaf, in whose hands he was not quite a free agent) remains the special subject of inquiry in this place. I think, however, that both the minister and his master were quite justified in wishing to transfer the province of Rohilkand from the hands of Rahmat to those of the Vazir. It has been already seen that the Páthan usurpers of that province had always been foes of the Moghul power, since the first rebellion of Ali Mohammad, with the solitary exception of the campaign of 1761, when they joined their Abdáli kinsman at Pánipat. It has also been seen that the fords by which the Ganges could be crossed in the cold weather were in their country, but that they could never hold them; and that, lastly, they were known to have been lately in treaty with the Mahrattas, without reference to the interests of the Empire. Eastern politicians are not usually or especially scrupulous; but, when it is remembered that the Rohillas were feudatories who had neither the will nor the power to be faithful, it must follow that here were substantial considerations of vital importance to the Dehli Government, sufficient to give them a fair inducement to sanction the enterprise of one who was their chief minister and most powerful supporter.

Of Shujäá's own motives there is not so much palliation to offer. He had often received aid from the Rohillas, and was under personal obligations to them, which ought to have obliterated all earlier memories of a hostile character;[56] and, whatever grounds the Emperor may have had for consenting to an attack upon the Páthans, or the British for aiding the same, none such are likely to have seriously actuated the Vazir in his individual character. If he thought the Rohillas were inclined to negotiate with the Mahrattas, he must have seen how those negotiations had been broken off the instant he came to their assistance; and if he wished to command the movements of the Mahrattas, he might first have endeavoured to strengthen the hands of the Imperial Government, and to cordially carry out his share of the treaty of 1772.

It must, however, be added—although the Vazir's character was not such as to render him altogether entitled to such justifications—that the latter of those engagements had been better fulfilled by himself than by the Páthans. For while, on the one hand, he had driven the Mahrattas out of the country, the Protector Rahmat Khán, on his part, had neither collected the wage of that service from the other chiefs, nor paid it himself. Moreover, the Vazir's proceedings were only directed against the usurping Protector and his actual adherents; and he was joined by Zábitá and some minor Rohilla chiefs, while others, among whom were the sons of the late Dundi Khán, held aloof altogether, and Faizula Khán, the son of the first founder of the Rohilla power, Ali Mohammad, and in every way the most respectable of the clan, though he would not desert an old friend in his hour of need, yet strongly disapproved of his proceedings, and urged him to fulfil his compact and pay the Vazir's claim. The bribe by which Zábitá had been detached from the confederacy, was an assignment of the district in the neighbourhood of Meerut, which had cleared itself of Mahratta occupation under the late Vazir's rule.

1774.—In October, 1773, the fort of Etáwa fell, and the last Mahratta forces were driven from the Doáb. The next two or three months were occupied in vain negotiations on the part of the Vazir with the Rohillas; and in more serious combinations with the Imperial Government, and with the British. And in January, 1774, the allied armies moved forward. On the 12th of April the British entered Rohilkand;[57] the Protector, when finally summoned to pay what he owed, having

[56] *Vide* Chap. i. p. 43.

[57] This is the date given by Captain Hamilton, who adds the following singular account of the condition of the Rohillas at the time, from a native Rohilla source:— "A surprising degree of animosity and discord had long since arisen in Rohilkand, and each person was earnestly bent upon the eradication of his neighbour: and, in order to effect that object, ready to enter into league with foreigners and invaders." Meanwhile, we have it

replied by a *levée en masse* of all who would obey his summons. At the same time, the Emperor ordered out a column which he accompanied for a few marches; and issued patents confirming the Vazir Shujää-ud-daulah in his Doáb conquests, as also in the grant already made by the British of Korah and Alláhábád. This latter circumstance removes all ground for calling in question the cession of those provinces by their temporary masters, and shows that the Emperor was conscious of his own inability to hold them, or to grant them to enemies of Áudh and of England.

On the 23rd of the same month (April) the British army completely surprised the camp of the Protector, who was defeated and slain, after a brave but brief resistance at Kattra. Faizula was pardoned and maintained in his own patrimonial fief of Rámpur (still held by his descendants), while the rest of the province was occupied, with but little further trouble, by the Vazir, in strict conformity to an Imperial firmán to that effect.[58]

The army of the Empire, under Mirza Najaf Khán, the Deputy Vazir, had not arrived in time to participate actively in this brief campaign; but the Vazir acknowledged the importance of the moral support that he had received from the Empire by remitting to court a handsome fine, on his investiture with the administration of the conquered territory. He also gave the Mirza some reinforcement, to aid him in his pending operations against the Játs of Bhartpur. Zábitá Khán was at the same time expelled from his lately acquired fief at Meerut, but was again put in charge next year; a proof, were proof required, of the weakness of the Home administration of Majad-ud-daulah, who (it need hardly be said) received a bribe on the occasion.

Anticipating a little, we may notice that the Viceroy of Áudh, at the very climax of his good fortune, met the only enemy whom neither force can subdue nor policy deceive. Shujää-ud-daulah died in January, 1775; and as it was not possible for so conspicuous a public character to pass away without exciting popular notice, the following explanation of the affair was circulated at the time; which, whether a fact or a fiction, deserves to be mentioned as the sort of ending which was considered in his case probable and appropriate. It was believed that, the family of Rahmat Khán having fallen into his hands, Shujää-ud-daulah sent for one of the fallen chief's daughters, and that the young lady, in the course of the interview, avenged the death of her father by stabbing his conqueror with a poisoned knife. "Although," says the author of the *Siar-ul-Mutákharin*, who is the authority for the story, "there may be no foundation of truth in this account, yet it was at the time as universally believed as that God is our Refuge."

The editor of the Calcutta translation of 1789 asserts that he had satisfactory

---

from the same authority that the original (non-Rohilla) population of the country was rack-rented, while life and property were without protection.

[58] Hamilton.—This writer, who professes to follow Rohilla historians, as far as possible, states that there are no records of the people being ill-used, further than that seventeen or eighteen thousand of the soldiery were deported and settled in the neighbouring territories of Zábita Khán. "The Hindoo inhabitants, about 700,000, were in no way effected." So much for the alleged depopulation of Rohilkand.

proof of the truth of this story. The Viceroy died of a cancer in the groin; and the women of his *Zanána*, who were let out on the occasion, and with one of whom he (the translator) was acquainted, had made a song upon the subject. They gave full particulars of the affair, and stated that the young lady—she was only seventeen—had been put to death on the day the Viceroy received the wound. (*S. U. M.*, III. 268.)

The death of the Viceroy-Vazir, however occasioned, was a serious blow to the reduced Empire of Dehli, which was just then beginning to enjoy a gleam of sunshine such as had not visited it since the day when Mir Mannu and the eldest son of Mohammad Sháh defeated the Abdáli, in 1748. Had the career of Shujäá-ud-daulah been prolonged a few years, it is possible that his ambitious energy, supported by British skill and valour, and kept within bounds by Mirza Najaf Khán's loyal and upright character, would have effectually strengthened the Empire against the Mahrattas, and altered the whole subsequent course of Indian history.

But Shujäá's son and successor was a weak voluptuary, who never left his own provinces; and although the Mirza, his deputy in the Vazirship and real *locum tenens*, received for his lifetime the reward of his merits, yet he was unable of himself to give a permanent consolidation to the tottering fabric.

It has been seen that he was meditating a campaign against the Játs, whom Zábitá's recent fall had again thrown into discontent, when summoned to Rohilkand, in 1774. In fact, he had already wrested from them the fort of Agra, and occupied it with a garrison of his own, under a Moghul officer, Mohammad Beg, of Hamadán. Not daunted by this reverse, Ranjit Singh, the then ruler of that bold tribe the Játs, advanced upon the capital, and occupied Sikandrabad with 10,000 horse. The forces left in Dehli consisted of but 5,000 horse and two battalions of sepoys; but they sufficed to expel the intruder. He shortly afterwards, however, returned, reinforced by the regulars and guns under Sumroo; but by this time the Mirza was returned from Rohilkand, and after the rains of 1774, marched against them, aided by a chief from Hariána, named after himself Najaf Kuli Khán, who brought into the field some 10,000 troops. This man, who was a good soldier and a faithful follower of the minister, was a converted Hindu, of the Rathur tribe; a native of the Bikanir country bordering on Rajputána Proper to the south, and to the north on Hariána and other states immediately surrounding the metropolis. Having been in service at Alláhábád, under the father of Mohammad Kuli, the connection and early patron of the Mirza, he became a Mohammadan under the sponsorship of the latter, and ever after continued a member of his household. At the time of which I write, he had been appointed to the charge of districts returning twenty lakhs a year, with the title of Saif-ud-daulah.

The departure of the Mirza for this campaign was extremely agreeable to the Diwán, Majad-ud-daulah, for he never lost an opportunity of prejudicing the Emperor's mind against this powerful rival, in whose recent appointment to the office of Naib Vazir, moreover, he had found a special disappointment. Indeed, Sháh Alám, between these two ministers, was like the hero of mediæval legend between his good and evil angels; only differing in this, that in his case the good influence was also, to a great extent, the most powerful. What the wily Kashmirian might have done in the way of supplanting the Mirza, if the latter had been signally worsted, and he himself had been otherwise fortunate, cannot now be certainly conjectured, for a fresh revolt of Zábitá's summoned the Diwán to the northward, whilst his rival was successfully engaged with the Játs. In this expedition Majad-ud-daulah displayed a great want of spirit and of skill, so that Zábitá became once more extremely formidable. Fortunately at this crisis Dehli was visited by an envoy, soliciting investiture for the new Viceroy of Áudh, Asaf-ud-daulah. Accompanying the embassy was a force of 5,000 good troops, with a train of artillery, the whole under command of the deceased Shujäá's favourite general, Latáfat Khán.[59] This timely reinforcement saved the metropolis, and allowed of a settlement being made with the incorrigible Zábitá, which preserved, to some extent at least, the dignity of the Government (*vide* next chapter).

Meanwhile the Imperialists had found the Játs, under their chieftain, intrenched near Hodal, a town sixty miles from Dehli, on the Mathra road. Dislodged from this, they fell back a few miles, and again took up a position in a fortified village called Kotban, where the Mirza endeavoured to blockade them. After amusing him with skirmishes for about a fortnight, they again fell back on Dig, a stronghold, to become the scene of still more important events a few years later. Dig—the name is perhaps a corruption of some such word as Dirájgarh—is a strong fort, with a beautiful palace and pleasure-grounds adjoining, on the shores of an artificial lake, fed by the drainage of part of the Alwar Highlands.[60] Observing that the sallies of the Játs had ceased, the Mirza left their camp at Dig in his rear, and marched to Barsana, where a pitched battle was fought.

1775.—The van of the Imperialists was commanded by Najaf Kuli. In the centre of the main line was the Mirza himself, with battalions of sepoys and artillery, under officers trained by the English in Bengal, on the two wings. In the rear was the Moghul cavalry. The enemy's regular infantry—5,000 strong, and led by Sumroo—advanced to the attack, covered by clouds of Ját skirmishers, and supported by a heavy cannonade, to which the Mirza's artillery briskly replied, but from which he lost several of his best officers and himself received a wound. A momentary confusion ensued; but the Mirza, fervently invoking the God of Islám, presently charged the Játs at the head of the Moghul horse, who were, it will be remembered, his personal followers. Najaf Kuli, accompanied by the regular infantry, following at the double, the Játs were broken; and the resistance of Sumroo's battalions only sufficed to cover the rout of the rest of the army, and preserve some appearance of order as he too retreated, though in somewhat better order, towards Dig. An immense quantity of plunder fell into the hands of the victors, who soon reduced the open country, and closely invested the beaten army. Such, however, was the store of grain in the Fort of Dig, that the strictest blockade proved fruitless for a twelvemonth; nor was the Fort finally reduced till the end of March, 1776, when the garrison found means—not improbably by connivance—to escape to the neighbouring castle of Kumbhair with portable property on

[59] Francklin's "Sháh Alum," pp. 68, 69.

[60] Here, on the 13th November, 1804, the army of Holkar was defeated by General Fraser; and the Játs having fired on the victors, the fort was stormed in the following month.

elephants. The rest of the Thákur's wealth was seized by the victors—his silver plate, his stately equipages and paraphernalia, and his military chest, containing six lakhs of rupees—which may perhaps be regarded as not very inferior, in relative value, to a quarter of a million sterling of our modern money.

In the midst of these successes, and whilst he was occupied in settling the conquered country, the Mirza received intelligence from Court that Zábitá Khán, emboldened by his easy triumph over the Diwán, Majad-ud-daulah (Abdul Ahid Khán), had taken into his pay a large body of Sikhs, with whom he was about to march upon the metropolis.

The enterprising minister returned at once to Dehli, where he was received with high outward honour. He was, on this occasion, attended by the condottiere Sumroo, who, in his usual fashion, had transferred his battalions to the strongest side soon after the battle of Barsana. Sumroo's original patron, Mir Kásim,[61] died about the same time, in the neighbourhood of Dehli, where he had settled, after years of skulking and misery, in the vain hope of obtaining employment in the Imperial service. The date of his death is given by Broome (*Hist. of Beng. Army*, p. 467) as 6th dune, 1777: it is added that his last shawl was sold to pay for a winding-sheet, and that his family were plundered of the last wreck of their possessions. But the detail of this year's events and their consequences requires a fresh chapter.

Note.—The following is the text of the supplemental treaty of 1772, as given by Captain Hamilton. (The former portion having provided in general terms for an alliance, offensive and defensive.) "The Vuzeer of the Empire shall establish the Rohillas, obliging the Mahrattas to retire, either by peace or war. If at any time they shall enter the country, their expulsion is the business of the Vuzeer. The Rohilla Sirdars, in consequence of the above to agree to pay to the Vuzeer forty lakhs of rupees, in manner following—viz., ten lakhs, in specie, and the remaining thirty lakhs in three years from the beginning of the year 1180 *Fussulee*." Only redundant or unimportant phrases have been omitted: there is not a word of payment to the Mahrattas. The contention that the Vazir of Oudh was only surety for the payment to the Mahrattas is not very pertinent. For the Mahrattas did not quit Rohilcand till the Vazir expelled them, and the money was not paid. But, as we have seen, the gloss is unsupported. Besides Hamilton, *Tárikh-i-Mozafari* and Francklin's "Sháh Alum" have been the chief authorities for this chapter.

[61] The Nawáb of Bengal (it will be remembered) who caused, with Sumroo's aid, the Patna massacre of 1763. *Vide sup.*, Chap. i.

CHAPTER IV.

A.D. 1776-85.

Vigour of Mirza Najaf—Zábitá rebels—Emperor takes the Field, and the Rebellion is suppressed—Sumroo's Jaigir—Abdul Ahid takes the Field—Unsuccessful Campaign against the Sikhs—Dehli threatened, but relieved by Najaf—Mirza's arrangements—Popham takes Gwalior—Begum Sumroo—Death of Mirza Najaf—Consequent Transactions—Afrásyáb Khán becomes Premier—Mirza Shaffi returns to Dehli—Is it Peace?—Murder of Shaffi—Action of Mr. Hastings—Flight of Sháhzáda—Mádhoji Sindhia goes to Agra—Afrásyáb's Death—Tribute claimed from British—Death of Zábitá Khán—Sindhia supreme—*Chálisa* famine—State of Country—General distress.

1776.—The splendid exertions of Mirza Najaf, though not yet at an end, might have been expected to give the Empire a breathing-time wherein to recover its strength. If we except the British in Bengal, it was now the most formidable military power on this side of India. No more than three fortified places remained to the Játs of all their once vast possessions. The Mahrattas had been occupied in the Deccan by the events that followed upon the death of their Peshwa, Mádho Rao; and the whole of their forces were temporarily withdrawn during the course of the year, by order of his successor. Najaf held viceregal state at Agra, surrounded not only by his faithful Moghuls and Persians, but by two brigades of foot and artillery, under the command, respectively, of Sumroo and of Médoc. The Mirza's chief Asiatic subordinates were Najaf Kuli Khán his adopted son, the converted Hindu,[62] otherwise Saif-ud-daulah; and Mohammad Beg of Hamadán: two officers of whom frequent mention will be found in the progress of this narrative. Mirza Shaffi, the minister's nephew, also held a high command. Sháh Alám lived the life of ease which had become a second nature to him, at Dehli, surrounded by able servants of the Mirza's selection. One of these, indeed, soon obtained an apparent ascendency over the indolent monarch, which was destined to afford another instance of the wisdom of that maxim invented of old in the East, "Put not your trust in Princes."[63] The only enemy who could disturb the repose of what may be termed the Home Districts was Zábitá Khán, who still exhibited all the faithlessness so common with his race, and a turbulent disposition peculiar to himself. Finding all present hope of aid from the Játs and Mahrattas at an end

[62] *Vide* last Chapter, p. 65.

[63] *V. sup.*, p. 61 for a notice of this man, Manzur Ali, the Nazir, or Comptroller.

(and instigated, it was suspected, by his late unsuccessful opponent, the Financial Minister, Abdul Ahid Khán), Zábitá, as stated at the close of the preceding chapter, turned to the Sikhs: a people who, in the decay of the Empire, had established themselves in the Sirhind territory, notably in Pattiala, and in Jhind. These pushing warriors—of whose prowess, both against and for the British, modern history tells so much—gladly accepted the invitation of the Páthan insurgent, and, crossing the Jamna in considerable numbers, joined his force at Ghausgarh, the fort between Saháránpur and Muzafarnagar, of which mention has been already made. It is even stated by Francklin (though, as usual, without specification of authority) that the Páthan on this occasion embraced the religion of the Sikhs, a sort of eclectic Monotheism tinctured with Hindu doctrine.

1777.—This conduct was justly regarded by the Mirza as a gross instance, not merely of disloyalty, but—what in his eyes was even worse—of impiety. In the opinion of a stern soldier of Islám, such as the Persian Prince had always shown himself to be, the act of joining with unbelievers was unpardonable. He therefore despatched a strong force against the combined rebels, under the command of an officer named Abdul Kásim Khán. Nothing daunted, the Confederates drew out their troops in front of the fort of Ghausgarh, and at once engaged the Imperial troops, whom they at the same time outflanked with a large body of horse, who got into the rear of the Imperialists without being perceived. Placed between two attacks, and deprived of their leader by a stray shot, the latter soon gave way, and Zábitá, having pursued them for some distance, returned to his stronghold triumphant. On this Mirza Najaf Khán resolved to take the field with all his power, and ere long presented himself before Ghausgarh, accompanied by the Emperor in person. The Mirza was aided in this campaign by the force of 5,000 men, with artillery, contributed by the new Viceroy of Áudh, as part of the *peshkash*, or fine for the investiture, and for the succession to the office of Vazir of the Empire, which had been held by his father, and which he desired to retain against the counter-claims of the Nizám and of other competitors. (*Vide* last chapter, p. 66.) The Páthan had, however, evacuated the fort on receiving notice of their approach, and retreated with his allies to their country beyond the Jamna, closely followed by the Imperial forces. An attempt at negotiation having been contemptuously rejected by the Captain-General, Mirza Najaf Khán, the two armies engaged on the famous field of Pánipat, and the action which ensued is described (with manifest exaggeration) as having been only less terrible than the last that was fought on the same historic ground, between the Mahrattas and the Musalmans, in 1761. Beyond this the native historians give no particulars of the battle, which raged till night, and with not unequal fortunes, if we may judge from the result—for on the following morning Zábitá Khán's renewed applications to treat were favourably received; on which occasion his estates were restored, and a double matrimonial alliance concluded. The Mirza himself condescended to take the Páthan's sister as his wife, while his godson (so to speak), Najaf Kuli, was promised the hand of Zábitá's daughter. The pardon of this restless rebel was attributed to the intercession of Latafat, the General of the Áudh Vazir, who is said to have had a large bribe on the occasion. (Francklin, *chap*. v.)

Peace being thus restored to Hindustan, the Minister revisited Agra, where he proceeded to provide for the administration of the country.

The English sought his alliance; but the negotiation failed because he would not surrender Sumroo. Asaf-ud-daulah, Viceroy of Áudh, was recognized as titular Vazir; a trustworthy chief, Maulah Ahmad Dád, was appointed to the charge of Sirhind; Najaf Kuli Khán held the vast tract extending from that frontier to the borders of Rajputána; and Sumroo was placed in charge of the country adjoining Zábitá Khán's lands, in the centre of which he fixed his capital at Sardhana, long destined to remain in the possession of his family, and where a country house and park, familiar to the English residents at Meerut, still belong to the widow of his last descendant. This territory, nominally assigned for the maintenance of the troops under the adventurer's command, was valued in those days at six lakhs of rupees annually; so that the blood-stained miscreant, whose saturnine manners had given him a bad name,[64] even among the rough Europeans of the Company's battalion, found his career of crime rewarded by an income corresponding to that of many such petty sovereigns as those of his native country.

1778.—The beginning of this year was marked by a bloodless campaign, to which Majad-ud-daulah led the Emperor. The Rájputs were the object of the attack, and they were rigorously mulcted. The Mirza's personal share in this matter was confined to that of a peacemaker. He probably disapproved of the campaign, which had been undertaken in a spirit of rivalry to himself; and by obtaining terms for the Rájputs he made new ties while displaying his own power. He accompanied the return of the expedition to Dehli, where his daughter was married to Najaf Kuli in the presence of the Emperor.

Mirza Najaf Khán then departed once more to Agra, the seat of his administration and his favourite abode. But his repose was not of long continuance, and he was soon called upon for fresh exertions; the Sikhs having risen against Maulah Ahmad Dád, the Faujdár of Sirhind, whom they defeated and slew. On the receipt of this intelligence the Emperor had deputed Abdul Ahid Khán—known to us by his title of Nawáb Majad-ud-daulah—with an army nominally under the command of one of the Imperial Princes, to inflict signal chastisement upon obstinate offenders. If the surmise of the native historians be correct—that Abdul Ahid Khán had been privy to the late combination between the Sikhs and Zábitá Khán against Mirza Najaf—the fact of his being sent against them, without any objection from so wise and loyal a minister as the Mirza, can only be accounted for by citing it as a proof of the peculiar danger to which great men are exposed, under an Eastern despotism, of reposing their confidence in secret enemies. That Abdul Ahid was even then plotting against his patron will be seen to be likely from his subsequent conduct, and certainly derives no confutation from the circumstance of his being a native of Kashmir, a country the faithlessness of whose inhabitants is proverbial, even in Indian story.

The Prince, whose standard was the rallying point of the army, is variously

[64] His comrades called him "Sombre," a sobriquet which, after adhering to him through life, became the family name of his descendants. Colonel Skinner is my authority for the tenure of his estates.

named as Jawan Bakht, Farkhanda Bakht, and Akbar; the former being the name of the Prince whom we saw acting as Regent during the Emperor's residence under English protection at Alláhábád, the later that of the future successor to the titular Empire. Whoever it may have been, the outset of the expedition promised him success, if not distinction. The Imperial host, 20,000 strong and with an efficient park of artillery, came in contact with the enemy at Karnál; but Majad-ud-daulah preferred negotiation to fighting, and induced the Sikhs to pay down a sum of three lakhs, and pledge themselves to the payment of an annual tribute. Joining the Sikh forces to his own, the Majad-ud-daulah next proceeded northwards, but was brought to a check at Pattiala by Amar Singh, the Ját chief of that state. Here fresh negotiations ensued, in which the perfidious Kashmirian is said to have offered to allay himself with the Sikhs for the destruction of Mirza Najaf Khán, on condition of being supported by them in his endeavours to be made Prime Minister in the room of that statesman. Whether the Ját leader had profited by the lesson lately read to his brethren of Bhartpur, or whether he was merely actuated by a desire to try conclusions with the Kashmirian, having penetrated the cowardice of his character, is matter for conjecture. Whatever the intrigue may have been, it was soon frustrated. A large Sikh reinforcement profited by the time gained in the negotiation to advance from Láhor; the Karnál force deserted the Imperial camp, and a general onset was made upon it the following morning. Led by a half-hearted commander and an inexperienced Prince, the Imperialists offered but a faint resistance; but their retreat was covered by the artillery, and they contrived to escape without suffering much in the pursuit, and indeed without being very closely followed up. It is interesting to observe, among the names of the Sikh Sirdars, who played this game of "diamond cut diamond" with the Kashmirian, that of Ranjit Singh, afterwards the wily Egbert of the Panjáb Heptarchy, and the firm friend of Britain for nearly forty years.

This disastrous campaign occurred in the cold weather of 1778-79, and the victorious Panjábis poured into the Upper Doáb, which they forthwith began to plunder.

1779.—Meanwhile, Mirza Najaf Khán remained in contemptuous repose at Agra, only interrupted by a short and successful dash at some Rájput malcontents, who had been stirred up, it is thought, at the instigation of his rival Majad-ud-daulah. That inefficient but unscrupulous intriguer is also shown by Captain Grant Duff to have been at the same time engaged in a correspondence with Mádhoji Sindhia, in view to joining, when once he should have gained possession of the power of the Empire, in an attack on the British Provinces. Duff gives this story on the authority of Sindhia's own letters, which that chief's grandson had placed in his hands; but he does not say whether the fickle Emperor was or was not a party to this iniquitous conspiracy for the ruin of his faithful servant and his long-established friends.

Certain it is that Sindhia was at that time very far from the statesmanlike views and reasonable aims which he ultimately adopted. Towards the close of the year, indeed, he took the ill-judged step of joining with Haidar Ali and the Nizám with the object of expelling the British from every part of the Indian Continent. But Mr.

Hastings soon disturbed the plans of the confederates and ere long rendered them hopeless. Some were conquered by force of arms, others were conciliated; and Sindhia in particular, received a lesson which made upon his sagacious mind a permanent impression.

1780.—There was, in the country now known as Dholpur, between Agra and Gwalior, a local Ját landholder who had in the decay of the Empire followed the example of Suraj Mal (of Bhurtpore) and assumed independence. In 1771, when Sháh Alám was returning to the throne of his ancestors, Chatr Singh, the then *Zemindar*, advanced money to the Treasury, and was soon after created a peer by the title of *Maháráj Rána*. Henceforth he figures in history as the "Rána of Gohad." Having a hereditary feud against the Mahrattas and a hereditary claim, such as it was, to the fortress of Gwalior, then in Sindhia's hands, he seemed to Hastings a useful instrument for causing a diversion. Major Popham, one of the best of the local officers, was accordingly sent to assist the Rána and stir up a confederation of Ját and Rájput powers to aid against the Musalman-Mahratta alliance by which British interests were threatened. The situation of the fort of Gwalior on a scarped and isolated rock over 200 feet high, need not here be more than mentioned; the manner of its capture, however, cannot be too often referred to as an instance of what resolution and conduct can effect in Asiatic warfare.[65] Having prepared scaling ladders in such secrecy that even his European officers were ignorant of what was being done or planned, Popham sent a storming party of sepoys, backed by twenty Europeans, to a place at the foot of the rock pointed out to him by some thieves. It was the night of the 3rd August, 1780, and the party, under the command of Captain Bruce, were shod with cotton to render their approach inaudible. The enemies' rounds were passing as they came near the spot; so the assaulting column lay down and waited until the lights and voices had ceased; then the ladders were placed against the cliff, and one of the robber guides mounting returned with intelligence that the guard had gone to sleep. The next moment the first ladder was mounted by Lieutenant Cameron, the engineer officer, and the others followed in silence, Captain Bruce having reached the rampart with twenty sepoys, a scuffle ensued which lasted till Popham arrived with the Europeans and made good the entrance. Thus was this strong place captured, and without the loss of one single life on the British side. The fort was made over to the Rána, but he did not long retain it, Sindhia having recaptured it. He soon afterwards took Gohad also (1784), and the descendants of the Ját chief are now known as Ránas of Dholpur.[66]

We have seen how marked a feature of the Emperor's character was his inability to resist the pertinacious counsels of an adviser with whom he was in constant intercourse; and it is certain that he gave Majad-ud-daulah all the support which his broken power and enfeebled will enabled him to afford.

But the danger was now too close and too vast to allow of further weakness. The Emperor's eyes seem to have been first opened by his army's evident confusion,

---

[65] The capture by two young Bombay subalterns in June, 1858, may also be remembered. (Malleson, 227.)

[66] The present Rána, a young man who has been carefully trained by Col. Dennehy, was honoured by a visit from the Prince of Wales in 1876.

as it returned to Dehli, and by the prevaricating reports and explanations which he received from its commander. If Mirza Jawan Bakht was the prince who had accompanied the ill-stared expedition, we know enough of his prudence and loyalty to be sure that he would have done all in his power to make his father see the matter in its true light; and what was wanting to his firm but dutiful remonstrances, would be supplied by the cries of fugitive villagers and the smoke of plundered towns.[67]

Najaf Khán was urgently summoned from Agra, and obeyed the call with an alacrity inspired by his loyal heart, and perhaps also by a dignified desire for redress. As he approached the capita], he was met by the Prince and the baffled Kashmirian. To the former he was respectful, but the latter he instantly placed under arrest, and sent back under a strong guard. The fallen Minister was confined, but in his own house; and the Mirza, on reaching Dehli, confiscated, on behalf of the Imperial treasury, his wealth, stated to have amounted to the large sum (for those days) of twenty lakhs, reserving nothing for himself but some books and a medicine chest. This was the second time he had triumphed over an unworthy rival, and signalized his own noble temper by so blending mercy with justice as has seldom been done by persons situated as he was. Abdul Ahid Khán—or Majad-ud-daulah—was a fop, very delicate in his habits, and a curiosity-seeker in the way of food and physic. It is said by the natives that he always had his table-rice from Kashmir, and knew by the taste whether it was from the right field or not.

Fully restored to the Imperial favour, the Mirza lost no time in obeying the pressing behests of his Sovereign, and sending an adequate force under his nephew, Mirza Shafi, to check the invaders. Their army, which had been collected to meet the Imperialists, drew up and gave battle near Meerut, within forty miles of the metropolis; but their unskilled energy proved no match for the resolution of the Moghul veterans, and for the disciplined valour of the Europeanized battalions. The Sikhs were defeated with the loss of their leader and 5,000 men, and at once evacuated the country.

1780.—It cannot have escaped notice we have been here reviewing the career of one whose talents and virtues merited a nobler arena than that on which they were displayed, and who would have indeed distinguished himself in any age and country. Profiting by experience, the successful Minister did not repeat the former blunder of retiring to Agra, where, moreover, his presence was no longer required; but continued for the brief remainder of his life to reside in the metropolis, and enjoy the fruit of his laborious career in the administration of the Empire, to which he had restored something of its old importance. Mirza Shafi commanded the army in the field; while Mohammad Beg, of Hamadán, was Governor of the Fort and District of Agra. Najaf Khán himself was appointed *Amir-ul-Umra* (Premier Noble); his title, as it had long been, was Zulfikár-ud-daulah—"Sword of State."

I have not thought it necessary to interrupt the narrative of the Mirza's successes by stopping to notice the death of Sumroo. This event occurred at

[67] Francklin says unhesitatingly that it was Farkhanda who accompanied the expedition. This prince died the following year. (Shah Alum, Chap. vi.)

Agra on the 4th of May, 1778, as appears from the Portuguese inscription upon his tombstone there.[68] He appears to have been a man without one redeeming quality—"stern and bloody-minded, in no degree remarkable for fidelity or devotion to his employers"—the one essential virtue of a free lance. This character is cited from the memoirs of Skinner, where it is also added that he cannot have been devoid of those qualities which attach the soldiery to their officer. But even this becomes doubtful, when we find the late Sir W. Sleeman (who was in the habit of moving about among the natives, and is an excellent authority on matters of tradition), asserting that he was constantly under arrest, threatened, tortured, and in danger at the hands of his men.

The force was maintained by his widow, and she was accordingly put in charge of the lands which he had held for the same purpose.

This remarkable woman was the daughter (by a concubine) of a Mohamadan of Arab descent, settled in the town of Kotána, a small place about thirty miles north-west of Meerut, and born about 1753. On the death of her father, she and her mother became subject to ill-treatment from her half-brother the legitimate heir; and they consequently removed to Dehli about 1760. It is not certain when she first entered the family of Sumroo, but she did not become his wife till some time afterwards. It has even been doubted if any formal marriage-ceremony ever took place, for Sumroo had a wife living, though insane; and the fact was probably sufficiently notorious to prevent any Catholic clergyman in that part of the country from celebrating a bigamous alliance with the rites of the Church.

1781.—At his death he left a son, baptized as "Aloysius," who was still in his minority; and the Minister, observing the Begum's abilities, saw fit to place her in charge, as has been already said. The ultimate result amply justified his choice. In 1781—under what influence is not recorded—she embraced Christianity, and was baptized, according to the ritual of the Latin Church, by the name of Johanna.[69] Her army is stated to have consisted, at this time, of five battalions of Sepoys, about 300 Europeans, officers and gunners, with 40 pieces of cannon, and a body of Moghul horse. She founded a Christian Mission, which grew by degrees into a convent, a cathedral, and a college; and to this day there are some 1,500 native and Anglo-Indian Christians resident at Sardhana.

1782.—On the 26th April[70] died Mirza Najaf Khán, after a residence in India of about forty-two years, so that he must have been aged at least sixty. He appears to have been an even greater and better man than his predecessor, Najib-ud-daulah, over whom he had the advantage in point of blood, being at once a descendant of the Arabian prophet, and a member of the Saffavi house, which had been removed from the throne of Persia by the usurpation of Nádir Sháh. Captain Scott—who was a good scholar and well-acquainted with Native politics, as Persian Secretary

[68] *Vide* Appendix B.

[69] Sleeman's "Rambles and Recollections," vol. ii. p. 384. The writer gives the Begum's age, at the time of her baptism, as forty. This is merely conjecture. By Francklin's computation, she was born about 1750.

[70] Mill says "late in the year;" the date in the text is that given by W. Hastings, who was Governor-General at the time.

to the Governor-General of British India—records of the Mirza that no one left his presence dissatisfied. If he could grant a request he would, and that with a grace as if it pleased him; if he could not, he could always convince the petitioner of his sorrow at being obliged to refuse. The faulty side of him appears to have been a love of money, and (towards the last part of his life, at least,) of pleasure. It will be seen in the sequel how soon his gains were dissipated, and his house overthrown. At his death he wielded all the power of the Empire which his energies and virtues had restored. He was Deputy Vazir of the absentee Viceroy of Áudh, and Commander-in-Chief of the army. He held the direct civil administration, with receipt of the surplus revenues, agreeably to Eastern usages, of the province of Agra and the Ját territories, together with the district of Alwar to the south-west and those portions of the Upper Doáb which he had not alienated in *Jaidad*. But he died without issue, and the division of his offices and his estates became the subject of speedy contests, which finally overthrew the last fragments of Moghul dominion or independence. The following notice of these transactions is chiefly founded on a Memorial, drawn up and submitted to the British Governor at Lucknow in 1784, by the Sháhzáda Jawan Bakht, of whom mention has been already made more than once, and who had, for the ten years preceding the Emperor's return to Dehli, in '71, held the Regency under the title of Jáhándár Sháh. After referring to the fact that Majad-ud-daulah (the title, it may be remembered, of Abdul Ahid Khán) had been and still was in custody, but that an equerry of the Emperor's procured the issue of patents confirming existing appointments, the Prince proceeds,—"The morning after the Mirza's death, I saw the attendants on His Majesty were consulting to send some persons to the house of the deceased, in order to calm disturbances; and at last the Wisdom enlightening the world resolved on deputing me to effect that object. [I] having departed with all speed, and given assurances to the afflicted, the friends of the departed had leisure to wash and dress the body, and the clamour began to cease. After necessary preparation, I attended the corpse to the Masjid, and the rites of Islám having been performed, sent it to the place of interment, under the care of Afrásyáb Khán, who was the cherished-in-the bosom" (adopted) "son" of the noble deceased; whose sister also regarded him as her adopted son.

"Afrásyáb Khán soon became ambitious of the dignities and possessions of the deceased, and the Begam (deceased's sister) petitioned his Majesty in his favour, with earnest entreaty; but this proved disagreeable to the far-extending sight of the royal Wisdom, as Mirza Shaffi Khán, who had a great army and considerable resources, looked to the succession, and would never agree to be superseded in this manner, so that contentions would necessarily ensue." There can be no doubt of the correctness of Sháh Alám's views. Mirza Shaffi was the nearest relative of the deceased, and in actual possession of the command of the army. He was thus not merely the most eligible claimant, but the best able to support his claims. But the Emperor—never, as we have seen, a man of much determination—was now enfeebled by years and by a habit of giving way to importunity.

"Instigated," proceeds Jawan Bakht, "by female obstinacy, the Begam would not withdraw her request, and her petition was at length, though reluctantly, honoured with compliance. The khillat of Amir-ul-Omra and acting Minister was conferred upon Afrásyáb by his Majesty, who directed this menial (though he [the writer] was sensible of the ill-promise of the measure) to write to Mirza Shaffi to hasten to the presence."

It is not quite clear whether the measure, to which this parenthesis represents the prince as objecting, was the appointment of Afrásyáb, or the summons to the Mirza. He was evidently opposed to the former, who was a weak young man, devoid of resources either mental or material. On the other hand, his own matured good sense should have shown him that no good consequences could follow the temporizing policy which brought the rivals face to face at Court. Afrásyáb's first measure was to release the Kashmirian Ex-Minister Majad-ud-daulah (Abdul Ahid Khán) from arrest, and by his recommendation this foolish and notorious traitor was once more received into the Imperial favour. In the meanwhile, Mirza Shaffi arrived at Dehli, and took up his quarters in the house of his deceased uncle, whose widow he conciliated by promising to marry her daughter, his first cousin. A period of confusion ensued, which ended for the time in the resignation of Afrásyáb, who retired to his estate at Ajhir, leaving his interests at Court to be attended to by Majad-ud-daulah and by the converted Rájput Najaf Kuli.[71] Shortly after his departure, Mirza Shaffi surrounded the houses of these agents, and arrested Majad-ud-daulah on the 11th September, 1782, and the Rájput on the following day, confining them in his aunt's house under his own eye. The Prince upon this received orders to negotiate with the Mizra, who was appointed to the office he had been so long endeavouring to compass. But Afrásyáb Khán, his absent competitor, had still allies at Court, and they succeeded in bringing over to his cause M. Paoli, the commander of Begam Sumroo's Brigade, together with Latafat Khán, commandant of the battalions that had been detached to the Imperial service by the Viceroy of Áudh. This took place a few days only after the arrest of the agents, and was almost immediately followed by the desertion from Mirza Shaffi of the bulk of the army. The Emperor put himself at the head of the troops, and proceeded to the Minister's house. Finding the premises had been evacuated the Sháh marched in triumph—not quite after the magnificent fashion of his ancestors—to the Jamma Masjid,[72] and Mirza Shaffi fled to Kosi, in the vicinity of Mathra, acting by the advice of the prince, as the latter informs us. The army did not pursue the fugitive, and the latter enlarged Majad-ud-daulah, who promised to intercede for him with the Emperor, and also made a friend in Mohamad Beg of Hamadán, whom we have already met with as Governor of Agra.

1783.—While the Moghuls were disturbing and weakening the empire by these imbecile contentions, Mádhoji Sindhia, the Patel, was hovering afar off, like an eagle on the day of battle. His position had just been greatly improved by the treaty of Salbai, an arrangement which was probably the result of the spirited policy pursued by Hastings, of which the storming of Gwalior was a specimen. Coote and Stuart too, in Madras, and Goddard in the Deccan, struck repeated blows at the confederacy. Peace, too, was concluded between the French and English in India as in Europe. Sindhia was one of the first to submit, and in 1782 acceded to that famous instrument, in which the British authorities had recognized him

[71] Otherwise Saif-ud-daulah. *Vide sup.*, p. 65.

[72] The Musulman Cathedral of Dehli.

as the representative chief of the Mahrattas, the Peshwa being still a minor, and the ostensible head of the Regency, Nána Farnavis, being a mere civilian, though otherwise an able man. The British Governor-General also, naturally alarmed at what was going on, and foreseeing danger from the interposition of the Mahrattas, with whom his Government had, till lately, been engaged in a deadly conflict, soon after sent two officers to the Imperial Court, being the first English Embassy that had visited the city of the Moghul since the memorable deputation from the infant Factory to the throne of Farokhsiar.[73]

But before these officials could arrive, further complications had occurred. Mirza Shaffi returning to Dehli, in company with Mohamad Beg, requested that his new opponents, Paoli and Latafat, might be sent to them with authority to treat, and the application was granted, much against the advice of the prince, who tells us that he proposed either that an immediate attack should be made upon the rebels before they had time to consolidate their power, or else that they should be summoned to the presence, and made to state their wishes there. To the envoys elect, he observed that, even were the concession made of sending a deputation to treat with refractory subjects, he would advise that only one should go at a time. "But," he continues, "as the designs of Providence had weakened the ears of their understandings, an interview appeared to them most advisable; a mutual suspicion rendering each unwilling that one should go and the other remain in camp, lest he who went should make his own terms without the other." What a glimpse this gives of the dissolution of all that we are accustomed to call society! The two envoys set out, but never returned: like the emissaries sent to the Jewish captain, as he drove furiously along the plain of Esdraëlon to ask, Is it peace? The European was slain at once, the Áudh general being imprisoned and deprived of sight. Mirza Shaffi and Mohamad Beg next began to quarrel with each other. The Emperor was now much perplexed, but matters were arranged for the time through the instrumentality of the prince and by the return of Afrásyáb, who became reconciled to his late competitor. The three nobles were presented with *khillats* (dresses of honour) and Mirza Shaffi became Premier, under the title of *Amir-ul-Umra,* while Majad-ud-daulah reverted to his ancient post of Intendant of the Home Revenues. We pursue the prince's narrative.

"It was at this period that much anxiety and melancholy intruding on the sacred mind of his Majesty, the Asylum of the World, and also on the breast of this loyal servant," their attention was turned towards the English alliance, which had been in abeyance for some years. On the 23rd of September, 1783, Mirza Shaffi, who had been to Agra, was shut out from the palace on his return, probably owing to Afrásyáb Khán's renewed desire to obtain the chief place in the State. On this the Mirza retired to Agra again, and naturally adopted a hostile attitude, an emissary was sent forth to treat with him, in the person of Mohamad Beg Hamadáni. The meeting took place in the open air in front of the main gate of the old Fort of Agra; and when the elephants, upon which the two noblemen were seated, drew near to each other, the Mirza held out his hand in greeting, when Mohamed Beg at once seized the opportunity, and pistolled him under the arm. It is asserted, indeed,

[73] *Vide sup.*, Part I. chap. i. p. 45.

by some that the actual crime was perpetrated by the attendant who occupied the back seat of the howdah; possibly Ismail Beg Khán, nephew of the Hamadáni.

Afrásyáb, who had instigated this murder, profited by it, and succeeded to the post of his ambition, while the mind of the prince became still more anxious, and still more bent upon opening his case, if possible, in a personal interview with the English Governor.

Meanwhile, the envoys of the latter were not less urgent on their employer to support the Emperor with an army. "The business of assisting the Sháh"—thus they wrote in December, 1783—"must go on if we wish to be secure in India, or regarded as a nation of faith and honour."[74] Mr. Hastings was not deaf to these considerations, and subsequent events proved their entire soundness. He desired to sustain the authority of the Empire, because he foresaw nothing from its dissolution but an alternative between Chaos and the Mahrattas; and, but for the opposition of his council in Calcutta, he would have interposed, and interposed after his fashion, with effect. Yet his not doing so was afterwards made the ground of one of the charges (No. 18) against him, and he was accused of having intrigued in the interest of Mádhoji Sindhia, the Patel. That Mr. Hastings, when overruled in his desire of anticipating Sindhia in Court influence at Dehli, preferred seeing the latter succeed, rather than the Empire should fall a prey to complete anarchy; that he "turned the circumstance to advantage"—to use Grant Duff's phrase—was neither contrary to sound statesmanship, nor to the particular views of the British Government, which was then occupied in completing the treaty of Salbai. Under this compact Central India was pacified, and the Carnatic protected from the encroachments of the notorious Haidar Ali Khán, and his son, the equally famous Tippu Sáhib. It is important here to observe that the *Calcutta Gazettes* of the day contain several notices of the progress of the Sikhs, and the feeble opposition offered to them by the courtiers. All these things called for prompt action.

1784.—On the 27th March, the British Governor arrived at Lucknow, and Jawan Bakht resolved to escape from the palace, and lay before him an account of Dehli politics, such as should induce him to interpose. The design being communicated to his maternal uncle, a body of Gujars,[75] from the prince's estate, was posted on the opposite bank of the river, and everything fixed for the 14th of April. About 8 P.M., having given out that he was indisposed, and on no account to be disturbed, the prince disguised himself, and, secretly departing from his chamber in the palace, passed from the roof of one building to the roof of another, until he reached the aqueduct which crossed the garden of the palace. The night was stormy, and the prince was suffering from fever, but he found a breach where the canal issued, by which he got to the rampart of the Salimgarh. Here he descended by means of a rope, and joined his friends on the river sands; and, with a considerable mixture of audacity and address, found means to elude the sentries and get across the river. One trait is worth preserving, as illustrative of the characteristic clemency of the

[74] Mill, Book VI. chap. i.

[75] A tribe claiming to be descended from Rájput fathers, and long famous in Hindustan for their martial and predatory character. They are regarded by Elliot as Scythian immigrants.

house of Timur. "I believe," said the prince, in talking of this night's adventure to Mr. Hastings, "I ought to have killed the guide who showed me where to ford the river; but my conscience disapproved, and I let him go, preferring to trust myself to the care of Providence. In effect, the man justified my suspicions, for he instantly went to the nearest guard and gave him information of my route, as I learned soon after; but I made such speed that my pursuers could not overtake me."[76]

His Highness reached Lucknow, where he impressed all who met him with a highly favourable opinion of his humanity, his intelligence, and his knowledge of affairs; but the only consolation he received, either from the Viceroy or from Mr. Hastings, hampered as the latter was by the opposition of his council, was the advice to turn to Mádhoji Sindhia. Captain Jonathan Scott (who was on Hastings' staff) says that the prince received an allowance of £40,000 a year from the British Government (Scott's Ferishta, vol. ii. 242.)

In the meanwhile Mohamad Beg, who had returned to his old residence at Agra, continued to trouble the repose of the new minister Afrásyáb, so that he also turned to the redoubted Patel, and this successful soldier who had barely escaped four-and-twenty years before from the slaughter of Pánipat, now found himself master of the situation. The movements of the Mahratta chief began, indeed, to be all-important. They were thus noticed in the *Calcutta Gazette* for 18th April:—"We learn that Sindhia is going on a hunting party. . . . We also learn that he will march towards Bundelkund." He marched in the direction, as it proved, of Agra.[77]

He sent an envoy to Lucknow to treat with the Governor-General, and proceeded in person to Hindustan, proposing to meet the Emperor, who was on his way to dislodge Mohamad Beg from the fort of Agra.

The *Calcutta Gazette* for May 10th says, "His Majesty has signified by letters to the Governor-General and Sindhia that he will march towards Agra."

The Emperor's desire to put himself into the hands of Sindhia was very much increased by the violent conduct of Afrásyáb towards one who, whatever his faults, had endeared himself, by long years' association, to the facile monarch. Majad-ud-daulah, the Finance Minister, having attempted to dissuade his Majesty from going to Agra, the haughty Moghul sent Najaf Kuli Khán with a sufficient force to Majad's house, and seizing him, with the whole of his property, kept him in close arrest, in which he continued for the most part till his death, in 1788.[78]

On his arrival, Sindhia had an interview with Afrásyáb Khán, at which it was agreed to concert a combined attack upon Mohamad Beg forthwith. Three days after, the minister was assassinated, viz., 2nd November, 1784. The actual hand that struck this blow was that of Zain-ul-Ábidin, brother of Mirza Shaffi, who, no doubt, was not unwilling to have an opportunity of punishing the supposed author of his uncle's murder; but there were not wanting those who, on the well-known maxim, *cui bono*, attributed the instigation to Sindhia. Francklin records, on the authority of one Said Razá Khán, that Zain-ul-Ábidin found shelter with Sindhia

[76] Appendix to Mr. Hastings's "Narrative."

[77] S. Karr's "Selections," vol. i. p. 13.

[78] Francklin's "Shah Alum," p. 118.

immediately after the murder, which was effected in the very tent of the victim. Rájah Himmat Bahádur (the Gosain leader)[79] at once proceeded to Sindhia's tent, accompanied by the chief Moghul nobles, where all joined in congratulations and professions of service.

1785.—The latter, at all events, immediately stepped into the dead man's shoes, leaving the title of Vazir to the Áudh Viceroy; and contenting himself with the substance of authority. Calling the Peshwa of Puna—the head of the Mahrattas—by the revived title of Plenipotentiary of the Empire, formerly borne (it may be remembered) by the first Nizám,[80] he professed to administer as the Peshwa's deputy. He assumed with the command of the army, the direct management of the provinces of Dehli and Agra, and allotted a monthly payment of sixty-five thousand rupees for the personal expenses of Sháh Alám. In order to meet these expenses, and at the same time to satisfy himself and reward his followers, the Patel had to cast about him for every available pecuniary resource. Warren Hastings having now left India, the time may have been thought favourable for claiming some contribution from the foreign possessors of the Eastern Subahs. Accordingly we find in the *Calcutta Gazette* the following notice, under the date Thursday, 12th May, 1785:—

> "We have authority to inform the public that on the 7th of this month the Governor-General received from the Emperor Sháh Alám and Maha Rájah Madagee Sindia an official and solemn disavowal, under their respective seals, of demands which were transmitted by them, on Mr. Macpherson's accession to the Government, for the former tribute from Bengal.
>
> "The demands of the tribute were transmitted through Major Brown,[81] and made immediately upon his recall from the Court of Sháh Alám, but without any communication of the subject to Mr. Anderson.[82]
>
> "Mr. Anderson was immediately instructed to inform Sindhia that his interference in such demands would be considered in the light of direct hostility, and a breach of our treaty with the Mahrattas; and Sháh Alám was to be informed that the justice of the English to his illustrous house could never admit the interference or recommendation of other powers, and could alone flow from their voluntary liberality.
>
> "A disavowal of claims advanced unjustly and disrespectfully was insisted upon; and we are authorized to declare that Mr. Anderson's conduct in obtaining that disavowal was open and decided, highly honourable to him as a public minister. He acted in conformity to the orders of Government even before he

[79] These Gosains were a sect of fighting friars, much valued at this period. *Vide inf.* Note to p. 93.

[80] *Vide sup.*, p. 16. The Persian word is *Vakil-i-Mutlak.*

[81] Major Brown was the head of the Dehli Mission already mentioned.

[82] Mr. Anderson was the British Resident in Sindhia's camp.

received them. He founded his remonstrances on a short letter which he had received from the Governor-General, and upon circumstances which passed in the presence of Sindhia, at Sháh Alám's Darbár, as Major Brown was taking his leave.

"The effects which Mr. Anderson's remonstrance produced are very satisfactory and creditable to Government, and such explanations have followed upon the part of Sindhia, as must eventually strengthen our alliance with the Mahrattas, expose the designs of secret enemies, and secure the general tranquillity of India."

The revolution begun by the Patel was soon completed. Zábitá Khán died about this time; and Mohamad Beg, being deserted by his troops, had no resource but to throw himself upon the mercy of the Mahratta chief. The fort of Agra surrendered on the 27th of March, 1785; and all that remained of the power of the Moghul party was the fort of Aligarh, where the widow and brother of the late minister, Afrásyáb Khán, still held out, in the hope of preserving the property of the deceased, the bulk of which was stored there. This stronghold, which the late Najaf Khán had wrested from the Játs, had been fortified with great care, and it had a strong garrison, but, having held out from July to November, the Governor was at last prevailed upon, by the entreaties of the ladies, to avert from them the horrors of a storm, and make terms with the besiegers. The result of the capitulation was that the eldest son of the deceased Afrásyáb received an estate, yielding a yearly revenue of a lakh and a half of rupees. The rest of the property—valued at a crore, a sum then corresponding to a million of money, but really representing much more of our present currency—was seized by Sindhia.

The latter was now supreme in Hindustan; the disunited Moghul chiefs, one and all, acknowledged his authority; and a Mahratta garrison, occupying the Red Castle of Sháh Jahán, rendered the Emperor little more than an honourable pageant. He joined, however, personally in all the operations of 1785, and did not return to Dehli until the middle of the following year. Sindhia did not at the time accompany him, but retired to his favourite cantonment of Mathra.

It has been already mentioned that there is little or nothing recorded of the condition of the country or of the people by native historians. It must not, however, be thought that I am satisfied with recording merely the dates of battles, or the biographies of prominent men. On the contrary, the absence of information upon the subject of the condition of the nation at large, is a great cause of regret and disappointment to me. A few particulars will be found in the concluding chapter.

In 1783, when Afrásyáb Khán was distracting the country by his ambitious attempts, occurred a failure of the periodical rains, followed by one of those tremendous famines which form such a fearful feature of Indian life.[83] In Bengal, where the monsoon is regular, and the alluvial soil moist, these things are almost as unknown as in England: but the arid plains of Hindustan, basking at the feet of the vastest mountain-chain in the world, become a perfect desert, at least once

[83] *Vide* Preliminary Observations, p. 2.

in every quarter of a century. The famine of 1783-4 has made a peculiarly deep impression upon the popular mind, under the name of the "Chalisa," in reference to the Sambat date 1840, of the era of Vikram Adit. An old Gosain, who had served under Himmat Bahádur, near Agra, once told the author that flour sold near Agra that year 8 seers for the rupee; which, allowing for the subsequent fall in the value of money, is perhaps equivalent to a rate of three seers for our present rupee—a state of things partly conceivable by English readers, if they will imagine the quartern loaf at four shillings, and butcher's meat in proportion.[84]

These famines were greatly intensified by the want of hands for field-labour, that must have been caused by the constant drafting of men to the armies, and by the massacre and rapine that accompanied the chronic warfare of those times. The drain on the population, however, combined with the absence of the tax-gatherer, must have given this state of things some sort of compensation in the long run. Some few further particulars regarding the state of the country will be found in the concluding chapter.

> Note.—Besides the *Mozafari,* the principal authorities for this chapter have been *Francklin's* "Sháh Alum" (*v. inf.,* p. 108), the narrative of the Sháhzádah published by Warren Hastings, and the continuation of Ferishta by Captain Jonathan Scott. This gentleman has already been mentioned (*v. sup.,* p. 74); he was assisted in compiling his narrative by Maj. Polier, who was at Dehli at the time. All these authorities are strictly original and contemporaneous; and in general agree with each other. The Memoirs of Irádat Khán have also been consulted—a Dehli noble of the period. A traditional account of the Famine by an "*Old Resident*" of Aligarh may not be without interest. It is taken from the *Dehli Gazette* of 6th June, 1874. "As told by many persons who witnessed it, the disastrous circumstance which occurred during Sindiah's rule and prior to Du Boigne's administration known by the people as the 'Chaleesa Kaut,' the severe famine of A.D. 1783 in a considerable degree desolated the country, and the many ruinous high mounds still visible in the district owe their origin to this calamity. The inhabitants either fell victims, or fled to other parts where they met a similar fate, for the famine was a general one. It was described to me by those who lived then, that for the two previous years the rains were very unfavourable, and the produce very scanty; the third year, A.D. 1783, the people entertained strong hopes that the season would be a propitious one: but sad was their condition when they found the rainy months, 'Assaur and Sawun, passing off with a scorching sun. In 'Bhadoon' they had clouds but no rain, and when the calamity came, all hopes

[84] *Vide Calcutta Gazette,* for Thursday, 13th May, 1784.—"The 12th.—Wheat is now selling at Battalah, 9 seers; at Láhore, 4 seers; and Jumoo, 3 seers per rupee."—Seton Karr's "Selections," I. 14.

were gone, the price of grain was enormous and with difficulty it could be procured, thousands died of sheer starvation within their walls and streets, and the native governments rendered no assistance to ameliorate or relieve the wants of their unfortunate subjects. Children were left to go astray and find their sustenance in the wild berries of the peepul, burrh, and goolur, and thus became an easy prey to the wild beasts who in numbers roved round the country in open day, living on carcases. About the middle of September, or 'Kooar,' the rains fell, and so regularly that the grain which was thrown in the fields in the two previous years and did not generate for want of moisture, now came up profusely, and abundant was the produce. The state of things gradually changed for the better in October and November. An old Brahmin of Secundra Rao narrated that some years before 1810 the harvest was so plentiful that on the occasion he built a house which was on a very high plinth: he filled the plinth instead of with mud with an inferior course of small grain called 'kodun,' selling at that time uncommonly cheap, much lower than the cost of mud would be; when the famine came he dug up the coarse grain, which was found good, and sold it, and with the money he made his house a *pucka* one, besides gaining a large sum in coin."

CHAPTER V.

A.D. 1786-88.

Gholám Kádir—Pillars of the State—Siege of Rághogarh—British policy—Measures of Sindhia—Rájput Confederacy—Battle of Lálsaut—Muhammad Beg's death—Defection of Ismail Beg—Greatness of Sindhia—Gholám Kádir enters Dehli—Is checked by Begam Sumroo and Najaf Kuli Khán—Gholám Kádir pardoned; joins Ismail Beg—Battle of Chaksána—Rájput Embassy—Emperor takes the field—Sháhzáda writes to George III.—Najaf Kuli rebels—Death of Sháhzáda—Emperor's return—Battle of Firozábád—Confederates at Dehli—Their difficulties—Sindhia inactive—Benoit de Boigne.

1786.—The eldest son of the deceased chief of the Báwani Mahál was that Gholám Kádir, whom we have seen already in the character of a captive and a page.[85] It does not appear under what circumstances he had recovered his liberty; but, on the death of Zábitá Khán, he at once succeeded to his estates, under the title of "Najib-ud-daulah Hoshyár Jang." As in the lower empire of Byzantium, so in the present case, in proportion as the State crumbled, the titles of its unserviceable supporters became more sonorous, until at last there was not a pillar of the ruinous fabric, however weak and however disengaged from the rest of the body, but bore some inscription equally "imposing" in both senses of the word. *Daulah* or *Daulat* means "The State," and the Musalman nobles were called *Arkán-i-Daulat*—"Columns of the Commonwealth." Of these one was its Sword, another its Asaph (the "Recorder" of David and Solomon), a third its Hero, and a fourth its Shield. The young "Najib" Gholám Kádir Khán, was now the most prominent representative of the Hindustáni Afgháns. Among the Moghuls the leading spirit was Mohamad Beg of Hamadán, for whom the Patel provided employment by sending him with an army into Málwa, where he was for some time occupied by the siege of Rághogarh. This was a very strong fort, held by a colony of Kachwáha Rájputs since the times of Najaf Khán, and commanding one of the main roads between Hindustan and the Mahratta country. It had resisted the Mahrattas when they first invaded Málwa, and it was destined to resist Sindhia's successors almost down to our own times. It is now a peaceful market town, and the traces of its former strength are all that it retains of a military character.

Sindhia's progress in the Doáb was more rapid, nor was it long before Musalman jealousy began to be aroused. The Patel opened negotiations with Mirza

[85] *Vide sup.* Chap. iii.

Jawan Bakht, having the object of inducing that prince to return to the capital; but from this he was strongly dissuaded by the Viceroy Vazir, acting under the advice of Major Palmer, the British Resident at Lucknow. That gentleman considered the interests of the Company and of the Vazir as deeply bound up in the fate of the prince. Whilst he remained under their joint protection, the Mahratta usurpation must be incomplete; should he fall into the power of the Patel, a permanent Mahratta occupation would be established, which would be a serious danger indeed.[86]

1787.—Under these circumstances the acting Governor-General Macpherson, who, as already noted, had succeeded Mr. Hastings when the latter left India, resolved on retaining a British Brigade in the Doáb; and Lord Cornwallis, on taking office the following year, confirmed the measure. That a change began to come over the policy of the British in India about this time is well known, however the English might strive to hide it from others—or even from themselves: see, for instance, the following passage from the *Calcutta Gazette* for March 8th, 1787:—

> "Though the Mussulmans dwindle into insignificance, we have nothing to apprehend from the Hindus. Many have urged the necessity of upholding the influence of Moghuls to counterbalance the power of Hindus; but this should seem bad policy, as we would causelessly become obnoxious, and involve ourselves in the interests of a declining State, who are at the same time our secret enemy and rivals."

The new Governor, likewise, further alarmed Sindhia by sending a minister to reside at the Peshwa's Court at Punah, and the Patel anxiously set himself to work to consolidate his power in Hindustan, so as to be ready for the storm, from whatever quarter it might break. Impressed with the success which had attended his predecessor, Mirza Najaf, Sindhia's first care was to organize a body of regular troops—a measure repugnant to the old politics of the Mahrattas, but, none the less approving itself to his judgment on that account.

The nucleus of this force was the corps raised and organized, in 1785, by Benoit de Boigne, an officer whose history, as it forms an excellent illustration of the condition of Hindustan in the latter part of the last century, will be given briefly in a note at the end of this chapter. The General in command of Sindhia's forces was a Mahratta, named Appa Khándi Rao, of whom we shall hereafter have occasion to make further mention.

In civil matters, the first step taken by the Patel was the sequestration of a number of the Jaigirs[87] of the Musalman nobles—a cause of discontent to the sufferers, and of alarm to the remainder; but even this step had a military character, for the Jaigirs were fiefs bestowed for military service, and their reduction formed part of the system under which he was endeavouring to organize a standing army. With this view he at the same time recalled Mohamad Beg from the siege of Rághogarh and attempted, vainly, to induce that Chief to disband his levies.

[86] Letter from Lucknow, dated 1st April, 1785. Ap. Mill.

[87] The "Jaghire" of old writers. The spelling of the text is the correct one, "Jai" *place*, and "gir" *holding*.

Amongst other unpopular measures must also be enumerated the removal of Rájá Naráyan Dáss, who had for some time been in charge of the Home Revenues, and who was replaced by Sháh Nizám-ud-din, a creature of Sindhia's. At the same time the Gosain leader, Himmat Bahádur, went into open rebellion in Bundelkand, on being called upon to give an account of the management of his Jaigir, a measure which he construed as portending resumption.

Nor was it an easy matter, at this particular juncture, to set about military reforms, for the Rájputs, emboldened perhaps by the resistance of Rághogarh, now began to organize a combination, which not only implied a considerable loss of power and of revenue, but likewise threatened to cut off the Patel's communications with Punah. Rájá Partáb Singh (head of the Kachwáhas, and Dhiráj of Jaipur), called for the aid of the head of the Ráthor clan, Mahárájá Bijai Singh of Jodhpur, who had married his daughter, and who adopted his cause with alacrity. Joined by the Rána of Udaipur, and by other minor chiefs, the Rájput leaders found themselves at the head of a force of 100,000 horse and foot, and 400 pieces of artillery, and with this array they took post at Lálsot, a town forty-three miles east from Jaipur, and there awaited the attack of the Imperial forces, with the more confidence that they were aware of the growing disaffection of the Moghul nobles.

Here they were encountered at the end of May, 1787, by an enormous force under Sindhia in person, with Ambáji Inglia, Appa Khándi, M. de Boigne, and other trusty lieutenants. The Moghul horse and the regular infantry in the Imperial service were under the general direction of Mohamad Beg and his nephew. The latter, a young man who will play a conspicuous part in the succeeding pages, was named Ismail Beg, and was the son of Nahim Beg, who had accompanied his brother Mohamad from Hamadán, the two attaching themselves to their Persian countryman, Mirza Najaf, during that minister's later prosperity. Ismail Beg had married his uncle's daughter, and was a person of great spirit, though not, as it would seem, of much judgment or principle.

The battle, as described by Native history, began by a reconnaisance of Ismail Beg at the head of 300 Moghul horse. A large body of Rájput horse made way before him, but the Mahrattas not following up, and nearly half his men being slain, he was forced to retreat to his uncle's division. This terminated the fighting for that day, but the next morning Ismail renewed the fight, leading on his artillery on foot, and followed by his uncle on an elephant with the rest of the corps. They were throughout the day engaged with the bulk of the Rájput army, but a heavy storm arose from the westward, as evening came on. The Mahrattas, having been in the meantime severely handled by a body of Rájput swordsmen mad with opium, the battle degenerated into a cannonade, at long ranges and at fitful intervals. Suddenly a chance round-shot dropped into the Moghul ranks, which, after overthrowing two horsemen, made a bound and struck Mohamad Beg on the right arm. He fell from his elephant, and, coming in contact with a small stack of branches of trees that had been piled at hand for the elephants' fodder, received a splinter in his temple which proved instantly mortal. Ismail, hearing of this event, exclaimed, "I am now the leader!" and immediately addressed the troops, and concluded the action for that day with a brisk cannonade. The next day (the 1st of June, and the third of this protracted engagement) both sides continued to fight till towards evening, when a body of some 14,000 infantry surrounded Sindhia's tents and clamorously demanded an issue of pay—very probably in arrear—and sent a message at the same time to the Jaipur Rájá, offering to join him on receipt of two lakhs of rupees. The Rájá readily accepting these terms, the battalions joined his camp and received their money on the spot.

Meanwhile, such was the distress in the Moghul-Mahratta camp, isolated, at it was, in an enemy's country, that wheat was selling at four seers the Rupee,[88] and there was every prospect of the scarcity increasing; while the countless camp-followers of the Rájputs were engaged in nightly depredations, stealing the elephants and horses from the midst of the sentries. Under these circumstances, the Patel broke up his quarters the next evening, and fell back upon Alwar, whence Ismail Beg marched off without leave towards Agra, taking with him 1,000 horse, four battalions, and six guns. Sindhia, justly regarding this as an open act of defection, instantly made terms with Ranjit Singh, the leader of the Játs, and pushed on all his forces to the pursuit, at the same time throwing a strong reinforcement into the fort of Agra, the garrison of which was placed under the command of Lakwá Dádá, one of his best officers.[89]

The following version of the affair appears in the *Calcutta Gazette*:—

> "Reports are various respecting the particulars of an engagement between Scindia and the Rájahs of Joynaghur[90] and Jeypore; it is certain a very bloody battle was fought near Joynaghur about the end of last month, in which, though the enemy were repulsed in their attack on his advanced body by Scindia's troops, with much gallantry, they were ultimately in a great measure victorious, as Scindia lost a part of his artillery during the engagement, which was long and obstinate, and in which upwards of 2,000 men were killed on either side. Both armies, however, still kept the field. Among the chiefs of note who fell on the part of Scindia, is *Ajeet Roy*. On that of the Joynaghur Rájah, is *Mohamed Beg Humdanee*, a very celebrated commander, much regretted by that party, and, but for whose loss, it is said that the Mahrattas would have been totally defeated. Several of Scindia's battalions, with a considerable corps of artillery, went over to the enemy on the 1st instant, but the intelligence we have

[88] Probably about twelve times the average price current of those days.

[89] This, it must be remembered, is a Musalman account of the campaign; and though it bears general marks of veracity, and is from the *Tárikh-i-Mozafari,* usually an accurate authority, yet one sees that it slurs over the details of Ismail Beg's defection. Grant Duff, writing from Mahratta sources, says that he and his uncle deserted before the battle of Lálsaut, which is the opposite extreme. Perhaps, we shall not be far wrong in supposing that Ismail Beg went off after his uncle's death, on the third day, when the mutinous corps deserted as stated in the text.

[90] *q. d.* "Jodhpur," which was sometimes called Jainagar. Lálsaut was near Jaipur (*v. sup.*). See also Jawan Bakht's letter (*inf.* 92), where the word is apparently used for Jaipur.

yet received does not enable us to account for this revolt."

Francklin says, in general terms, that Mohamad Beg went over at the commencement of the action, and that it was Partáb Singh who conferred the command of the Moghuls upon Ismail Beg. But Partáb Singh would have no voice in such a matter, and Francklin inconsistently adds that the trained battalions of the late Afrásyáb's force went over later in the day. Where no authorities are given, it is inevitable that we should judge for ourselves. And, after all, the point is not of much importance. It is, however, pretty clear that the Moghul nobles were grievously discontented; that their discontents were known to the Rájputs before they provoked a collision; and that the latter were joined by them as soon as a likelihood appeared of Sindhia's being defeated.

General de Boigne used to relate that this was the hour of Sindhia's moral greatness. He made vast efforts to conciliate the Játs, appealing to the Thâkur's rustic vanity by costly presents, while he propitiated the feeling of the Bhartpur army, and the patriotism of the country at large, by restoring to the Játs the fortress of Dig, which had been held for the Emperor ever since its conquest by Najaf Khán. He likewise placed his siege-train in the charge of his new allies, who stored it in their chief fort of Bhartpur. At the same time he wrote letters to Poona, earnestly urging a general combination for the good cause.

Ismail Beg, on his part was not idle. His first effort was to procure the co-operation of the Rájputs, and had they not been too proud or too indolent to combine actively with him, it is possible that Mahratta influence might have been again overthrown, and the comparatively glorious days of Mirza Najaf Khán renewed in the Empire of Hindostan. A fresh associate, too, in these designs are now to appear upon the scene, which, for a brief but terrible period, he was soon after to fill. This was Gholám Kádir,[91] who hastened from Ghausgarh to join in the resuscitation of Mohamadan interests, and to share in the gains. The Emperor, moreover, was known to be in private correspondence with the Rájput chiefs, who shortly after this inflicted another defeat on the Mahrattas under Ambáji.

Unable to resist this combination, Sindhia fell back upon Gwalior, and Ismail Beg hotly pressed the siege of Agra.

Towards the end of the rainy season of 1787, Gholám Kádir approached Dehli, and encamped on the Sháhdara[92] side of the river; his object at this time being, in all probability, a renewal of his father's claims, and attempts to obtain the dignity of *Amir-ul-Umra* or Premier Noble. He is always understood to have been acting under the direction of Manzur Ali Khán, Controller of the Imperial Household, who thought to secure a valuable support for the cause of Islám by introducing the young Páthan chief into the administration. The Mahratta garrison was commanded by a son-in-law of the Patel, known in Musalman History as the Desmukh—which is interpreted "Collector of Land Revenue,"—and by a member of the Imperial Household, on whom, from some unexplained reason, had been bestowed the title of the great Aulia Saint Sháh Nizám-ud-din,[93] and who had

[91] *Vide sup.*, p. 84.

[92] Sháhdara was the scene of Suraj Mal's defeat and death.—*Vide sup.*, Chap. ii.

[93] *Vide inf.*, p. 99, Note.

lately been placed in charge of the Home Revenues, as stated above (p. 86.) These officers immediately opened fire from the guns on the riverside of the fort, and the young Rohilla replied from the opposite bank. At the same time, however, he did not fail to employ the usual Eastern application of war's sinews; and the Moghul soldiers of the small force being corrupted, the Mahrattas made but a feeble resistance. Gholám Kádir crossed the river, and the Imperial officers fled to the Ját Fort of Balamgarh, leaving their camp and private effects to the mercy of the victor.

It need hardly be observed that the firing on the palace was an act of gross disrespect, and, unless explained, of rebellion. Nor was the young chief blind to the importance of basing his proceedings on an appearance of regularity. He accordingly entered into a correspondence with the above mentioned Manzur Ali (a nominee, it may be remembered, of the late Mirza Najaf Khán).[94] By the agency of this official, Gholám Kádir was introduced to the Diwán Khas, where he presented a *Nazar* of five gold mohurs, and was graciously received. He excused his apparent violence by attributing it to zeal for the service of his Majesty, formally applied for the patent of *Amir-ul-Umra*, and with professions of implicit obedience withdrew to cultivate the acquaintance of the courtiers, retiring at night to his own camp. Matters remained in this condition for two or three days, when Gholám Kádir, impatient perhaps at the non-occurrence of any circumstance which might advance his designs, re-entered the Palace with seventy or eighty troopers, and took up his abode in the quarters usually occupied by the *Amir-ul-Umra*.

Meanwhile, Begam Sumroo, who was with her forces operating against a fresh rising of the Cis-Satlaj Sikhs, hastened from Pánipat and presented herself in the palace. Awed by this loyal lady and her European officers, and finding the Moghul courtiers unwilling to enter into any combination against them, the baffled Rohilla retired across the river, and remained for some time quiet in his camp. Francklin, indeed, states that the cannonade was renewed immediately on Gholám Kádir's return to his camp; but it is more probable that, as stated above, this renewal did not occur until the arrival of Najaf Kuli Khán. The Emperor showed on this occasion some sparks of the temper of old time, before misfortune and sensual indulgence had demoralized his nature. He sent Moghul chiefs to keep an eye on the Páthan, while he increased his household troops by a levy of 6,000 horse, for the pay of whom he melted a quantity of his personal plate. He also despatched messengers to the converted Ráthor, Najaf Kuli Khán, who was on his estate at Rewári, urging his immediate attendance in Dehli.

Rewári is in what is now the district of Gurgaon, and lies about fifty miles S.W. of Dehli. It is a country of mixed mountain and valley; the former being a table-land of primitive rocks, the latter the sandy meadow land on the right bank of the river Jamna. Here, in a district wrested by his former patron from the Játs,[95] Najaf Kuli had been employed in endeavours to subjugate the indigenous population of Mewátis, a race professing Islám like himself, but mixing it with many degrading superstitions, and resembling their neighbours the Minas of Rajputána and the

[94] *Vide sup.*, p. 61.
[95] *Vide* Chap. i. *in fin.*

Bhattis of Hariána in habits of vagrancy and lawlessness, which above half a century of British administration has even now failed to eradicate.

Najaf Kuli Khán obeyed the Imperial summons, and reached Dehli, where he encamped close to the Begam Sumroo, in front of the main gate of the Palace, on the 17th November, 1787. The general command of the Imperial troops was conferred upon the Emperor's second son, Mirza Akbar, who, since the flight of his elder brother, had been considered as heir apparent, and who now received a khillat of seven pieces. The son of a Hindu official, named Rám Rattan, was appointed the Prince's deputy (although he was by descent nothing but a *modi* or "chandler"); and a cannonade was opened on the camp of Gholám Kádir, who replied by sending round shot into the palace itself, some of which fell on the Diwán Khas.

Sindhia's conduct at this juncture has never been explained. He was himself at Gwalior, and his army under Lakwá Dádá, shut up in the fort of Agra, was defending itself as well as it might against the forces under Ismail Beg. At the same time the author of the *Tárikh-i-Mozafari* assures us that Ambáji Inglia—one of Sindhia's most trusty lieutenants, arrived in Dehli with a small force, and that his arrival was the signal for a reconciliation between the Emperor's principal adherents and Gholám Kádir, who was then introduced to the presence, and invested with the dignity of Premier Noble (Sháh Alám himself binding upon his head the jewelled fillet called *Dastar-u-Goshwára*). It is probable that a compromise was effected, in which Gholám Kádir, by receiving the desired office at the hands of the Mahratta minister, was supposed to have acknowledged the supremacy of the latter. The whole story is perplexing. When cannonaded, the Páthan chief suddenly appears within the palace; when Sindhia's troops arrive, he receives the investiture that he was seeking in opposition to Sindhia; and at the moment of success he marches off to Aligarh. This latter movement is, however, accounted for by Francklin, who attributes it to the news of Prince Jawan Bakht being at hand with the forces of Himmat Bahádur, who had joined the cause of Ismail Beg. At all events, if Gholám Kádir owed this sudden improvement in his position to the good offices of the man whose garrison he had so lately chased from Dehli, he did not evince his gratitude in a form that could have been expected; for he lost no time in marching against Sindhia's late conquest of Aligarh, which fort almost immediately fell into his hands. He then proceeded to join his forces to those of Ismail Beg, before Agra; and remained for some months assisting at the siege of that fort; these operations being subject to constant annoyance from the Játs, and from the troops of Sindhia, who finally crossed the Chambal at the end of the cold season of 1787, having received large reinforcements from the Deccan. Ismail Beg and Gholám Kádir immediately raised the siege of Agra, turned upon the advancing army, and an obstinate battle took place at Chaksána, eleven miles from Bhartpur, on the 24th April. The particulars of this action are not given by the native historian, whom I here follow,[96] but they are detailed by Grant Duff, who probably had them from General de Boigne, who was present at the action, and with whom that writer had frequent conversations at Chambéri after the General's

[96] *Tárikh-i-Mozafari.*

retirement to his native country.[97] The Mahratta army was commanded by Rána Khán, a man who, having in the capacity of a water-carrier been the means of assisting Sindhia to escape from the carnage of Pánipat in 1761, had been much protected by him; and being otherwise a man of merit, was now become one of the chief officers of the army. Besides M. de Boigne there was another French officer present, whose name is given by Duff as Listeneaux, perhaps a mistake for some such word as Lestonneaux. John Hessing was also in this campaign, as may be gathered from the epitaph on his tomb, which is close to that of Sumroo at Agra. (See Appendix.) The Musalman leaders fought well, Gholám Kádir threw himself upon the infantry of the right wing, and broke them. Ismail Beg with all the impetuosity of his character vigorously attacked the battalions of M. de Boigne, but was received with *sang froid* and resolution. The Mahratta horse supported the infantry fairly, but were overmatched for such severe duty by the weight of the Moghul cavalry and their superior discipline. It is probable, however, that the infantry, formed and led by Europeans, would have been more than a match for all their attempts, had not three of the battalions deserted and joined the enemy, while the Ját cavalry failed to sustain the efforts of the remaining sepoys. The army of Rána Khán, under these circumstances, withdrew under cover of night to Bhartpur; and Ismail Beg renewed the siege of Agra, while Gholám Kádir moved northward in order to protect his own possessions from an incursion of the Sikhs, with which he was then just threatened.

While these transactions were going on to the south and south-east of the capital, the Emperor had been occupied by a campaign which he conducted personally in the west, and which might have given Sindhia much anxiety had it been directed by a more efficient leader. As events turned, this expedition is chiefly remarkable as being the last faint image of the once splendid operations of the great military monarchy of Akbar and of Aurangzeb.

At the end of 1787, and probably in consequence of Ismail Beg's attempts to secure the co-operation of the Rájputs, an embassy from Jodhpur had presented itself at the Court of Sháh Alám, bearing a handsome *nazar* (gift of homage or respect) and a golden key. The envoy explained that he was instructed by his master Bijai Singh, the Ráthor leader, to present this, the key of the Fort of Ájmir, in token of his wish that an Imperial army under his Majesty in person might march thither and take possession of that country; adding that Partáb Sing, the Kachwáha Dhiráj of Jaipur, joined in the application.

It seems plain that principle and prudence should have combined to deter the Emperor from consenting to this invitation, whereby he took an active step of hostility towards Sindhia, his minister, and at this time perhaps his most powerful and best disposed supporter. But the dream of a Musalman restoration, even with Hindu aid, will always have a fascination for the sons of Islám; and the weak Sháh Alám adopted the proposal with an alacrity such as he had not shown for many years. On the 5th of January, 1788, he marched from Dehli, accompanied by several of the princes and princesses of his family. From the fact of Mirza Akbar continuing to be regarded as heir apparent, and from some other considerations, it

[97] Vol. iii. p. 19. Bombay Edition.

may be gathered that the last attempt of Jawan Bakht in the Emperor's favour, and its eventual defeat, must have already taken place; for such is the confused manner in which these events are related by my authorities—some leaving out one part, and some another, while the dates shine few and far, like stars in a stormy night—that the relative position of events is sometimes left entirely open to conjecture. But it is certain that the excellent prince whom we have heretofore encountered more than once, did about this time make his appearance at the capital, with a small contingent supplied him by the Viceroy of Áudh, adding to his force such irregular troops as he was able to raise upon the way; and that on this occasion it was that he addressed to George III. of Britain the touching yet manly appeal from which I make the following extract:—"Notwithstanding the wholesome advice given from the throne to Sindhia, to conciliate the attachment of the ancient nobility, and to extend protection to the distressed peasantry, that ungrateful chief, regardless of the royal will, has established himself in continued and unvaried opposition; until he, having by his oppressions exasperated the Rájás and Princes of the Empire, particularly the most illustrious prince of Jainagar, Rájá Partáb Singh, as likewise the ruler of Jodhpur, both of whom are allied by blood to our family, these chiefs united to chastise the oppressor, gave him battle, and defeated him; but the machinations of the rebellious increased. On one side, Gholám Kádir Khán (son of the detested Afghán Zábitá Khán) has raised the standard of rebellion. His example having encouraged others, the disturbance became so formidable as to penetrate even to the threshold of the Imperial palace; so that our august parent was compelled to make use of the most strenuous exertions."

This statement of the condition of the Empire is interesting, as being given by a contemporary writer in all respects the best able to judge. He concludes by an urgent appeal to the British monarch for assistance "to restore the royal authority, punish the rebellious and re-establish the house of Timur, and, by this kind interposition, to give repose to the people of God, and render his name renowned among the princes of the earth."

Among the pressing disturbances noted by the prince was undoubtedly the defection of Najaf Kuli Khán, whom we have lately seen combined with the Begam in the protection of the Emperor against the insults of Gholám Kádir, but who had since gone into open rebellion, upon an attempt made by the faction in temporary power to supplant him in his government by one Murád Beg. This Moghul officer having been put in charge of some part of the convert's territorial holding, the latter not unnaturally regarded the act as a menace to his whole power, waylaid the Moghul on his way to his new post, and put him in confinement at Rewári.

But the men who had given the advice which led to this misfortune did not stop there, but proceeded to strike at the prince himself, whom they accused to the Emperor of designs upon the throne. He obtained however the titular office of Governor of Agra, and seriously attempted, with the aid of Ismail Beg, to obtain possession of the fort and province. Foiled in this, and escaping narrowly an attempt upon his person by Gholám Kádir, he ultimately retired to the protection of the British at Benares, where he died a mortified and heartbroken man on the 31st May, in the eventful year 1788. It is not quite clear, from the records of these transactions, why the prince, experienced statesman as he was, attempted to ally himself to those Musalman malcontents rather than to the Mahratta Chief, whose ability and resources must have been well known to him. It must, however, be admitted that Sindhia was just then showing an inaction which was calculated to arouse Jawan Bakht's suspicions, and we can trace, in the letter quoted a short time back, signs of hostility in his mind against that wily politician. Idle as the speculation may now appear, it is difficult to refrain from a passing thought on the manner in which his choice of associates affected the fate not merely of his royal Father, but of Hindustan and the British power there. United with Sindhia he would in all probability have drawn off Gholám Kádir and changed the whole fortunes of the country. *Dis aliter visum.*

The prince, who was known to the English as Jáhándár Sháh, is described as "an accomplished gentleman, irreproachable in his private character, constant, humane, and benevolent" (Francklin, p. 162). He was about forty at the time of his death, which was caused by a fit, and is narrated in detail at p. 256 of the selections from the *Calcutta Gazettes,* in a manner somewhat more minute than that of Francklin, whose account (taken as usual from Razá Khán) appears inaccurate as well as incomplete.

Unattended therefore by this, his best and nearest friend, the poor old Emperor began his march to the westward. On the way it appeared well to take the opportunity of reducing Najaf Kuli, who, confident in his stronghold of Gokalgarh, would make no submission unless he were appointed premier. As we know that the Controller Manzur Ali, who was at present all-powerful, was in favour of the claims of Gholám Kádir, we may suppose that these terms were rejected with scorn, and the trenches were accordingly opened and the fort invested. The Emperor's army on this occasion consisted, according to Francklin, of some battalions of half-drilled infantry (called Najibs), the body guard, called the "Red Battalion," a very considerable body of Moghul horse, and three disciplined regiments which had been raised and drilled by the deceased Sumroo, and now with a detail of artillery and about two hundred European gunners, served under the well-known Begam; with these forces Sháh Alám sate down before Gokalgarh.[98] On the 5th April, 1788, the besieged made a vigorous sally, and charged close up to the tents of the Emperor. Such was the unprepared state of the royal camp, that the whole family were in imminent danger of being killed or captured; the imperial army was already in commotion, when, at this moment, three battalions of the Begam's Sepoys and a field piece dashed up, under the command of her chief officer Mr. Thomas. The infantry deployed with the gun in the centre, and threw in a brisk fire of musketry and grape, which checked the sortie, and gave the Imperialists time to form. The Moghul horse lost their leader: on the other side the *Chela* (adopted son) of the chief was shot dead; Himmat Bahádur, at the head of his Gosains (a kind of fighting friars who were then beginning to be found useful as mercenaries),[99]

[98] The Emperor was also accompanied by Hira Singh, the Ját chief of Ballamgarh, and by a small detachment from Ismail Beg's army under the command of Himmat Bahádur.

[99] Strictly, *Gosain* is the denomination of the lay-brother or apprentice, who is allowed to hold property, and to mingle in the world. That is not the case with the three higher orders of Hindu devotees.

delivered a frantic charge, in which they lost 200 men; and Najaf Kuli was finally driven in with the loss of his field-guns. He soon after opened negotiations through the inevitable Manzur Ali; and, the Begam Sumroo joining in his favour, he was admitted to the presence and fully pardoned. In the same Darbár, the Begam was publicly thanked for her services, and proclaimed the Emperor's daughter, under the title of Zeb-un-Nissa—"Ornament of her sex."

The expedition, however, exhausted itself in this small triumph. Whether from mistrust of the Rájputs, or from fear of Sindhia, who was just then hovering about Bhartpur, the Emperor was induced to turn back on the 15th April, and reached the capital by a forced march of twenty-four hours, accompanied by Himmat Bahádur. The Begam retired to Sirdhana, and Gholám Kádir and Ismail Beg parted, as we have already seen, after the indecisive action of Chaksána, a few days later. Though disappointed in their hopes of aid from Dehli, the Rájput chiefs fought on, and the tide of Sindhia's fortunes seemed to ebb apace. After the last-named fight he had fallen back upon Alwar, but only to be encountered by Partáb Singh, the Kachwáha prince, of Jaipur, who drove him back once more upon Agra. Here Ismail Beg met him again and chased him across the Chambal. Meanwhile Ambáji Inglia was prevented from rendering aid to his master by the persistence of the Ráthors of Jodhpur, who put him to flight after an obstinate engagement. Thus cut off, Sindhia remained under the friendly protection of the Chambal until the month of June, when Rána Khán joined him with a fresh body of troops that he had received from the Deccan. Thus reinforced Sindhia once more marched to the relief of his gallant follower Lakwá Dádá, who still held out in the Fort of Agra. The attack was made on this occasion from the eastward, near the famous ruins of Fatihpur-Sikri, and was met by Ismail Beg with one of his furious cavalry charges. De Boigne's infantry and artillery however repulsed him, before Gholám Kádir, who was returning to the Moghul's aid, had been able to cross his forces over the Jamna, or effect a junction. Ismail Beg, who was severely wounded, did not hesitate to plunge his horse into the stream, swollen and widened as it was by the melting of the Himalayan snows. The Mahrattas, satisfied with having raised the siege, did not pursue him, and the two Mohammadan chiefs once more united their forces at Firozábád. Francklin (who very seldom gives a date) says that this final battle took place on the 22nd August. He also states that Gholám Kádir had already joined Ismail Beg, but drew off on the approach of the Mahratta army. The former statement is easily seen to be erroneous, as both the noblemen in question were in a very different scene in August of that year.[100] The latter is possible, but the weight of authorities, Mahratta and Musalman, is in favour of the account given above. Francklin carelessly adds:—"Agra *surrendered*," the fact being that the gallant governor Lakwá Dádá was a brother officer of Rána Khán's, and his relief had been the object of the battle. About this time de Boigne retired from Sindhia's employ and went to Lucknow, where he entered into a business partnership with the famous Claude Martine, or Martin. Whether this step was caused by weariness, by doubts of ultimate success, or by hopes of more material advantage, is not known. But the immediate consequence that followed was, that the Patel went into cantonments at Mathra, and remained there watching events

[100] *Vide inf.*, p. 99 ff.

throughout the whole of that eventful autumn.

There is reason to believe that Gholám Kádir—whether from avarice, from ambition, from a desire to avenge some personal injury, or from a combination of any two or of the whole of these motives—had by this time formed a project, vague perhaps at first, of repeating the career of crime with which Ghâzi-ud-din had startled Asia nearly thirty years before. Meantime he spoke Ismail fair, seeing in him a chief, worsted indeed for the moment, but a rallying-point for the Moghuls, on account as much of his proved valour as his high birth; one who would be alike useful as a friend, and dangerous as a foe. He accordingly explained, as best he could, his late defection, and persuaded the simple soldier to lose no time in collecting his scattered forces for an attack upon the capital. No sooner had the Beg left for this purpose, than Gholám Kádir also departed, and proceeding to Dehli renewed his hypocritical professions of loyalty through the instrumentality of Manzur Ali Khán. He asserted that Ismail Beg, who had arrived before him, and who now joined forces with him, was like himself actuated by the sole desire to save the Empire from the usurpations of the Mahratta chief; and, as far as the Beg was concerned, these professions were possibly not without foundation. At present the conduct of both leaders was perfectly respectful. In the meantime a small force was sent to Dehli by Sindhia and entered the palace, upon which the confederates, whose strength was not yet fully recruited, retired to their former encamping ground at Sháhdara—the scene, it may be remembered, of Surajmal's fall in the days of Najib-ud-daulah. In this situation the confederates began to be straitened for provisions, for it was now the month of July, and the stock of winter crops, exhausted as were the agriculturists by years of suffering and uncertainty, was running low, whilst the lawless character of the young Páthan and his Rohillas was not such as to encourage the presence of many grain-dealers in their camp. Desertions began to take place, and Gholám Kádir prepared for the worst by sending off his heavy baggage to Ghausgarh. He and his companions renewed to the Emperor their messages of encouragement in the project of throwing off the yoke of Sindhia; but the Emperor, situated as he was, naturally returned for answer, "That his inclinations did not lie that way." Sháh Alám was sustained in this firm line of conduct by the presence of the Mahratta troops under Himmat Bahádur, and by the ostensible support of Gul Mohammad, Bádal Beg Khán, Sulaimán Beg, and other Moghul courtiers whom he believed to be faithful; and it seemed for the moment as if the confederates' cause was lost.

Thus pressed, these desperate men at length dropped all disguise and opened fire on the palace with all their heavy guns. The Emperor on this invited the aid of his Mahratta minister, who was now at Mathra, only a week's hard marching from the capital. It was Mádhoji Sindhia's undoubted duty to have hastened to the relief of him whom he professed to serve; but it must be admitted that the instances he had already witnessed of Sháh Alám's want of resolution and of good faith may have furnished the minister with some excuse for wishing to read him a severe lesson. He had also had sufficient taste of the fighting powers of the Musalmans to lead him to avoid a general engagement as long as possible, since every day would increase the probability of their quarrelling if left to themselves, while external attacks would only drive them to cohere.

Sindhia accordingly pursued a middle path. He sent to the Begam Sumroo, and urged her to hasten to the Emperor's assistance; but the prudent lady was not willing to undertake a task from which, with his vastly superior resources, she saw him shrink. He likewise sent a confidential Brahmin, who arrived on 10th July, and five days after, appeared a force of 2,000 horse under Ráyáji, a relation of Sindhia's. The Ballamgarh Játs likewise contributed a small contingent.

Note.—The following account of de Boigne's early career is from Captain Duff, who knew him at Chambéri, about the year 1825:—

After describing his adventures as a youthful soldier of fortune, first as an ensign in the French army, and then in the Russian service in the Levant, whence he reached Cairo, and finally got to India by what is now called the Overland Route,—the writer proceeds to state that M. de Boigne was appointed an ensign in the 6th Native Battalion under the Presidency of Madras, from whence he, not long after, proceeded to Calcutta, bearing letters of recommendation to Mr. Hastings, the Governor-General. He was then permitted to join Major Browne's Embassy to Dehli (in 1784, *vide sup*.), when he took the opportunity of visiting Sindhia's camp, on the invitation of Mr. Anderson, the British resident. Gohad being at this time besieged by Sindhia (who had treated de Boigne very scurvily), the latter communicated a plan for its relief to a Mr. Sangster, who commanded 1,000 sepoys and a train of artillery in the service of the Gohad Rána. The scheme broke down, because the Rána could not or would not advance the required sum of money.

De Boigne next made overtures to the Rájá of Jaipur, and was commissioned by him to raise two battalions; but Mr. Hastings having meanwhile recalled him to Calcutta, the Rájá was induced to alter his intentions. De Boigne finally entered the service of his original enemy, Mádhoji Sindhia, on an allowance of Rs. 1,000 a month for himself, and eight all round for each of his men. To the privates he gave five and a half, and paid the officers proportionately from the balance. M. de Boigne gradually got European officers of all nations into his corps. Mr. Sangster, from the service of the Rána of Gohad, joined him, and became superintendent of his cannon foundry.

Some account of the further proceedings of General de Boigne will appear in the succeeding pages: and some notes regarding the close of his life will be found in the Appendix. Though moving in an obscure scene he was one of the great personages of the World's Drama; and much of the small amount of the civil and military organization upon which the British administration in Hindustan was ultimately founded is due to his industry, skill, and valour.

CHAPTER VI.

A.D. 1788.

Defection of Moghuls—Confederates obtain possession of Palace—Emperor deposed—Palace plundered—Gholám Kádir in the Palace—Emperor blinded—Approach of Mahrattas—Apprehensions of Spoiler—The Moharram—Explosion in Palace—Flight to Meerut—Probable Intentions—Capture of Gholám Kádir—His Punishment—Excuse for his Deeds—Sindhia's Measures—Future nature of Narrative—Poetical Lament—Col. Francklin.

Alarmed by these various portents, Gholám Kádir lost no time in summoning all his adherents from Ghausgarh, stimulating their zeal with the promise of plunder. At the same time he deputed Ismail Beg across the river to practise upon the fidelity of the garrison; and such was the Beg's influence that the Moghul portion of the Imperial troops joined him immediately, and left the unfortunate Emperor to be protected exclusively by unbelievers, under the general direction of the Gosain leader, Himmat Bahádur. This mercenary, not perhaps having his heart in the cause, terrified by the threats of the Páthan, and (it is possible) tampered with by traitors about the emperor's person, soon withdrew; and the confederate chiefs at once crossed the river, and took possession of the city.

The Emperor now became seriously anxious, and, after a consultation with his attendants, resolved on deputing Manzur Ali to seek a personal explanation with Gholám Kádir and Ismail Beg. It has always been customary to tax this official with the responsibility of this measure, and of the appalling results which followed; but it does not appear absolutely necessary to impute his conduct to complicity with the more criminal part of Gholám Kádir's designs; and his subsequent fate is perhaps some sort of argument in his favour. But, be this as it may, he went to the chiefs by order of the Emperor, and demanded, "What were their intentions?" In the usual style of Eastern manners they replied, "These slaves are merely in attendance for the purpose of presenting their duty in person to his Majesty." "Be it so," said the Controller; and his acquiescence seems to have been unavoidable. "But," he added, "you surely need not bring your army into the palace: come with a small retinue, lest the Governor should shut the gates in your faces." Upon this advice the two noblemen acted, and entered the *Am Khás* on the forenoon of the following day (18th of July) with some half hundred men-at-arms. Each received a *khilat* of seven pieces, together with a sword and other presents; Gholám Kádir also receiving a richly-jewelled shield. They then returned to their respective residences in the town, where Ismail Beg spent the rest of the day in making arrangements in order to preserve the safety and confidence of the inhabitants. Next day, he removed his quarters permanently to the house formerly occupied by Mohammad Sháh's Vazir, Kammar-ud-din Khán; and his men were quartered a couple of miles south of the city, in and about the celebrated monumental tomb of the ancient Saint, Sháh Nizám-ud-din.[101] Gholám Kádir's men were nearer the palace, where the present Native Infantry cantonment is, in Dariaoganj; while his officers occupied the vast premises formerly belonging successively to the Ministers Ghází-ud-din and Mirza Najaf, outside of the Cabul Gate. The ostensible state of Dehli politics was now this; Gholám Kádir was Premier (an office he swore upon the Korán faithfully to discharge), vice Mádhoji Sindhia, dismissed; and the combined armies were the troops of the Empire, commanded by Ismail Beg.

Under these circumstances Gholám Kádir did not want a pretext, and at seven in the morning of Friday, the 29th July, he returned to the palace, where he had an interview with the Emperor in the Diwán Khas. Francklin is at fault again here; making his second interview one with that which occurred more than a week before. Citing the authority of Ismail Beg, who stood by, he represented that the army was prepared to march on Mathra, and to chase the Mahrattas from Hindustan; but that they first demanded a settlement of their arrears, for which the Imperial treasury was alone responsible, and alone sufficient.

This harangue, at its conclusion, was warmly echoed by the Controller, by his Deputy, and by Ramrattan *Modi*. On the other side. Lálla Sital Dás, the Treasurer, who was at once summoned, declared that, whatever might be the responsibility of the Treasury for an army in whose raising it had had no share, and by whose service it had not hitherto at all profited, at least that its chests contained no means for meeting the claims. He boldly urged that the claims should be resisted at all hazards.

Gholám Kádir replied by an assumed fit of ungoverned anger, and producing an intercepted letter from Sháh Alám, calling upon Sindhia for help, ordered the Emperor to be disarmed, together with his personal guard, and removed into close arrest; and then, taking from the privacy of the Salim Garh a poor secluded son of the late Emperor Ahmad Sháh, set him on his throne, hailed him Emperor, under the title of Bedar Bakht, and made all the courtiers and officials do him homage. It is but just to record, in favour of one whose memory has been much blackened, that Manzur Ali, the Controller, appears on this occasion to have acted with sense, if not spirit. When Bedar Bakht was first brought forward, Sháh Alám was still upon the throne, and, when ordered to descend, began to make some show of resistance. Gholám Kádir was drawing his sword to cut him down, when the Controller interposed; advising the Emperor to bow to compulsion, and retire peacefully to his apartments.[102] For three days and nights the Emperor and his

[101] Sháh Nizám-ud-din Aulia was an influential adventurer in the reign of Alá-ud-din Khilji, circ. 1300 H.D. He is supposed by some to have been a sorcerer, by others an assassin of the Secret Society of Khorásán. His tomb is to this day maintained in perfect preservation, and with all possible respect.

[102] Francklin's "Sháh Alum," p. 176.

family remained in close confinement, without food or comfort of any sort; while Gholám Kádir persuaded Ismail Beg to return to his camp, and devoted himself to wholesale plunder during the absence of his associate. The latter's suspicions were at length aroused, and he soon after sent an agent to remind Gholám Kádir that he and his men had received nothing of what it had been agreed to pay them. But the faithless Páthan repudiated every kind of agreement, and proceeded to defend the palace and apply all that it contained to his own use.

Ismail Beg, now sensible of his folly, lost no time in sending for the heads of the civic community, whom he exhorted to provide for their own protection; at the same time strictly charging his own lieutenants to exert themselves to the very utmost should the Páthans attempt to plunder. For the present, Gholám Kádir's attention was too much taken up with the pillage of the Imperial family to allow of his doing much in the way of a systematic sack of the town. Dissatisfied with the jewellery realised from the new Emperor, to whom the duty of despoiling the Begams was at first confided, he conceived the notion that Sháh Alám, as the head of the family, was probably, nay, certainly, the possessor of an exclusive knowledge regarding the place of a vast secret hoard. All the crimes and horrors that ensued are attributable to the action of this monomania. On the 29th, he made the new Titular, Bedar Bakht, inflict corporal chastisement upon his venerable predecessor. On the 30th, a similar outrage was committed upon several of the ladies of Sháh Alám's family, who filled the beautiful buildings with their shrieks of alarm and lamentation. On the 31st, the ruffian thought he had secured enough to justify his attempting to reconcile Ismail Beg and his men by sending them a donative of five lakhs of rupees. The result of this seems to have been that a combined, though tolerably humane and orderly attempt was made to levy contributions from the Hindu bankers of the city.

On the 1st of August a fresh attempt was made to wrest the supposed secret from the Sháh, who once more denied all knowledge of it, employing the strongest figure of denial. "If," said the helpless old man, "you think I have any concealed treasures, they must be within me. Rip open my bowels, and satisfy yourself." The tormentor then tried cajolery and promises, but they were equally futile. "God protect you, who has laid me aside," said the fallen Monarch. "I am contented with my fate."

The aged widows of former Emperors were next exposed to insult and suffering. These ladies were at first treated kindly, their services being thought necessary in the plunder of the female inhabitants of the *Imtiáz Mahál*, whose privacy was at first respected. But on the failure of this attempt, the poor old women themselves were plundered and driven out of the palace. When other resources had been exhausted, the Controller fell under the displeasure of his former *protégé*, and was made to disburse seven lakhs. On the 3rd August, Gholám Kádir gave proof of the degraded barbarity of which Hindustáni Páthans[103] can be guilty, by lounging on the throne on the Diwán Khas, side by side with the nominal Emperor, whom he covered with abuse and ridicule, as he smoked the *hookah* in his face. On the 6th,

[103] "Páthan," as has been already observed, is the usual designation of the Rohillas and other Hindustánis of Afghán descent.

he destroyed the same throne for the sake of the plating which still adhered to it, which he threw into the melting-pot; and passed the next three days in digging up the floors, and taking every other conceivable measure in pursuit of his besetting chimera—the hidden treasure. During this interval, however, he appears to have been at times undecided; for, on the 7th he visited the Emperor in his confinement, and offered to put on the throne Mirza Akbar, the Emperor's favourite son—who did in fact ultimately succeed. The only answer to these overtures was a request by Sháh Alám that he might be left alone, "for he was weary," he said, "of such state as he had lately known, and did not wish to be disturbed with public business."

At length arrived the memorable 10th of August, which, perhaps, as far as any one date deserves the distinction, was the last day of the legal existence of the famous Empire of the Moghuls. Followed by the Deputy Controller, Yákub Ali, and by four or five of his own most reckless Páthans, Gholám Kádir entered the Diwán Khas, and ordered Sháh Alám to be brought before him. Once more the hidden treasure was spoken of, and the secret of its deposit imperiously demanded; and once more the poor old Emperor—whom we not long ago saw melting his plate to keep together a few troops of horse—with perfect truth replied that if there was any such secret he for one was in total ignorance of it. "Then," said the Rohilla, "you are of no further use in the world, and should be blinded." "Alas!" replied the poor old man, with native dignity, "do not so: you may spare these old eyes, that for sixty years have grown dim with the daily study of God's word."[104] The spoiler then ordered his followers to torture the sons and grandsons of the Emperor, who had followed, and now surrounded their parent. This last outrage broke down the old man's patience. "Take my sight," he cried, "rather than force upon it scenes like these." Gholám Kádir at once leaped from the throne, felled the old man to the ground, threw himself upon the prostrate monarch's breast, and, so some historians relate, struck out one of his eyes with his own dagger. Then rising, he ordered a byestander—apparently a member of the household, Yákub Ali himself—to complete the work. On his refusing, he slew him with his own hand. He then ordered that the Princes should share the fate of their father and be deprived of eyesight, but desisted from this part of his brutality on the pressing remonstrance of the Treasurer, Lálla Sital Dás. The Emperor was, however, completely blinded by the Páthans, and removed to Salimgarh, amid the shrill lamentations of women, and the calmer, but not less passionate curses of men, who were not scourged into silence without some difficulty and delay. Francklin, following his usual authority, the MS. narrative of Saiyid Razá Khán, says that, under these accumulated misfortunes, the aged Emperor evinced a firmness and resignation highly honourable to his character. It is pitiable to think how much fortitude may be thrown away by an Asiatic for want of a little active enterprise. There were probably not less than half-a-dozen points in Sháh Alám's life when a due vigour would have raised him to safety, if not to splendour; but his vigour was never ready at the right moment. There is a striking instance in Khair-ud-din's *Ibratnáma*. Gholám Kádir asking the blind Emperor in mockery "If he saw anything?" was answered, "Nothing but the Korán between thee and me."

[104] Kalám Ullah, the name by which Musalmans designate the Korán.

The anxious citizens were not at once aware of the particulars of this tragedy; but ere long rumours crept out to them of what crimes and sufferings had been going on all day in the Red Castle,—behind those stern and silent walls that were not again to shield similar atrocities for nearly seventy years. Then another day of horror was to come, when one of the princes who were tortured on the 10th of August, 1788, was to see women and children brutally massacred in the same once splendid courts; and to find himself in the hands of adherents whose crimes would render him a puppet if they succeeded, and a felon if they failed.

But on the 12th more money was sent to Ismail Beg; and, as before, the citizens were offered as the victims of the reconciliation. They now began to leave the city in large numbers; but on the 14th flying parties of Mahrattas began to appear from the southward, and somewhat restored confidence. Ismail Beg, who had long ceased to have any real confidence in Gholám Kádir, and who (let us hope for the credit of human nature) felt nothing but disgust at his companion's later excesses, now opened negotiations with Rána Khán. On the 17th a convoy of provisions from Ghausgarh was cut off, and a number of the Páthans who escorted it put to the sword or drowned in attempting to cross the river. On the 18th the Mahrattas came up in considerable force on the left bank of the Jamna, where they blockaded the approach from all but the side of the Musalman camp. In the city the shops were shut, and supplies began totally to fail. Scarcity even began to prevail in the palace, and the troops within to murmur loudly for their share of the spoil. Next day the spoiler condescended to argue with some who remonstrated with him on his treatment of the Royal Family. Their condition was in truth becoming as bad as it could well be; many of the women dying daily of starvation. It is almost with relief that we find, that the increasing scarcity compelling fresh acts of spoliation, the Controller, who had so much helped in bringing about this deplorable state of affairs, became himself its victim, being deprived of everything that he possessed. Thus passed the month of August, 1788, in Dehli.

The courage of Gholám Kádir did not at once yield to his growing perils and difficulties. He appropriated an apartment in the palace—probably the *Burj-i-Tilla* or "Golden Bastion." Here he caroused with his officers, while the younger members of the royal family played and danced before them like the common performers of the streets. And they were rewarded by the assurance on the part of their tormentor that, however deficient they might be in princely virtues, their talents would preserve them from wanting bread. Khair-ud-din adds a strange account of Gholám Kádir going to sleep among them; and on waking, he is represented as reviling them for their lack of courage in not stabbing him while thus at their mercy! Many of the younger princesses were exposed to insult and outrage, according to this writer. Gholám Kádir at the same time partially suppressed the discontents of his men, though not without risk to his life. At length, on the 7th of September, finding the Mahrattas increasing in numbers and boldness, and fearing to be surrounded and cut off, Gholám Kádir moved his army back to its old encampment across the river, and despatched part of his plunder to Ghausgarh, conciliating his followers by the surrender of what was less portable, such as the rich tents and equipage which had been lately used by the Emperor on his expedition to Rewári. On the 14th he paid a further visit to his camp, being under apprehensions from Ismail Beg, but returned to the palace soon after, in order to make one more attempt to shake what he considered the obstinacy of Sháh Alám about the hid treasure. Foiled in this, and hemmed in by difficulties, it may be hoped that he now began to perceive with horror the shadow of an advancing vengeance. His covering the retreat to the eastward of the palace and city favours the supposition.

Meanwhile the great ceremony of mourning for the sons of Ali[105] drew on; the Moharram, celebrated in Hindustan alike by the Shias, who venerate their memory, and by the Sunnis, who uphold their murderers. The principal features of this celebration are processions of armed men, simulating the battle of Karbala; and the public funeral of the saints, represented, not by an effigy of their bodies, but by a model of their tombs. Loving spectacle and excitement, with the love of a rather idle and illiterate population whose daily life is dull and torpid, the people of India have very generally lost sight of the fasting and humiliation which are the real essence of the Moharram, and have turned it into a diversion and a show. But there was no show nor diversion for the citizens of Dehli that year, menaced by contending armies, and awed by the knowledge of a great crime. At length, on the 11th October, the last day of the fast, a sense of deliverance began to be vaguely felt. It began to be known that Ismail Beg was reconciled to Rána Khán, and that the latter was receiving reinforcements from the Deccan. Lestonneaux, with the formidable "Telinga" battalions of de Boigne, had already arrived; all was movement and din in the Páthan camp at Sháhdara. Finally, as the short chill evening of the autumn day closed in, the high walls of the Red Castle blabbed part of their secret to those who had so long watched them. With a loud explosion, the powder magazine rose into the air, and flames presently spread above the crenellated parapets. The bystanders, running to the rampart of the town, facing the river, saw, by the lurid light, boats being rowed across; while a solitary elephant was moving down at his best pace over the heavy sands, bearing the rebel chief. Gholám Kádir had finally departed, leaving the Salimgarh by a sally-port, and sending before him the titular Emperor, the plundered controller of the household, and all the chief members of the royal family.

The exact events which had passed in the interior of the palace that day can never now be known. Whether, as is usually thought, Gholám Kádir tried to set fire to the palace, that his long crime might be consummated by the destruction of Sháh Alám among the blazing ruins of his ancestral dwelling; or whether, as the author of the *Mozafari* supposes, he meant to hold out against the Mahrattas to the last, and was only put to flight by the explosion, which he attributed to a mine laid by them, can only be a matter for speculation. To myself, I confess, the popular story appears the more probable. If Gholám Kádir meant to stand a siege, why did he send his troops across the river? and why, when he was retiring at the appearance of a mine—which he must have known was likely to be one of the siege operations—did he remove the royal family, and only leave his chief victim? Lastly, why did he leave that victim alive? Possibly he was insane.

[105] Ali was the son-in-law of the Prophet of Islám, and his sons were slain by rival claimants.—*Vide* Gibbon, &c.

The Mahratta general immediately occupied the castle; and the exertions of his men succeeded in extinguishing the flames before much injury had occurred. Sháh Alám and the remaining ladies of his family were set at liberty, provided with some present comforts, and consoled as to the future. Rána Khán then awaited further reinforcements from Sindhia, while the Páthans retired towards their own country.

The Court of Punah saw their advantage in strengthening the Patel, and sent him a strong body of troops, led by Takuji Holkar in person, on condition that both that chief and the Peshwa should participate in the fruits of the campaign. The arrival of these forces was welcomed alike by Rána Khán and by the long harassed citizens of Dehli; and after the safety of the palace had been secured, the rest of the army, commanded by Rána Khán, Appa Khándi Rao, and others, started in pursuit of Gholám Kádir, who found himself so hard pressed that he threw himself into the Fort of Meerut, three marches off, and about equi-distant from Dehli, from Ghausgarh, and from the frontiers of Rohilkand. Why he did not, on leaving Dehli, march due north to Ghausgarh cannot be now positively determined; but it is possible that, having his spoil collected in that fort, he preferred trying to divert the enemy by an expedition in a more easterly direction; and that he entertained some hopes of aid from his connection, Faizula Khán of Rámpur, or from the Bangash of Farrukhábád.

Be this as it may, the fort of Meerut sheltered him for the time, but in that fort he was ere long surrounded. The investing army was large, and, as the chances of escape diminished, the Páthan's audacity at length began to fail, and he offered terms of the most entire and abject submission. These being sternly rejected, he prepared for the worst. On the 21st of December a general assault was delivered by the Mahratta army, against which Gholám Kádir and his men defended themselves with resolution throughout the short day. But his men in general were now weary, if not of his crimes at all events of his misfortunes, and he formed the resolution to separate from them without further delay. He accordingly stole out of the fort that night, mounted on a horse, into whose saddle-bags he had stuffed a large amount of the most valuable jewellery from the palace plunder, which he had ever since retained in his own keeping, in view of an emergency. He rode some twelve miles through the winter night, avoiding the haunts of men, and apparently hoping to cross the Jamna and find refuge with the Sikhs. At last, in the mists of the dawn, his weary horse, wandering over the fields, fell into a slope used for the descent of the oxen who draw up the bucket from the well, for the purposes of irrigation. The horse rose and galloped off by the incline made for the bullocks, but the rider was either stunned or disabled by his bruises, and remained where he fell. As the day dawned the Brahmin cultivator[106] came to yoke his cattle and water the wheat, when he found the richly-dressed form of one whom he speedily recognized as having but lately refused him redress when plundered by the Páthan soldiery. "*Salám, Nawáb Sáhib!*" said the man, offering a mock obeisance, with clownish malice, to his late oppressor. The scared and famished caitiff sate

[106] His name is said to have been Bhikka; the village is not far from the Begam Sumroo's home at Kotána, and is called Jáni; where, I believe, Bhikka's descendants still enjoy a piece of freehold land that was bestowed upon him by Sháh Alám for this service.

up and looked about him. "Why do you call me Nawáb?" he asked. "I am a poor soldier, wounded, and seeking my home. I have lost all I have, but put me in the road to Ghausgarh, and I will reward you hereafter." Necessarily, the mention of this fort would have put at rest any doubt in the Brahmin's mind; he at once shouted for assistance, and presently carried off his prize to Rána Khán's camp. Hence the prisoner was despatched to Sindhia, at Mathra, while the Páthans, left to themselves, abandoned the Fort of Meerut and dispersed to their respective homes. Bedar Bakht, the titular Emperor, was sent to Dehli, where he was confined and ultimately slain, and the unfortunate controller, Manzur Ali, who had played so prominent a part in the late events as to have incurred general suspicion of treacherous connivance, was tied to the foot of an elephant and thus dragged about the streets until he died.

For the Rohilla chief a still more horrible fate was prepared. On his arrival at Mathra, Sindhia inflicted upon him the punishment of *Tashhir*, sending him round the bazaar on a jackass, with his face to the tail, and a guard instructed to stop at every considerable shop and beg a *cowree*, in the name of the Nawáb of the Báwani. The wretched man becoming abusive under the contemptuous treatment, his tongue was torn out of his mouth. Gradually he was mutilated further, being first blinded, as a retribution for his treatment of the Emperor, and subsequently deprived of his nose, ears, hands and feet, and sent to Dehli. Death came to his relief upon the road, it is believed by his being hanged upon a tree 3rd March, 1789,[107] and the mangled trunk was sent to Dehli, where it was laid before the sightless monarch, the most ghastly *Nazar* that ever was presented in the *Diwán Khás*.

Perhaps, if we could hear Gholám Kádir's version of the revolution here described,[108] we might find that public indignation had to some extent exaggerated his crimes. It is possible that the tradition which imputes his conduct to revenge for an alleged cruelty of Sháh Alám[109] may be a myth, founded upon a popular conception of probability, and only corroborated by the fact that he died childless. Perhaps he merely thought that he was performing a legitimate stroke of State, and imitating the vigorous policy of Gházi-ud-din the younger; perhaps the plunder of the palace was necessary to conciliate his followers; perhaps the firing of the palace was an accident. But the result of the combination of untoward appearances has been to make his name a bye-word among the not over-sensitive inhabitants of Hindustan, familiar, by tradition and by personal experience, with almost every form of cruelty, and almost every degree of rebellion. It is said that during moments of reaction, after some of his debauches in the palace (*v.* p. 102),

[107] S. Karr's *Selections* from the *Calcutta Gazette*, Vol. ii. p. 202.

[108] I made an attempt to ascertain what this might be some years ago; and Gholám Kádir's nephew, Nawáb Mahmud Ali Khán, of Najibábád, promised to send me papers. But the troubles of 1857 arising before he had fulfilled his promise, the Nawáb did according to all that his fathers had done: he rebelled under circumstances of peculiar selfishness and treachery; and being captured by the British column in the following year, died shortly after, a prisoner in the Central Jail at Meerut. In all likelihood, the family papers perished in these transactions.

[109] *Vide* Chap. ii. *sup.*

Gholám Kádir attempted to justify his conduct by representing himself as acting under supernatural inspiration. "As I was sleeping," he averred, "in a garden at Sikandra, an apparition stood over me and smote me on the face, saying, Arise, go to Dehli, and possess thyself of the palace." It may be that at such times he experienced some feelings of remorse. At all events, his punishment was both immediate and terrible, and his crimes proved the ruin of his house. Ghausgarh was forthwith razed to the ground, so that—as already mentioned[110]—no vestige but the mosque remains. The brother of the deceased fled to the Panjáb.

The first care of the Patel, after these summary vindications of justice, was to make provision for the administration of Hindustan, to which he probably foresaw that he should not be able to give constant personal attention, and in which he resolved to run no further risks of a Musalman revival. The fallen Emperor was restored to his throne, in spite of his own reluctance, "in spite of his blindness," as the native historian says, who knew that no blind man could be a Sultán; and at the enthronement, to which all possible pomp was lent, the agency of the Peshwa, with Sindhia for his deputy, was solemnly renewed and firmly established. We also learn from Francklin that an annual allowance of nine lakhs of rupees was assigned for the support of the Emperor's family and Court, an adequate civil list if it had been regularly paid. But Sháh Nizám-ud-din, who had been restored to office, was an unfit man to be entrusted with the uncontrolled management of such a sum; and during the Patel's frequent and protracted absences, the royal family were often reduced to absolute indigence. Sáyid Razá Khán, on whose authority this shocking statement rests, was the resident representative of the British Minister at Lucknow, and was the channel through which the aged Emperor received from the British Government a monthly allowance of 2,000 rupees. This, together with the fees paid by persons desirous of being presented, was all that Sháh Alám could count on in his old age for the support of his thirty children and numerous kinsfolk and retainers. Captain Francklin was an eye-witness of the semblance of State latterly maintained in the Red Castle, where he paid his respects in 1794. He found the Emperor represented by a crimson velvet chair under an awning in the *Diwán Khás*, but the Sháh was actually in one of the private rooms with three of his sons. The British officers presented their alms under the disguise of a tributary offering, and received some nightgowns, of sprigged calico, by way of honorific dresses.

The so-called Emperor being now incapable of ruling, even according to the very lax political code of the East, and all real power being in the hands of a Hindu headborough supported by mercenary troops, the native records, to which I have had access, either cease altogether, or cease to concern themselves with the special story of Hindustan. And, indeed, as far as showing the fall of the empire, my task is also done. I do not agree with those who think that the empire fell with the death of Aurangzeb, or even with the events that immediately preceded the campaign of Pánipat, in 1761. I consider the empire to have endured as long as "the king's name was a tower of strength"; as long as Nawábs paid large fines on succession, and contending parties intrigued for investiture; as long as Shujáá-ud-daulah could need its sanction to his occupation of Kattáhir, or Najaf Khán led its armies to the

[110] *Sup.*, p. 56.

conquest of the Játs. We have seen how that state of affairs originated, and how it came to an end; there is nothing now left but to trace briefly the concluding career of those who have played their parts in the narrative, and to introduce their successors upon the vast and vacant theatre. In so doing it must be borne in mind that, although we, from our present standpoint, can see that the Moghul Empire was ended, it did not altogether so appear to contemporaries. Whether federation or disintegration be the best ideal destiny, for a number of Provinces whose controlling centre has given way, is a question which may admit of more than one answer. But it is, in any case, certain that in the year 1789 the Provinces of which the Empire had been composed, were not ripe for independent and organic existence. There was still, therefore, a craving for a paramount power; and that craving was to be finally met by the British. In the meanwhile the almost effete machinery of the Empire, directed and administered by Sindhia, made the best available substitute; General de Boigne—who had the most complete information on the subject—bears unequivocal testimony on this subject. His words will be found at the beginning of the next chapter.

NOTE.—It would be curious to know what became of Gholám Kádir's jewel-laden horse after the rider fell into the pit. In Skinner's life, it is conjectured that he came into the hands of M. Lestonneaux. It is certain that this officer abruptly abandoned Sindhia's service at this very time. Perhaps the crown jewels of the Great Mughal are now in France. The Emperor (who composed poetry with estimation under the name of "Aftáb") solaced his temporary captivity by writing verses, which are still celebrated in Hindustan, and of which the following is a correct translation. The resemblance to the Psalms of David is noticeable:—

"The storms of affliction have destroyed the Majesty of my Government: and scattered my State to the winds.

I was even as the Sun[111] shining in the firmament of the Empire: but the sun is setting in the sorrowful West.

It is well for me that I have become blind; for so I am hindered from seeing another on my throne.

Even as the saints were afflicted by Yazid[112]; so is the ruin that has fallen upon me, through the appointment of Destiny.

The wealth of this world was my sickness; but now the Lord hath healed me.

I have received the just reward of mine iniquities; but now He hath forgiven me my sins.

I gave milk to the young adder; and he became the cause of my

[111] Aftáb, "Sun" was Sháh Alám's *nom de plume*.

[112] Yazid is the name of him whose troops slew Imam Hossain son of Ali.—*Vide Not. sup*. p. 103.

destruction.

The Steward[113] who served me thirty years compassed my ruin; but a swift recompense hath overtaken him.

The lords of my council who had covenanted to serve me; even they deserted me, and took whatsoever in thirty years I had put by for my children.

Moghuls and Afgháns alike failed me; and became confederates in my imprisonment.

Even the base-born man of Hamadán, and Gul Mohammad, full of wickedness; Alláh Yár also, and Solaimán and Bádal Beg[114] all met together for my trouble.

And now that this young Afghán[115] hath destroyed the dignity of my empire; I see none but thee, O Most Holy! to have compassion upon me.

Yet peradventure Timur Sháh[116] my kinsman may come to my aid; and Mádhoji Sindhia, who is even as a son unto me he also will surely avenge my cause.

Asaf-ud-daula and the chief of the English; they also may come to my relief.

Shame were it if Princes and People gathered not together; to the end that they might bring me help.

Of all the fair women of my chambers none is left to me but Mubarik Mahál.

O Aftáb! verily thou hast been this day overthrown by Destiny; yet God shall bless thee and restore thy fallen brightness."

Francklin's *Sháh Alum* has been constantly referred to. He was an officer of great diligence, who had large local opportunities, having been in Dehli, the Doáb, and Rohilkand, from 1793 to 1796, on a survey ordered by the British Government. He had access to many native sources of information; but unfortunately never cites any in the margin but Sáyid Razá's MS. I have not hesitated to combat his views on several points; but there are few English writers on the subject to whom we are more indebted. Besides this work, and one to be hereafter noticed, he was the author of books on Ancient Palibothra and on snake-worship. He died a lieutenant-colonel in the Bengal army.

[113] Manzur Ali Khán, whom Sháh Alám had much reason to execrate, even though his conduct was only due to a mistaken policy.

[114] Courtiers on whom he had relied. (*Sup.*, p. 95.)

[115] Gholám Kádir, Rohilla, Páthan, Indian Afghán.

[116] The son of Ahmad Abdáli, king of Kábul, who had married Sháh Alám's daughter.

PART III.

CHAPTER I.

A.D. 1789-94.

Sindhia as Mayor of Palace—British Policy—Augmentation of Army under General de Boigne—Ismail Beg joins the Rájput rising—Battle of Pátan—Sindhia at Mathra—Siege of Ájmir—Jodhpur Rájah—Battle of Mirta—Rivals alarmed—French Officers—Progress to Puna—Holkar advances—Ismail Beg taken—Battle of Lakhairi—Sindhia rebuked—Power of Sindhia—Rise of George Thomas—Thomas quits Begam—Sindhia at Puna—Death and character of Mádhoji Sindhia—Koil in the last Century.

From the time of the revolution of 1788 each of the dismembered provinces has its separate history; and the present record naturally shrinks to the contracted limits of a local history of the capital, and of the districts more especially connected with it by proximity or by political ties. Still, since the country is one that has long been occupying our attention, and the persons who have made it do so are still upon the scene, it may be interesting to those who have followed the narrative thus far if a brief conclusion is presented to them. The story of the empire's fall will thus be completed, and the chasm between the Moghul rule and the English rule will be provisionally bridged. It must, moreover, be remembered that the visible centre of authority is a thing for which men will always look. And, even in the fallen state of the Dehli monarchy this was still in the palace of the descendant of Bábar. To use de Boigne's words, written in 1790:—"le respect . . . . envers la maison de Timour regnait à tel point que, quoique toute la péninsule se fût sucessivement soustraite à son autorité, aucun prince . . . . de l'Inde ne s'était arrogé le titre de souverain. Sindhia partageait le respect, et Sháh Alám était toujours assis sur le Trône Mogol, et tout se faisait en son nom."

It has been already shown how "Mahárájá Patel," as Mádhoji Sindhia is called by the native writers, assumed the actual government, whilst he secured for the youthful chief of the Mahratta confederacy the titular office of "Agent Plenipotentiary," which had been once or twice previously used to designate mighty Viceroys like the first Nizám.

In providing this distinction for his native superior, the usually shrewd old minister intended to blind his countrymen and his rivals; and by another still more clumsy *coup de théâtre*, he assumed to himself the position of a servant, as harmonizing with the rural dignity of Beadle or Headborough, which, as we have seen, he persisted in affecting. Decorated however by the blind old Emperor with the more sonorous appellations of *Madár-ul-Mahám, Ali Jáh, Bahádur* ("Exalted and valorous Centre of Affairs"), he played the Mayor-of-the-Palace with far more effect at Dehli than it would have been possible for him to do at Punah. Circumstances, moreover, were now far more in his favour than they had been since 1785. During the three years that followed, the Rohillas of Ghausgarh were broken, Muhammad Beg was dead, the strength of the brave but indolent Rájputs was much paralyzed, and Najaf Kuli Khán—who never had opposed him, but might have been formidable if he pleased—had succumbed to a long attack of dropsy.[117] Ismail Beg, it is true, was still in existence, and now more than ever a centre of influence among the Moghuls. But Ismail Beg was at present conciliated, having joined the Patel's party ever since his former associate, Gholám Kádir, had proceeded to such criminal excesses in the palace. As a further means of attaching to him this important, even if not very intelligent chief, the Patel about this time conferred upon him a portion of Najaf Kuli's fief in the Mewát country south of Dehli. By this he not only pleased the Moghul noble, but trusted to furnish him with occupation in the reduction and management of the wild mountaineers of that district. It was indeed idle to hope that Ismail Beg would remain faithful in the event of any future resurrection of the Musalman power; and it could not be denied that something of the kind might at any time occur, owing to the menacing attitude of the Afgháns, who were still very powerful under the famous Ahmad Abdáli's son, Timur Sháh. Indeed, this was a ceaseless difficulty during the whole of Mádhoji's remaining life; and one that would have been still more serious, but for the anxiously pacific policy which, for the most part, characterized the British administration during that period. Nor did the Minister at this time enjoy the advantage of being served by European commanders. Lestonneaux retired suddenly in the beginning of 1789;[118] and de Boigne, as above-mentioned, had also left the army, and was engaged in commercial pursuits at Lucknow. But the army continued to comprise a certain proportion of regular troops; nor was it long before M. de Boigne, being earnestly solicited by Mádhoji, and offered his own terms, resumed his command, augmented this portion of the force, and assumed a position of confidence and freedom which had not previously been allowed him. The skeletons of his two original battalions remained to form the nucleus of the new force. The battalion of Lestonneaux—or whatever the name—was deserted by its commandant, with eight months' arrears due to it, was disorganized and mutinous; and Sindhia meditated an attack upon it with an overwhelming body of horse. De Boigne however interceded, representing that the soldiers were not to blame for their colonel's defection; and that their demand, though it might not be expressed with due respect, was after all founded on justice. Sindhia relented so far as to award a present payment of half the arrears, and a permission that the men should be absorbed in the brigade about to be formed; but the astute Savoyard took care first to make them pile their arms, so that their future entertainment should be as individuals only. The officers were at the same time cashiered; and thus the mutiny of a battalion was patiently and ingeniously suppressed without

[117] He was in his sixtieth year when he died. His death took place at Kanaund, *vide inf.*, p. 117.

[118] *Vide* Foot Note at the end of last Chapter.

its precious material being lost to the service. The requisite new recruits were principally raised from Rohilkand and Áudh—the future nurseries of the famous Bengal army. The officers were the most respectable Europeans that the General could collect; and the non-commissioned posts were given to picked men of the old battalions.[119]

The augmented force gradually reached the strength of three brigades, each brigade consisting of eight battalions of sepoys, each 700 strong; with 500 cavalry and forty fieldpieces. The General was allowed 10,000 rupees *per mensem* for his own pay, and a liberal scale was fixed for the European officers, whose number was from time to time increased, and the whole force, forming a small army in itself, marched under the white cross of Savoy,[120] the national colours of its honourable chief. A gratuity was secured to all who might be wounded in action, and it was guaranteed that their pay should go on while in hospital. Invalids were to have pensions in money and grants of land.

It soon had to take the field: for Ismail Beg's loyalty, already wavering in view of an Afghán invasion, gave way entirely in the beginning of 1790 before the solicitations of the Rájput chiefs. These high-spirited men, longing for an opportunity to strike another blow for national independence, fancied, and not without reason, that they could reckon upon the aid of the restless Ismail with whom they had already combined during the Lálsaut campaign in 1787.[121]

The corps of de Boigne formed part of the army sent under the command of Sindhia's Mahratta generals, Lakwá Dádá and Gopál Rao Bhao, to prevent if possible the junction of Ismail Beg with his Rájput allies. But the Moghul soldier of fortune was determined not to yield without a struggle. No sooner did he raise his standard than thousands of disbanded Afghán and Persian horsemen flocked to his headquarters. In March de Boigne left his employer at his favourite cantonment of Mathra, and sending before him a cloud of Mahratta horse, marched upon Ismail Beg with a complete brigade, including fifty pieces of artillery. On the morning of the 10th May they came upon him at a place called Pátan, in the rocky country between Ájmir and Gwalior, not many miles from the scene of the former battle at Lálsaut. For three weeks or more nothing was effected, but on the 19th June Ismail announced his intention of attacking the Mahratta lines. De Boigne sent a messenger to say that he would spare him the fatigue of the journey, and advanced to the encounter with all his force on the following morning.

The Rájputs had come up; but there was no longer union between them; for the Patel, taking advantage of a temporary soreness felt by the Kachwáhas of Jaipur on

[119] Mémoire sur la Carrière militaire et politique de M. le Général Cte. de Boigne. 2nd Edition. *Chambéry*, 1830.

[120] The pay of this force, and pay is always the chief difficulty in insuring the fidelity of Asiatic troops, was provided punctually from lands assigned to the General for that purpose, and managed by him. He thus guarded against the recurrence of those frequent mutinies for arrears by which others in his situation had been so often thwarted. In addition to his regulars, he maintained some light troops, known in the histories of those days by the barbarous designation of "Ally gools." These particulars are taken from Baillie Fraser's *Life of Skinner*, and Grant Duff's *History of the Mahrattas*, and the *Memoir* of M. de Boigne.

[121] *Vide sup.* Chapter V.

some trifling provocation, had contrived to secure their inaction before the battle began. Notwithstanding this defection, a large body of infantry still stood firm, but European skill and resolution conquered in the end. Ismail at the head of his Moghul cavaliers repeatedly charged de Boigne's artillery, sabring the gunners at their posts. Between the charges the infantry were thinned by well-directed volleys of grape, and the squares had to be formed with the greatest rapidity as the cavalry of the enemy once more attacked them. De Boigne's squares, however, resisted all attempts throughout the afternoon, and a general advance of the whole line at length took place, before which the enemy gradually broke. De Boigne placing himself at the head of one of his battalions, ordered the others to follow, and precipitated his foot upon the enemy's batteries. The first was carried with the shock; at eight in the evening he was master of the second; the third fell an hour later; the Moghuls' resistance was completely overpowered, and their leader was chased into the city of Jaipur. Ismail also lost in this engagement one hundred guns, fifty elephants, two hundred stand of colours and all his baggage; and on the following day a large portion of his army, amounting to seven battalions of foot and ten thousand irregular troops, went over to the victors. On this, as on many other occasions, the Mahratta cause was jeopardised by jealousies; Holkar holding aloof during the action, which would have begun earlier, and in all probability proved more decisive and with less loss, had he given due co-operation. There is a modest account of this action from de Boigne's pen in the *Calcutta Gazette* for 22nd July, 1790. The letter is dated 24th June—four days after the battle—and does not represent the exertions of the Mahrattas in anything like the serious light adopted in Captain Grant Duff's work, to which I have been principally indebted for my account of the action.[122] The gallant writer estimates Ismail Beg's Moghul horse, however, at 5,000 sabres; and admits that the Mahrattas would have sustained severe loss but for the timely firmness of the regular battalions. The fact appears to be that the diminished Rájput infantry, deficient in discipline and zeal, and wanting the prestige and coolness inspired among Asiatics by the presence of European leaders, did not support the cavalry, and that the latter become exhausted by their vain assaults upon the well-trained squares. Seeing this, de Boigne marched up his men (10,000 strong, by his own account), under the protection of a steady cannonade from his own guns, and stormed the enemy's camp. He estimates his own loss[123] at 120 killed and 472 wounded; the enemy's foot were not much cut up, because they were intrenched; "but they have lost a vast number of cavalry." He says of himself, "I was on horseback encouraging our men; thank God I have realized all the sanguine expectations of Sindhia; the officers in general have behaved well; to them I am a great deal indebted for the fortune of the day."[124] This was the most important victory that Sindhia had ever gained, and fully justified the increased confidence that he had shown his Savoyard General. The memoir above cited, estimates the whole combined forces of the enemy at 25,000 foot and 20,000 horse, but it is probable that they were not all engaged. Pátan, a fortress which has been compared to Gibraltar, was taken by

[122] S. Karr, *ut sup.*

[123] Referring to the regular infantry of his brigade alone.

[124] *Vide* also Tod, vol. i. pp. 760, 861.

storm after three days of open trenches, and Ismail Beg fled to the Panjáb.

The Patel himself was not present with the army during this campaign, but remained at Mathra, which was a favourite residence of his, owing to its peculiar reputation for holiness among the Hindus. This ancient city, which is mentioned both by Arrian and by Pliny, is the centre of a small district which is to the worshippers of Vishnu what Palestine is to Christians, and the Western part of Arabia is to the people of the Prophet. Here was born the celebrated Krishna, reported to be an incarnation of the Deity; here was his infant life sought by the tyrant Kans; hence he fled to Gujrát; returning when he came to man's estate, and partially adopting it as his residence after having slain his enemy.

We have seen how the general of Ahmad the Abdáli massacred the inhabitants, with a zeal partaking of the fanatic and the robber in equal proportions, in 1757.[125] Since then the place, standing at the head of the Bhartpur basin, and midway between Dehli and the Rájput country, had recovered its importance, and now formed Mádhoji's chief cantonment. Here it was that he received the news of the battle of Pátan, and of the temporary disappearance of Ismail Beg; and hence he proceeded to Dehli, and there obtained a fresh confirmation of the office of Plenipotentiary for the Peshwa, together with two fresh firmáns (or patents). One conferring upon himself the power to choose a successor in the Ministry from among his own family, and the other an edict forbidding the slaughter of horned cattle (so highly reverenced by the Hindus) throughout all the territory which still owned the sway, however nominal, of the Moghul sceptre.

Soon after he ordered his army, commanded as before, to return to Rajputána, and punish Bijai Singh, the Ráthor leader of Jodhpur, for abetting the resistance of Ismail Beg. On the 21st of August the General arrived at Ájmir, and took the town on the following day. He then sat down to form the regular siege of the citadel, called Táragarh (a fastness strong by nature, and strengthened still more by art, and situated on an eminence some 3,000 feet above sea-level). Bijai Singh, in Rájput fashion, was ready to try negotiation, and thought that he might succeed in practising upon one whom he would naturally regard in the light of a mercenary leader. He accordingly sent a message to de Boigne offering him the fort, with the territory for fifty miles round Ájmir if he would desert his employer. But the General sent him for answer that "Sindhia had already given him both Jodhpur and Jaipur, and that the Rájah could not be so unreasonable as to expect him to exchange the whole of those territories for the portion offered." After delivering himself of this grim piece of humour, and leaving a force to blockade the citadel, General de Boigne marched west to encounter the Rájah. Burning to retrieve the disgrace of Pátan, Bijai Singh was marching up from Jodhpur to the relief of Táragarh, when de Boigne met him at Mirta, a walled town about two marches distant from Ájmir and 76 miles N.E. of Jodhpur. It stands on high ground, the western wall being of mud, the eastern of masonry. On the 9th September the armies approached, and Gopál Rao was for attacking at once, but the General, with his accustomed coolness, pointed out that, not only were the men fatigued with marching and in need of repose, but that the day was too far advanced to

[125] *Vide sup.* Part I. Chap. iv.

allow of due pursuit being made should they—as was to be hoped—gain the action. It was therefore determined to try the effect of a surprise after the men had had a meal and a few hours repose. The forces on either side were not unequal. The Rájputs had the better in point of cavalry, their strength in this arm has been computed at 30,000 sabres. The Mahrattas had the advantage in artillery and in disciplined foot. The lines of the Rájputs were partially covered in rear by the walls of the town. But the spot was of evil omen. Bijai Singh had sustained a severe defeat on this very ground near forty years before. Nevertheless, years had not taught the Ráthors wisdom, nor misfortune schooled them to prudence. De Boigne came up in the grey of the morning, when the indolent Hindus were completely off their guard. And when the Rájah and his companions were roused from the drunken dreams of *Madhu*,[126] they already found the camp deserted, and the army in confusion. Fifty field pieces were piercing the lines with an incessant discharge of grape-shot, and Colonel Rohan who commanded de Boigne's right wing had, with unauthorised audacity, thrown himself into the midst of the camp at the head of three battalions. Rallying a strong body of horse—and the Rájput cavaliers were brave to a fault—the Rájah fell furiously upon the advanced corps of infantry, which he hoped to annihilate before they could be supported from the main army. But European discipline was too much for Eastern chivalry. Hastily forming hollow square the battalions of de Boigne awaited the storm; the infantry of Waterloo before the gendarmerie of Agincourt. The ground shook beneath the impetuous advance of the dust-cloud sparkling with the flashes of quivering steel. But when the cloud cleared off, there were still the hollow squares of infantry, like living bastions, dealing out lightnings far more terrible than any that they had encountered. The baffled horsemen wheeled furiously round on the Mahratta cavalry, and scattered them to the four corners of the field. They then attempted to gallop back, but it was through a Valley of Death. The whole of the regular troops of the enemy lined the way; the guns of de Boigne, rapidly served, pelted them with grape at point-blank distance; the squares maintained their incessant volleys; by nine in the morning nearly every man of the 4,000 who had charged with their prince lay dead upon the ground. Unfatigued and almost uninjured, the well-trained infantry of de Boigne now became assailants. The battalions rapidly deployed, and advancing with the support of their own artillery, made a general attack upon the Rájput line. By three in the afternoon all attempt at resistance had ceased. The whole camp, with vast plunder and munitions of war, fell into the hands of the victors. The middle-ages were over in India; and the prediction of Bernier was vindicated by the superiority of scientific warfare over headlong valour.[127] The town was easily taken, and the fall of Táragarh, the lofty and almost impregnable-looking citadel that frowns above Ájmir, followed soon after. The

[126] An intoxicating trance produced by drugs which the Hindus consider very divine. Krishna is called Mádhu Rao, and Sindhia appears to have been named after him.

[127] We learn from General de Boigne's own description of the battle that his battalions were only enabled to resist the furious charge of the Ráthor horse by forming themselves into hollow squares—the formation to be rendered so famous in after years at Quatre Bras and Mont St. Jean. More than a century before, in the most splendid period of Aurangzeb's career, Bernier had said that 25,000 of Turenne's troops would scatter the whole of the hosts of Hindustan.

echo of this blow resounded throughout native India. The Nána Farnavis heard it at Punah, and redoubled his Brahmin intrigues against his successful countryman. He likewise stimulated the rivalry of Takuji Holkar, who, with more of practical sagacity, resolved to profit by Sindhia's example, and lost no time in raising a force similarly organised to that which had won this great victory. De Boigne, almost worn out himself, allowed his victorious troops no time to cool, but marched on Jodhpur, and arrived at Kuarpur in the vicinity of the capital on the 18th of November. But his presence was enough. The Rajas of Udaipur and Jodhpur hastened to offer their submission to the chief who combined the prestige of the house of Timur with the glamour of the fire-eating Feringhee. Sindhia (to borrow a phrase from the gambling table) backed his luck. He gave de Boigne an increased assignment of territory; and authority to raise two more brigades, on which by express permission of the blind old Sháh was conferred the title of Army of the Empire. The territory assigned to the General extended from Mathra to Dehli, and over the whole Upper Doáb, yielding a total revenue of about twenty-two lakhs of rupees, a large sum for those days. After liquidating the pay of the troops it was estimated that this left a balance in his favour of about 40,000 rupees a year besides his pay, and very large perquisites. He also exercised unlimited civil and military jurisdiction. His headquarters were at Aligarh, where he exercised quasi-royal sway over the whole surrounding country. Some further work, however, awaited de Boigne before he finally retired into purely civil administration. Among the last to hold out against the good fortune and genius of Sindhia was the founder of the present state of Indore, Jeswant Rao Holkar, who resolved to try the effect upon his rival of a blow struck with his own weapons. The Duke of Wellington in 1803 took much the same view of this fondness on the part of the Mahrattas for European discipline and fashions in war as that vainly urged on Sheodásheo Rao by Malhár Ráo Holkar in 1760. "Sindhia's armies had actually," so wrote General Wellesley in 1803, "been brought to a very favourable state of discipline, and his power had become formidable by the exertions of European officers in his service; but, I think, it is much to be doubted whether his power—or rather that of the whole Mahratta nation—would not have been more formidable if they had never had a European or an infantry soldier in their service, and had carried on their operations in the manner of the original Mahrattas, only by means of cavalry." Malhár Ráo and Wellesley were two great authorities; but, in any case, when once any State had introduced the new system, all its rivals were compelled to do likewise, and the State which did it with the most energy prevailed. The citation above given is from Owen's *Selections*, p. 336.

This was the hey-day of European adventure in the East. France, still under the influence of feudal institutions, continued to send out brave young men who longed, while providing for themselves, to restore the influence of their country in India, shaken as it had been by the ill success of Dupleix, Lally, and Law. The native princes, on the other side, were not backward in availing themselves of this new species of wardog. A Frenchman was worth his weight in gold; even an Anglo-Indian—the race is now relegated to the office-stool—fetched, we may say, his weight in silver. But men of the latter class, though not deficient in valour, and not without special advantages from their knowledge of the people and their language, were not so fully trusted. Doubtless the French officers would be more serviceable in a war with England; and that contingency was probably never long absent from the thoughts of the native chiefs. With the exception of the Musalman Viceroys of Áudh and the Deccan, every native power dreaded the advance of the English, and desired their destruction. In fact, now that the Empire was fallen, a general Hindu revival had taken its place, the end of which was not seen till the Sikhs were finally subdued in 1849.

Holkar's new army was commanded by a French officer, whose name variously spelt, was perhaps du Drenec.[128] He was the son of an officer in the Royal navy of France, and is described as an accomplished and courteous gentleman. He usually receives from contemporary writers the title of Chevalier, and his conduct sustained the character of a well-born soldier.

1792.—The Patel lost no time in pushing his success in the only quarter where he now had anything to fear. The combination of the Nána in the cabinet and Holkar with an Europeanized army in the field, was a serious menace to his power; and with enterprising versatility he resolved at once to counteract it. With this view he obtained *khillats* of investiture, for the Peshwa and for himself, from the Emperor, and departed for Puna, where he arrived after a slow triumphal progress, on the 11th of June, 1792. On the 20th of the same month the ceremony took place with circumstances of great magnificence; the successful deputy endeavouring to propitiate the hostility of the Nána by appearing in his favourite character of the Beadle, and carrying the Peshwa's slippers, while the latter sate splendidly attired upon a counterfeit of the peacock throne. All men have their foibles, and Sindhia's was histrionism, which imposed on no one. The thin assumption of humility by a dictator was despised, and the splendid caparisons of the nominal chief were ridiculed by the Mahrattas and Brahmans of the old school.

Meanwhile Holkar saw his opportunity and struck his blow. Profiting by the absence of his rival, he for the first time since 1773, advanced on Hindustan; and summoning Ismail Beg like an evil spirit from his temporary obscurity, he hurled him upon the country round the capital, while he himself lost no time in forcing a rupture with Sindhia's civil deputy in Rajputána.

In the northern part of the Rewári country is a place called Kanaund; about equidistant from Dehli and Hánsi, to the south of both cities. Here Najaf Kuli Khán had breathed his last in a stronghold of earth faced with stone, on the borders of the great Bikanir desert, among sand-hills and low growths of tamarisk; and here his widow—a sister of the deceased Gholám Kádir[129]—continued to reside. A call to surrender the fort to Sindhia's officers being refused by the high-spirited Páthan lady, gave Ismail Beg occasion to reappear upon the scene. He hastened to her aid, but found the place surrounded by a force under the command of M. Perron, a French officer whose name will often recur hereafter. The Beg, as usual, attacked furiously, and, as usual, was defeated. He took refuge in the fort which he

[128] I find it written in the following ways:—Dudrenec, Doderneque, Dudernaig. The last is impossible. The spelling I have adopted is reconci'able with a Breton origin. But see App. F.

[129] *Vide sup.*, Part II. Chap. iv.

contrived to enter, and the defence of which he conducted for some time. But the lady being killed by a shell, the garrison lost heart, and began to talk of throwing overboard the Moghul Jonah. The latter, obtaining from Perron a promise of his life being spared, and having that strong faith in the truth of his promise which is the real homage that Asiatics pay to Europeans, lost no time in coming into camp, and was sent into confinement at Agra, where he remained till his death a few years later.[130] Francklin, writing about 1794, says that he had no chance of deliverance so long as Mahratta sway endured at Dehli; but that he might, otherwise, still live to play a conspicuous part. But I believe he died about four years later. His residence was in the quarters near the Dehli Gate of the Fort, popularly known as Dán Sáh Ját's house, still standing.

De Boigne meantime took the field in person against Holkar, who brought against him not only the usual host of Mahratta horsemen, but, what was far more formidable, four battalions of sepoys under Colonel du Drenec. The forces of the Empire, of somewhat inferior strength, brought Holkar to action at Lakhairi, not far from Kanaund, and on the road to Ájmir. The battle which ensued, which was fought in the month of September, 1792, was considered by M. de Boigne as the most obstinate that he ever witnessed. The ground had been skilfully chosen by du Drenec; he held the crest of a pass, his rear being partly protected by a wood; a marsh covered his front, while the sides were flanked by forests. The regular infantry was supported by a strong artillery, and guarded by 30,000 cavalry. Having reconnoitred this position from a rising ground, de Boigne advanced under a discouraging fire from Holkar's batteries; and as his own guns—whose advance had been unexpectedly impeded—came into action he hoped to silence those of the enemy. But his artillery officer was unlucky that day. A tumbril being struck in de Boigne's batteries, led to the explosion of ten or twelve others; and Holkar observing the confusion, endeavoured to extricate his cavalry from the trees, and charge, while du Drenec engaged the enemy's infantry. But the charge of Holkar's horse was confused and feeble (here Ismail Beg's absence must have been felt), and de Boigne sheltering his men in another wood, soon repulsed the cavalry with a well-directed and well-sustained discharge from 9,000 muskets. As they retreated, he launched his own cavalry upon them, and drove them off the field. It was now his turn once more to advance. Re-forming his infantry and guns in the shelter of the thick tree-growth, he fell upon the left of the enemy where the regulars still maintained themselves. Raw levies as they were, they fought bravely but unskilfully till they were annihilated; their European officers were nearly all slain, and their guns taken, to the number of thirty-eight. The battle was lost without retrieval, mainly owing to the inefficiency of Holkar's horse; thus vindicating the wise, if premature, confidence of Ibráhim Gárdi at Pánipat more than thirty years before. Holkar, with the remnant of his army, crossed the Chambal, and fell back on Málwa, where he revenged himself by sacking Ujain, one of Sindhia's chief cities.[131]

---

[130] I have been indebted for some information regarding Ismail Beg to Nawáb Mustafa Khán, of Jahángirabad, his grandson by the mother's side.

[131] The description of these two campaigns is a combination of the Mahratta account, as given by Duff; and the Rájput account given in Skinner's "Memoirs," chiefly from Tod;

While these things were taking place, a new rebuff was being prepared for himself by the Emperor, from whom neither age nor misfortune had taken that levity of character which, partly inherited from his ancestors, partly constitutional to himself, formed at once his chief weakness and his greatest consolation. In his dependent condition, enjoying but the moderate stipend of ninety thousand pounds a year for his whole civil list—and that not punctually paid—the blind old man turned envious thoughts upon the prosperity of the provinces which he had formerly ceded to his old protectors, the British. Accordingly, in July 1792, the Court newsman of Dehli was directed to announce that despatches had been sent to Punah, instructing Sindhia to collect tribute from the administration of Bengal. A similar attempt had been made, it will be remembered, though without success, in 1785 (*vide sup*., Pt. II. c. iv. *in fin*.) The present attempt fared no better. This hint was taken certainly, but not in a way that could have been pleasant to those who gave it; for it was taken extremely ill. In a state-paper of the 2nd of August, Lord Cornwallis, the then Governor-General, gave orders that information should be conveyed to Mádhoji Sindhia to the effect that in the present condition of the Dehli court he, Sindhia, would be held directly responsible for every writing issued in the name of the Emperor, and that any attempt to assert a claim to tribute from the British Government would be "warmly resented." Once more the disinclination of the British to interfere in the Empire was most emphatically asserted, but it was added significantly, that if any should be rash enough to insult them by an unjust demand or in any shape whatever, they felt themselves both able and resolved to exact ample satisfaction.

This spirited language, whether altogether in accordance with abstract right or not, was probably an essential element in the maintenance of that peaceful policy which prevailed in the diplomatic valley that occurred between Warren Hastings and the Marquess Wellesley. Sindhia (not unmindful of Popham's Gwalior performance just twelve years before) hastened to assure the British Government that he regarded them as supreme within their own territories; and that, for his part, his sole and whole object was to establish the Imperial authority in those territories that were still subject to the Emperor.

In this he had perfectly succeeded. The fame of his political sagacity, and the terror of General de Boigne's arms, were acknowledged from the Satlaj to the Ganges, and from the Himalayas to the Vindhyas. And for nearly ten years the history of Hindustan is the biography of a few foreign adventurers who owed their position to his successes. In the centre of the dominions swayed by the Dictator-Beadle were quartered two who had attained to almost royal state in the persons of General de Boigne and the Begam Sumroo: the one at Sardhana, the other at Aligarh. The Chevalier du Drenec, who had not been well used by Holkar, left (without the slightest blame) the service of that unprosperous chief, and joined his quasi-compatriot and former antagonist, the Savoyard de Boigne, as the commandant of a battalion. The "dignity of History" in the last century has not deigned to preserve any particulars of the private life of these gallant soldiers; but one can fancy them of an evening at a table furnished with clumsy

connected by reference to the Memoirs of de Boigne quoted above.

magnificence, and drinking bad claret bought up from the English merchants of Calcutta at fabulous prices; not fighting over again the battle of Lakhairi, but rather discussing the relative merits of the slopes of the Alps and the cliffs of the Atlantic; admitting sorrowfully the merits of the intermediate vineyards, or trilling to the bewilderment of their country-born comrades, light little French songs of love and wine.[132]

Among the officers of the Begam's army there would be few congenial companions for such men. The Brigadier, Colonel Levaissoult (or le Vasseur; it is impossible to be quite sure of these names as manipulated by the natives of India),[133] seems to have been a young man of some merit. Her only other European officer who was at all distinguished was an Irishman named George Thomas, who had deserted from a man-of-war in Madras Roads about ten years before, and after some obscure wanderings in the Carnatic, had entered the Begam's service, and distinguished himself, as we have seen, in the rescue of Sháh Alám before Gokalgarh, in 1788. The officers of the Begam's little army had never recovered the taint thrown over the service by its original founder, the miscreant Sumroo, and the merits of the gallant young Irishman, tall, handsome, intrepid, and full of the reckless generosity of his impulsive race, soon raised him to distinction. About his military genius, untaught as it must have been, there could be no doubt in the minds of those who had seen the originality of his movement at Golkalgarh;[134] his administrative talents, one would suppose, must have given some indication by this time of what they were hereafter to appear in a more leading character, and upon a larger stage.

Some time in 1792 the partiality of the Begam for M. Levaissoult began to show itself; and Mr. Thomas who was not only conscious of his own merits, but had all the hatred of a Frenchman which characterized the British tar of those days, resolved to quit her service and attempt a more independent career. With this view he retired, in the first instance, to Anupshahar on the Ganges, so often noticed in these pages, and now, for some time, the cantonment of the frontier brigade of the English establishment in the Presidency of the Fort William.[135] Here

[132] The translator of the *Siar-ul-Mutákharin* gives the following amusing contrast between two famous European chiefs of a somewhat earlier date as an illustration of "the different geniuses of the French and English nations."—"M. de Bussy always wore embroidered clothes or brocade. He was seen in an immense tent, about thirty feet high, at one end of which he sate in an armchair embroidered with his King's arms, on an elevation covered with a crimson cloth of embroidered velvet; over against him his French guard on horseback, and behind those his Turkish guard; his table was covered with three, and sometimes four services of plate. . . . Governor Hastings always wore a plain coat of English broadcloth, and never anything like lace or embroidery: his throne a plain chair of mahogany, with plenty of such thrones in the hall; his table sometimes neglected; his diet sparing, and always abstemious; his address and deportment *very d stant from pride and still more from familiarity.*" —Vol. iii. p. 150.

[133] His name is spelt Levaissoult upon the tombstone at Sardhana.

[134] Sumroo had taught his men to enter the field from the safest part, to deliver one volley and then to form square. Thomas introduced a very different system of tactics.—*Vide sup.*, pp. 93-94.

[135] It was from here that the brothers Daniell, the well-known landscape painters,

he found a hospitable welcome, and from this temporary asylum commenced a correspondence with Appa Khándi Rao, a chief whom he had formerly met in the Mahratta army, and whose service he presently entered with an assignment of land in Ismail Beg's former Jaigir of Mewát. In the Mewát country he remained for the next eighteen months, engaged in a long and arduous attempt to subjugate his nominal subjects; in which employment we must for the present leave him engaged.

In the meanwhile the Begam had been married to M. Levaissoult, according to the rites of the ancient Church to which both adhered. Unfortunately for the lady's present reputation and the gentleman's official influence, the marriage was private; the only witnesses of the ceremony being two of the bridegroom's friends, MM. Saleur and Bernier.[136]

All this time Sindhia was at Punah endeavouring to raise his influence in the Mahratta country to something like a level with his power in Hindustan. But the situation was one of much greater difficulty in the former instance than in the latter. In the one case he had to deal with a blind old voluptuary, of whom he was sole and supreme master; in the other the sovereign Mádhu Rao Peshwa was in the vigour of life, and had a confidential adviser in the Nána Farnavis, who was almost a match for the Patel in ability, and had an undoubted superiority in the much greater unity of his objects and the comparative narrowness of his field of action. It is no part of my task to trace the labyrinth of Mahratta politics in a work which merely professes to sketch the anarchy of Hindustan; it will be sufficient for our present purpose to state that the *Tárikh-i-Mozafari*, the Persian history to which we have heretofore been so largely indebted, notices an incident as occurring at this time which is not detailed in the usually complete record of Captain Grant Duff, though it is not at variance with the account that he gives of Punah politics in 1794. The Persian author briefly states that the Peshwa (whose mind was certainly at this time much embittered against Mádhoji Sindhia) sent assassins to waylay him at a little distance from the city, against whose attack the Patel defended himself with success, but only escaped at the expense of some severe wounds. From the situation of the writer, who appears always to have lived in Bihár or Hindustan, as well as from the vagueness with which he tells the story, it is evidently a mere rumour deriving some strength from the fact that Mádhoji died at Wanauli, in the neighbourhood of the Mahratta capital, on the 12th February of that year, in the midst of intrigues in which he was opposed, not only by the Nána, but by almost all the chiefs of the old Mahratta party.

An interesting and careful, though friendly analysis of the Patel's character will be found in the fifth chapter of Grant Duff's third volume. As evinced in his proceedings in Hindustan, we have found him a master of untutored statecraft, combining in an unusual manner the qualities of prudence in counsel and enterprise in action; tenacious of his purposes, but a little vulgar in his means of

accompanied by a few British officers, made their way about this time into the gorge of the Ganges in the Himalayas, above Hurdwar—the first Europeans who had ever seen or been seen in those regions.—S. Karr, vol. ii.

[136] On her baptism, 1781, the Begam had received the Christian name of Joanna. To this, on her marriage, she added that of Nobilis, which she ever after bore.

affecting opinion. He was possessed of the accomplishment of reading and writing; was a good accountant and versed in revenue administration; and thus able to act for himself, instead of being obliged, like most Mahratta leaders, to put himself into the hands of designing Brahmans. My valued friend Sir Dinkar Rao informs me that, among other traditions of high Mahratta society, he has been told by aged men that the Mahárájá was never known to evince serious displeasure save with cowards and men who fled in battle. To all others his favour was equal, and solely apportioned to merit, no matter what might be their creed, caste, or colour. He showed discrimination and originality in the wholesale reform that he introduced into the organization of the army, and the extensive scale on which he employed the services of soldiers trained and commanded by men of a hardier race than themselves. *Sic fortis Etruria crevit*; and it is curious to find the same circumstances which in the Middle Ages of Europe caused the greatness of the Northern Italian States thus reproducing themselves in the Italy of the East.

NOTE.—The following extract from the *Dehli Gazette* of June 5th, 1874, gives the existing tradition as to the domicile of the officers at Aligarh:—"De Boigne lived in his famous mansion, called Sáhib Bagh, between the fort and city, and on leaving for France he gave it to Perron, who considerably improved the building and garden, which was well laid out with all descriptions of fruit trees procured from distant climes. He so adorned the place that it was said by the French officers that the garden was next to that of Rám Bagh, on the Agra river, so beautiful was the scenery. Perron had a number of officers in his army, English, French, and Italian. Next to Perron was Colonel Pédron, who commanded the fortress of Allygurh; this officer had his mansion in an extensive garden, which at the British conquest was converted into the Judges' Court, and the site is the same where it now stands. There are still some old jamun trees of the said garden in the school compound. Chevalier Dudernaque was another officer of distinction in Perron's Brigade; his house was on the edge of the city, it still stands in the occupancy of Khooshwuk Allee, a respectable Mahomedan, who has an Illaqua in Sahnoul."—*History of Coel. Aligurhs, by an Old Resident.*

CHAPTER II.

A.D. 1794-1800.

Daulat Rao Sindhia—Thomas adopted by Appa Khándi Rao—Revolution at Sardhana—Begam Sumroo attacked but delivered—Begam Sumroo becomes a wiser Woman—Movements of Afgháns—De Boigne retires—General Perron—Musalman intrigues—Afgháns checked—Succession in Áudh—War of "The Bais"—Afgháns and British—Rising of Shimbunáth—Thomas independent—Revolt of Lakwá Dádá—Holkar's defeat at Indor—Power of Perron.

1794.—The powers and dignities of the old Patel were peaceably assumed by Daulat Rao, the son of the deceased's youngest nephew, whom he had, shortly before his death made preparations to adopt as a son. This new minister was only in his fifteenth year, but the chiefs of the Deccan soon becoming involved in war with their Musalman neighbours, and Takuji Holkar shortly afterwards becoming imbecile both in mind and in body, the young man had leisure to consolidate his power. He retained eight battalions always about him, under the command of a Neapolitan named Filose, and continued to reside at Punah; the Begam Sumroo and her new husband were at Sardhana; de Boigne at Aligarh; and Thomas still engaged in conquering the country which had been nominally conferred upon him by a chieftain who had no right to it himself. Nothing can better show the anarchy that prevailed than such a state of things as this last mentioned.

The news of Mádhoji's death, and the short suspense that followed on the subject of the succession, caused some little confusion at Dehli, and led Appa Khándi Rao to visit the metropolis, on which occasion Thomas attended him. Here they received investiture to their several fiefs from Sindhia's local representative, Gopál Rao Bhao; but it was not long before this chief, stirred up, says Thomas's biographer, by the Begam and her husband, begam to tamper with the fidelity of Appa Khándi's men, who mutinied and confined their chief. Thomas retaliated by plundering the Begam's estates to the south of Dehli, and loyally escorted his master to Kanaund. On this occasion Appa (who seems not to have been destitute of good impulses) adopted him as his son, made him some handsome presents, and conferred upon him the management of several contiguous tracts, yielding in all an annual revenue of one lakh and a half of the money of those days.

One cannot wonder at the faith in the pagoda-tree which formed so prominent an article of the English social creed of those days, when we thus find a common sailor, at forty years of age, attended by a body-guard of chosen cavaliers, and managing districts as large and rich as many a minor kingdom. No doubt the price paid was high. Thomas's exertions were evidently prodigious and ceaseless; while his position—nay, his very existence—was extremely precarious. On the other hand, his prospect of realizing any part of his good fortune, and retiring to enjoy it in his native Tipperary—which must have sometimes presented itself to his mind—was certainly not hopeful. To the degenerate Europeans of the present day, whose programme involves constant holidays in a mountain climate, occasional furloughs to England, and, when resident in India, a residence made endurable by imported luxuries, and by every possible precaution against heat, there is something almost incredible in this long life of exile, where the English language would not be heard for years,[137] and where quilted curtains and wooden shutters would be all the protection of the most luxurious quarters, and an occasional carouse upon fiery bazaar spirits the chief excitement of the most peaceful intervals of repose. Such intervals, however, were very rare; and the sense of constant struggles in which one's success was entirely due to one's own merits, must have been the chief reward of such a life as Thomas was now leading.

Foremost among the difficulties with which he had to contend was the uncertain character of his chief: and he was at the time of which we are treating—1794—strongly tempted by Lakwá Dádá to enter the service of Sindhia, in which he was offered the command of 2,000 horse. This temptation, however, he manfully resisted, and continued true to Appa, even though that chief was neither true to his follower nor to himself. Whilst thus engaged in a cause of but small promise, he was once more exposed to the machinations of the Begam, who, influenced by her husband, marched into Thomas's new district and encamped about three marches S.E. from Jhajar, at the head of a force of four battalions of infantry, twenty guns, and four squadrons of horse. Thomas made instant preparations to meet the invasion, when it was suddenly rolled away in a manner which presents one of the characteristic dissolving views of that extraordinary period.

The ruffianly character of most of the officers in the Sardhana service has been already mentioned. With the exception of one or two, they could not read or write, and they had all the debauched habits and insolent bearing which are the besetting sins of the uneducated European in India; especially when to the natural pride of race are added the temptations of a position of authority for which no preparation has been made in youth. Among these men (whom Le Vaissoult, not unnaturally, refused to admit to his dinner-table) was a German or Belgian, now only known to us by the nickname of Liégeois, probably derived from his native place. With this man it is supposed that Thomas now opened a correspondence by means of which he practised on the disaffection of his former comrades. The secrecy which the Begam continued to preserve on the subject of her marriage naturally added to the unpopularity of Le Vaissoult's position; and the husband and wife hurried

[137] Thomas being on a subsequent occasion, applied to by Lord Wellesley for an account of the state of the country (which was then to the Government of British India something like what Kábul has been in more recent times), replied that he would be happy to oblige his lordship, but had forgotten English to such an extent that he hoped he might be allowed to write his memoir in Persian.

back to Sardhana on learning that the officers had commenced negotiations with Aloysius the son of the deceased Sumroo, who resided at Dehli with the title of Nawáb Zafaryáb Khán, and had carried over with them a portion of the troops. Finding the situation untenable, they soon resolved on quitting it and retiring into the territories of the British with their portable property, estimated at about two lakhs of rupees. With this view they wrote to Colonel McGowan, commanding the brigade at Anupshahar; and finding that officer scrupulous at participating at the desertion of an Imperial functionary, Le Vaissoult, in April, 1794, addressed the Governor-General direct. The result was that Sindhia's permission was obtained to a secret flitting; and Le Vaissoult was to be treated as a prisoner of war, allowed to reside with his wife at Chandarnagar.[138]

Towards the end of 1795, Zafaryáb, at the head of the revolted soldiery set out from Dehli; determined, by what judicial stupidity I cannot tell, to cut off the escape of that enemy for whom, if he had been wise, he ought to have paved the road, had it been with silver. The intelligence of this movement precipitated Le Vaissoult's measures; and he set out with his wife—the latter was in a palankeen, the former armed and on horseback—with a mutual engagement between them that neither was to survive if certified of the death of the other. The troops who still remained at Sardhana, either corrupted by the mutineers, or willing to secure the plunder before the latter should arrive, immediately set out in pursuit. The sequel is thus told by Sleeman, who gathered his information from eye-witnesses on the spot:—"They had got three miles on the road to Meerut, when they found the battalions gaining fast upon the palankeen. Le Vaissoult drew a pistol from his holster and urged on the bearers. He could have easily galloped off and saved himself, but he would not quit his wife's side. At last the soldiers came up close behind them. The female attendants of the Begam began to scream, and looking into the litter, Le Vaissoult observed the white cloth that covered the Begam's breast stained with blood. She had stabbed herself, but the dagger had struck against one of the bones of her chest, and she had not courage to repeat the blow. Her husband put the pistol to his temple and fired. The ball passed through his head, and he fell dead to the ground." This tragedy is somewhat differently detailed in the account furnished by Thomas to his biographer, which is made to favour the suspicion that the Begam intentionally deceived her husband in order to lead him to commit suicide. Thomas says that Le Vaissoult was riding at the head of the procession, and killed himself on receiving a message from the rear attested by the sight of a blood-stained garment borne by the messenger: but it is hard to see why a man in his position should have been absent from his wife's side at such a critical moment. Thomas was naturally disposed to take an unfavourable view of the Begam's conduct; but the immediate results of the scene were certainly not such as to support the theory of her having any understanding with the mutineers. She was carried back to the Fort, stripped of her property, and tied under a gun. In this situation she remained several days, and would have died of starvation but for the good offices of a faithful *ayah*, who continued to visit her mistress, and supply her more pressing necessities.

[138] England was then at war with the French Republic. Readers remember Lord Howe's victory—"glorious 1st of June," 1794.

The new Nawáb was a weak and dissolute young man; and the Begam had a friend among the officers, Saleur, whom the reader may recollect as one of the witnesses of her marriage. She was ere long released, and M. Saleur lost no time in communicating with Thomas, whose aid he earnestly invoked. The generous Irishman, forgetful of the past, at once wrote strongly to his friends in the service, pointing out that the disbandment of the force would be the only possible result of their persisting in disorderly conduct, so detrimental to the welfare of the Emperor and his minister. He followed up this peaceful measure by a rapid march on Sardhana, where he surprised the Nawáb by dashing upon him at the head of the personal escort of horse, which formed part of the retinue of every leader of those days. The troops, partly corrupted, partly intimidated, tired of being their own masters, and disappointed in Zafaryáb, made a prisoner of their new chief. He was plundered to the skin, and sent back to Dehli under arrest; while the Begam, by the chivalry of one she had ill-used for years, recovered her dominions, and retained them unmolested for the rest of her life. The secret of her behaviour is probably not very difficult of discovery. Desirous of giving to her passion for the gallant young Frenchman the sanction of her adopted religion, she was unwilling to compromise her position as Sumroo's heir by a publicly acknowledged re-marriage. She had large possessions and many enemies; so that, once determined to indulge her inclinations, she had to choose between incurring scandalous suspicions, and jeopardising a succession which would be contested, if she were known to have made a fresh and an unpopular marriage.

M. Saleur was now appointed to the command of the forces; but the astute woman never again allowed the weakness of her sex to imperil her sovereignty; and from the period of her restoration by Thomas (who spent two lakhs of rupees in the business), to the date of her death in 1836, her supremacy was never again menaced by any domestic danger. Having, as far as can be conjectured, now arrived at the ripe age of forty-two, it may be hoped that she had learned to conquer the impulse that sometimes leads a female sovereign to make one courtier her master, at the expense of making all the rest her enemies. The management of her extensive territories henceforward occupied her chief attention, and they were such as to require a very great amount of labour and time for their effective supervision: stretching from the Ganges to beyond the Jamna, and from the neighbourhood of Aligarh to the north of Mozafarnagar. There was also a Jaigir on the opposite side of the Jamna, which has formed the subject of litigation between her heirs and the Government in recent times. Her residence continued to be chiefly at Sardhana, where she gradually built the palace, convent, school, and cathedral, which are still in existence. Peace and order were well kept throughout her dominions; no lawless chiefs were allowed to harbour criminals and defraud the public revenue; and the soil was maintained in complete cultivation. This is considerable praise for an Asiatic ruler; the reverse of the medal will have to be looked at hereafter.[139]

Death soon relieved her of all anxiety on the score of her undutiful stepson, who drank himself to death in his arrest at Dehli, leaving a daughter, who married a Mr. Dyce, and became the mother of Mr. D. O. Dyce-Sombre, whose melancholy

[139] *Vide* Appendix D.

story is fresh in the memory of the present generation. Zafaryáb Khán was buried like his infamous father at Agra. But his monument is not in the cemetery, but in a small church since secularized.

Thomas was now, for the moment, completely successful. The intrigues of his Mahratta enemy Gopál Rao ended in that officer being superseded, and Thomas's friend Lakwá Dádá became Lieutenant-General in Hindustan. Appa Khándi, it is true, commenced a course of frivolous treachery towards his faithful servant and adopted son, which can only be accounted for on the supposition of a disordered intellect; but Thomas remained in the field, everywhere putting down opposition, and suppressing all marauding, unless when his necessities tempted him to practise it on his own account.

About this time we begin, for the first time, to find mention of the threatening attitude of the Afgháns, which was destined to exercise on the affairs of Hindustan an influence so important, yet so different from what the invaders themselves could have anticipated. Timur Sháh, the kinsman to whom Sháh Alám alludes in his poem, had died in June, 1793; and after a certain amount of domestic disturbance, one of his sons had succeeded under the title of Zamán Sháh. The *Calcutta Gazette* of 28th May, 1795, thus notices the new ruler:—

> "Letters from Dehli mention that Zamán Sháh, the ruler of the Abdalees, meditated an incursion into Hindustan, but had been prevented, for the present, by the hostility of his brothers. . . . . We are glad to hear the Sikhs have made no irruption into the Doáb this season."

This Zamán Sháh is the same who died, many years later, a blind pensioner of the English at Ludiana; and for the restoration of whose dynasty, among other objects, the British expedition to Kábul in 1839 took place.

To this period also belongs the unsuccessful attempt to revive Musalman power in the South of India, in which the Nizám of the Deccan engaged with the aid of his French General, the famous Raymond. The battle fought at Kardla, near Ahmadnagar, on the 12th March, 1795, is remarkable for the number of Europeans and their trained followers who took part on either side. On the Nizám's side, besides a vast force of horse and foot of the ordinary Asiatic kind, there were no less than 17,000 infantry under Raymond, backed by a large force of regular cavalry and artillery. The Mahrattas had 10,000 regulars under Perron, 5,000 under Filose, 3,000 under Hessing, 4,500 under du Drenec and Boyd. An animated account of this battle will be found in Colonel Malleson's excellent book, *The Final Struggles of the French in India,* in which, with admirable research and spirit, the gallant author has done justice to the efforts of the brave Frenchmen by whom British victory was so often checked in its earlier flights. The power of the Musalmans was completely broken by Perron and his associates on this occasion. It is further remarkable as the last general assembly of the chiefs of the Mahratta nation under the authority of their Peshwa (Grant Duff, ii. 284-8). The Moghul power in the Deccan was only preserved by the intervention of the British, and has ever since been dependent on their Government.

Early in 1796 a change was perceptible in the health of General de Boigne, which time and war had tried for nearly a quarter of a century in various regions. He had amassed a considerable fortune by his exertions during this long period, and entertained the natural desire of retiring with it to his native country. Sindhia had no valid ground for opposing his departure, and he set out for Calcutta somewhere about the middle of the year, accompanied by his personal escort—mounted upon choice Persian horses—who were afterwards taken into the British Governor's body-guard. In the profession of a soldier of fortune, rising latterly to almost unbounded power, de Boigne had shown all the virtues that are consistent with the situation. By simultaneous attention to his own private affairs he amassed a fortune of nearly half a million *sterling*, which he was fortunate enough to land in his own country, where it must have seemed enormous. He lived for many years after as a private gentleman in Savoy, with the title of Count, and visitors from India were always welcome and sure of being hospitably entertained by the veteran with stories of Mahratta warfare. On the 1st February, 1797, he was succeeded, after some brief intermediate arrangements, by M. Perron, an officer of whom we have already had some glimpses, and whom de Boigne considered as a steady man and a brave soldier. Like Thomas, he had come to India in some humble capacity on board a man-of-war, and had first joined the native service under Mr. Sangster, as a non-commissioned officer. De Boigne gave him a company in the first force which he raised, with the title of Captain-Lieut. On the absconding of Lestonneaux, in 1788, as above described—when that officer was supposed to have appropriated the plunder taken by Gholám Kádir on his flight from Meerut—Perron succeeded to the command of a battalion, from which, after the successes of the army against Ismail Beg, he rose to the charge of a brigade. He was now placed over the whole regular army, to which the civil administration, on de Boigne's system, was inseparably attached, and under him were brigades commanded by Colonel du Drenec and by other officers, chiefly French, of whom we shall see more hereafter. De Boigne, while entertaining a high opinion of Perron's professional ability, seems to have misdoubted his political wisdom, for both Fraser and Duff assert that he solemnly warned Daulat Rao Sindhia against those very excesses into which—partly by Perron's counsel—he was, not long after, led. "Never to offend the British, and sooner to discharge his troops than risk a war," was the gist of the General's parting advice.[140]

Sindhia remaining in the Deccan, in pursuance of his uncle's plan of managing both countries at once, the ex-Sergeant became very influential in Hindustan, where (jealousies with his Mahratta colleagues excepted) the independent career of George Thomas was the only serious difficulty with which he had to contend.

For the present the two seamen did not come in contact, for Thomas confined his operations to the west and north-west, and found his domestic troubles and the resistance of the various neighbouring tribes sufficient to fully occupy his attention. Scarcely had he patched up a peace with his treacherous employer, and brought affairs in Mewát to something like a settlement, when his momentary quiet was once more disturbed by the intelligence that Appa had committed suicide

[140] For a few more particulars regarding Count de Boigne, see Appendix C.

by drowning himself, and that his son and successor, Váman Rao, was showing signs of an intention to imitate the conduct of the deceased in its untruthful and unreliable character. With the exception of a brief campaign in the Upper Doáb, in which the fortified towns of Shámli and Lakhnaoti had rebelled, Thomas does not appear to have had any active employment until he finally broke with Váman Rao.

The rebellion of the Governor of Shámli (which Thomas suppressed with vigour) seems to have been connected with the movements of the restless Rohillas of the Najibábád clan, whose chief was now Bhanbu Khán, brother of the late Gholám Kádir, and an exile among the Sikhs since the death of his brother and the destruction of the Fort of Ghausgarh. Profiting by the long-continued absence of Sindhia, he re-opened that correspondence with the Afgháns which always formed part of a Mohamadan attempt in Hindustan, and appealed, at the same time, to the avarice of the Sikhs, which had abundantly recovered its temporary repulse by Mirza Najaf in 1779.[141] The grandson of the famous Abdáli soon appeared at Peshawar at the head of 33,000 Afghán horse. But the Sikhs and Afgháns soon quarrelled; a desperate battle was fought between them at Amritsar, in which, after a futile cannonade, the Sikhs flung themselves upon Zamán's army in the most reckless manner. The aggregate losses were estimated at 35,000 men. The Sháh retreated upon Láhor;[142] and the disordered state of the Doáb began to be reflected in the only half-subdued conquests of the Viceroy of Áudh in Rohilkand.

At this crisis 'Asaf-ud-daulah, the then holder of this title, died at Lucknow, 21st September, 1797, and it was by no means certain that his successor, Vazir 'Ali,[143] would not join in the reviving struggles of his co-religionists. It must be remembered that, in virtue of its subjugation to the Sindhias, the Empire was now regarded as a Hindu power, and that Shia and Sunni might well be expected to join, as against the Mahrattas or the English, however they might afterwards quarrel over the spoil, should success attend their efforts. Furthermore it is to be noted that in this or the following year the Afgháns, under Zamán Sháh, were known to be advancing again upon Láhor.

This state of things appeared to the then Governor-General of the British possessions sufficiently serious to warrant an active interposition. The calm courage of Sir John Shore, who held a local investigation into what, to most politicians, might have appeared a very unimportant matter—namely, whether the heir-apparent was really 'Asaf-ud-daulah's son or not; the grave decision against his claims (the claims of a *de facto* prince); his deposition and supersession by his eldest uncle, Säädat 'Ali the Second; and Vazir 'Ali's subsequent violence, when, too late to save his throne, he contrived, by the gratuitous murder of Mr. Cherry, the British resident at Benares, to convert his position from that of a political martyr to that of a life-convict, are all amply detailed in the well-known History of Mill, and in the Life of Lord Teignmouth by his son. Shore, at the same

[141] *Vide* Part II. Chap. iv.

[142] *Calcutta Gazette,* 9th February, 1797.

[143] Thus referred to in the *Calcutta Gazette*:—"Meerza Vuzeer Alee, the newly-appointed Vuzeer" (such was still the form), "is a youth of about eighteen years of age, of very promising disposition. A salute was fired at Fort William in his honour."—S. Karr, *ut sup*. p. 486. For his subsequent conduct and fate, *v.* next page.

time, sent an embassy to Persia under Mahdi 'Ali Khán, the result of which was an invasion of Western Afghánistan and the consequent retirement of the Sháh from the Panjáb. The events referred to only so far belong to the History of Hindustan, that they are a sort of crepuscular appearance there of British power, and show how the most upright and moderate statesmen of that nation were compelled, from time to time, to make fresh advances into the political sphere of the Empire.

About this time died Tákaji Holkar, who had lately ceased to play any part in the politics, either of Hindustan or of the Deccan. He was no relation, by blood, of the great founder of the house of Holkar, Malhár Ráo; but he had carried out the traditionary policy of the clan, which may be described in two words—hostility to Sindhia, and alliance with any one, Hindu or Musalman, by whom that hostility might be aided. He was succeeded by his illegitimate son Jaswant Rao, afterwards to become famous for his long and obstinate resistance to the British; but for the present only remarkable for the trouble that he soon began to give Daulat Rao Sindhia.

1798.—The latter, meanwhile, as though there were no such persons as Afgháns or English within the limits of India, was engaging in domestic affairs of the most paltry character. His marriage (1st March) with the daughter[144] of the Ghatgai, Shirji Rao, put him into the hands of that notorious person, whose ambition soon entangled the young chief in the obscure and discreditable series of outrages and of intrigues regarding his uncle's widow, known as the War of the Bais. The cause of these ladies being espoused by Mádhoji's old commander, Lakwá Dádá, whom the younger Sindhia had, as we have seen, raised to the Lieutenant-Generalship of the Empire, a serious campaign (commenced in May) was the result. Sindhia's army (nominally the army of the Emperor) was under the chief command of Ambáji Inglia, and in 1798 a campaign of some magnitude was undertaken, with very doubtful results.

The ladies first retreated to the camp of the Peshwa's brother, Imrat Rao, but were captured by a treacherous attack ordered by Sindhia's general, and undertaken by M. Drugeon, a French officer, at the head of two regular brigades, during the unguarded hours of a religious festival. This was an overt act of warfare against Sindhia's lawful superior, the Peshwa, in whose protection the ladies were, and threw the Peshwa into the hands of the British and their partizans.

Sindhia, for his part, entered into negotiations with the famous usurper of Mysore, Tippu Sultán, who was the hereditary opponent of the British, and who soon after lost his kingdom and his life before the Mahrattas could decide upon an open espousal of his cause.

1799.—The glory of the coming conquerors now began to light up the politics of Hindustan. The Afgháns retired from Láhor in January, and were soon discovered to have abandoned their attempts on Hindustan for the present. But it was not known how long it might be before they were once more renewed. The celebrated

[144] This was the lady known in later times as the "Baiza Bai" (*v. Up the Country*, by the Hon. Emily Eden). Her brother, Rájá Hindu Rao, will be remembered by Anglo-Indians who knew Dehli before the Mutiny; and his house upon the ridge played a well-known part in the siege of that time.

treaty of "subsidiary alliance" between the British and the Nizám (22nd June, 1799), occupied the jealous attention of Sindhia, who had accommodated matters with the Peshwa, and taken up his quarters at Punah, where his immense material resources rendered him almost paramount. Still more was his jealousy aroused by the knowledge that, as long as the attitude of the Afghâns continued to menace the ill-kept peace of the Empire, the British must be of necessity driven to keep watch in that quarter, in proportion, at least, as he, for his part, might be compelled to do so elsewhere. To add to his perplexities, Jaswant Rao Holkar, the hereditary rival of his house, about this time escaped from the captivity of Nágpur, to which Sindhia's influence had consigned him. Thus pressed on all sides, the Minister restored Lakwá Dádá to favour, and by his aid quelled a fresh outbreak in the Upper Doáb, where Shimbunáth, the officer in charge of the Báwani Mahál, had called in the Sikhs in aid of his attempts at independence. Shimbunáth was met and repulsed by a Moghul officer, named Ashraf Beg; and, hearing that Perron had sent reinforcements under Captain Smith, retired to the Panjáb.[145]

At the same time the Mahratta Governor of Dehli rebelled, but Perron reduced him after a short siege, and replaced him by Captain Drugeon, the French officer already mentioned in reference to the war of the Bais.

Thomas was for the present quite independent; and it may interest the reader to have a picture, however faint, of the scene in which this extraordinary conversion of a sailor into a sovereign took place. Hánsi is one of the chief towns of the arid province curiously enough called *Hariána*, or "Green land," which lies between Dehli and the Great Sindh Deserts. When Thomas first fixed on it as the seat of his administration, it was a ruin among the fragments of the estates which had belonged to the deceased Najaf Kuli Khán. His first care was to rebuild the fortifications and invite settlers; and such was his reputation, that the people of the adjacent country, long plundered by the wild tribes of Bhatiána, and by the Játs of the Panjáb, were not slow in availing themselves of his protection. Here, to use his own words, "I established a mint, and coined my own rupees, which I *made current* (!) in my army and country . . . . cast my own artillery, commenced making muskets, matchlocks, and powder . . . . till at length, having gained a capital and country bordering on the Sikh territories, I wished to put myself in a capacity, when a favourable opportunity should offer, of attempting the conquest of the Panjáb, and aspired to the honour of placing the British standard on the banks of the Attock."[146]

His new possessions consisted of 14 Pargannas, forming an aggregate of 250 townships, and yielding a total revenue of nearly three lakhs of rupees,—Thomas being forced to make very moderate settlements with the farmers in order to realize anything. From his former estates, acquired in the Mahratta service, which he still retained, he derived nearly a lakh and a half more.

Having made these arrangements, Thomas consented to join Váman Rao, the son of his former patron, in a foray upon the Rájá of Jaipur; and in this was nearly slain, only escaping with the loss of his lieutenant, John Morris, and some

[145] Skinner, i. 166.
[146] Francklin's "George Thomas."

hundreds of his best men. He then renewed his alliance with Ambáji Sindhia's favourite general, who was about to renew the war against Lakwá Dádá in the Udaipur country.

This new campaign was the consequence of Lakwá having connived at the escape of the Bais, a trait of conduct creditable to his regard for the memory of Mádhoji Sindhia, his old master, but ruinous to his own interests. For the moment, however, the Dádá was completely successful, routing all the detachments sent against him, and taking possession of a considerable portion of Rajputána.

Thomas did not join this campaign without undergoing a fresh danger from the mutiny of his own men. This is a species of peril to which persons in his position seem to have been peculiarly open; and it is related that the infamous Sumroo was sometimes seized by his soldiers, and seated astride upon a heated cannon, in order to extort money from him. In the gallant Irishman the troops had a different subject for their experiments; and the disaffection was soon set at rest by Thomas seizing the ringleaders with his own hands, and having them blown from guns on the spot. This is a concrete exhibition of justice which always commands the respect of Asiatics; and we hear of no more mutinies in Thomas's army.

1800.—In 1800 the sailor-Rájá led his men once more against their neighbours to the north and northwest of his territories, and gathered fresh laurels. He was now occupied in no less a scheme than the conquest of the entire Panjáb, from which enterprise he records that he had intended to return, like another Nearchus, by way of the Indus, to lay his conquests at the feet of George the Third of England. But the national foes of that monarch were soon to abridge the career of his enterprising subject, the Irish Rájá of Hánsi. For the present, Perron marched into the country of the Dattia Rájá, in Bundelkhand, and entirely defeated Lakwá Dádá, who soon after died of his wounds. His success was at first balanced by Holkar, who routed a detachment of the Imperial army, under Colonel Hessing, at Ujain. Hessing's four battalions were completely cut up; and of eleven European officers, seven were slain and three made prisoners. This event occurred in June, 1801. But it was not long before the disaster was retrieved at Indor (the present seat of the Holkar family), by a fresh force under Colonel Sutherland. Holkar lost ninety-eight guns, and his capital was seized and sacked by the victors, about four months after the former battle.

The French commander of the regular troops was indeed now master of the situation. Victorious in the field, in undisturbed possession of the Upper Doáb, and with a subordinate of his own nation in charge of the metropolis and person of the sovereign, General Perron was not disposed to brook the presence of a rival—and that a Briton—in an independent position of sovereignty within a few miles of Dehli. The French sailor and the English sailor having surmounted their respective difficulties, were now, in fact, face to face, each the only rival that the other had to encounter in the Empire of Hindustan.

Note.—Thomas describes the Begam as small and plump; her complexion fair, her eyes large and animated. She wore the

Hindustáni costume, made of the most costly materials. She spoke Persian and Urdu fluently, and attended personally to business, giving audience to her native employés behind a screen. At darbars she appeared veiled; but in European society she took her place at table, waited on exclusively by maid-servants. Her statue, surmounting a group in white marble by Tadolini, stands over her tomb in the Church at Sardhana.

CHAPTER III.

A.D. 1801-3.

Feuds of the Mahrattas—Perron attacks Thomas—End of Thomas—Treaty of Bassein—Lord Wellesley—Treaty of Lucknow—Wellesley supported—Fear of the French—Sindhia threatened—Influence of Perron—Plans of the French—The First Consul—Wellesley's Views—War declared—Lake's Force—Sindhia's European Officers, English and French—Anti-English Feelings and Fall of Perron—Battle of Dehli—Lake enters the Capital—Emperor's Petition—No Treaty made.

1801.—The end was now indeed approaching. Had the Mahrattas been united, it is possible that their confederacy might have retrieved the disasters of 1760-1, and attained a position in Hindustan similar to that which was soon after achieved by the Sikhs in the Panjáb. But this could not be. The Peshwa still assumed to be Vicegerent of the Empire, as well as head of the Mahrattas, under the titular supremacy of Satára, and Sindhia affected to rule in Hindustan as the Peshwa's Deputy. But the new Peshwa, Báji Rao—having dislodged the usurping minister Nána Farnavis—had proceeded to provoke the Holkars. Jeswant Rao, the present head of that clan, took up arms against the Peshwa, whose side was espoused by Sindhia; and Sindhia consequently found himself constrained to leave the provinces north of the Narbadda to the charge of subordinates. Of these the most powerful and the most arrogant was the promoted Quarter-Master Sergeant, now General Perron.

As long as the last-named officer was in a subordinate position, he evinced much honourable manhood. But the extremes of prosperity and adversity proved alike the innate vulgarity of the man's nature.

When every hereditary prince, from the Satlaj to the Narbadda, acknowledged him as master, and he enjoyed an income equal to that of the present Viceroy and the Commander-in-Chief of India combined; at this climacteric of his fortunes, when he was actually believed to have sent an embassy to the First Consul of the French Republic,[147] instead of seriously and soberly seeking to consolidate his position, or resign it with honour, his insolence prepared the downfall which he underwent with disgrace.

Not content with openly flouting his Mahratta colleagues, and estranging such of the Europeans as were not his connections or his creatures, he now summoned

[147] Skinner, i. 190.

George Thomas to Dehli, and called upon him to enter Sindhia's service—in other words, to own his (Perron's) supremacy. The British tar repudiated this invitation with national and professional disdain; upon which a strong Franco-Mahratta army invaded his territories under Louis Bourquin, one of Perron's lieutenants. Judgment formed no part of Thomas's character; but he acted with his wonted decision. Sweeping round the invading host, he fell upon the detachment at Georgegarh—one of his forts which was being beleaguered—and having routed the besiegers with great loss, threw himself into the place, and protected his front with strong outworks, resolving to await assistance from Holkar, or to seize a favourable opportunity to strike another blow.

Events showed the imprudence of this plan. No aid came; the French being reinforced, invested his camp, so as to produce a blockade: corruption from the enemy joined with their own distress to cause many desertions of Thomas's soldiers, till at length their leader saw no alternative but flight. About 9 P.M. therefore, on the 10th November, 1801, he suddenly darted forth at the head of his personal following, and succeeded in reaching Hánsi by a circuitous route, riding the same horse—a fine Persian—upwards of a hundred miles in less than three days. But his capital was soon invested by his relentless foes as strictly as his camp had been; and although the influence of his character was still shown in the brave defence made by the few select troops whom neither hope nor fear could force from his side, he was at last obliged to see the cruelty of taxing their fidelity any farther. M. Bourquin was much incensed against this obstinate antagonist; but the latter obtained terms through the mediation of the other officers, and was allowed to retire to British territory with the wreck of his fortune, on the 1st of January, 1802. He died in August, on his way down to Calcutta, and was interred at Barhampur. He left a family, of whom the Begam Sumroo at first took charge, but their descendants have now become mixed with the ordinary population of the country.[148]

This extraordinary man was largely endowed by Nature, both morally and physically. During the time of his brief authority he settled a turbulent country, and put down some crimes, such as female infanticide, with which all the power of Britain has not always coped successfully. It would have been profitable to the British Government had they supported him in his manful struggles against Mahratta lawlessness, and against French ambition and ill-will.

1802.—The overthrow of Thomas was nearly the last of Sindhia's successes. Having made a final arrangement with the Bais (from whom we here gladly part), he confined his attention to the politics of the Deccan, where he underwent a severe defeat from Holkar, at Punah, in October, 1802. The Peshwa, on whose side Sindhia had been fighting, sought refuge with the British at Bassein, and Holkar obtained temporary possession of the Mahratta capital. On the 31st of December the celebrated treaty of Bassein was concluded with the Peshwa. It appears from the *Wellington Dispatches*, published by Mr. Owen in 1880, that this treaty was certainly not conceived in a spirit of hostility to Daulat Rao. He was a party directly, to the preceding negotiations and, by the agency of his minister, "to

[148] Francklin's "Life of George Thomas." Skinner *ut sup*. Oral tradition.

the whole transaction." (Owen's *Selection*, p. 30.) Still, as Mr. Wheeler has pointed out, this instrument tended to substitute the British as the paramount power in Hindustan (*Short History*, p. 433), and "shut Sindhia out from the grand object of his ambition, namely, to rule the Mahratta empire in the name of the Peshwa." One of the articles of the treaty debarred the Mahrattas from entertaining French officers. Grant Duff had seen a secret letter written shortly after the date of the treaty by the Peshwa in which he summoned Sindhia to Punah. (II. *Grant Duff*, p. 384.) Then, not only supplanted by the British as Protector of the Mahratta State, but alarmed on the score of his position in Hindustan, Sindhia began to intrigue with the hitherto inactive Mahratta chief, Rághoji, the Bhonsla Rájá of Nágpur.

Aided by the British under the already famous Arthur Wellesley, the Peshwa soon regained his metropolis, which Sindhia was preparing to occupy. That chief was still further estranged in consequence of the disappointment.

Holkar now held aloof, wisely resolving to remain neutral, at least until his rival should be either overthrown or irresistible. The Governor-General, Marquis Wellesley, apprised by his brother and other political officers of the intrigues of Sindhia, demanded from the latter a categorical explanation of his intentions. And this not being given, General Wellesley was ordered to open the campaign in the Deccan, while General Lake co-operated in the Doáb of Hindustan.

In order to appreciate the grounds of this most important measure, it will be necessary to break through the rule by which I have been hitherto guided of keeping nothing before the reader besides the affairs of Hindustan proper. The motives of Lord Wellesley formed part of a scheme of policy embracing nearly the whole inhabited world; and whether we think him right or wrong, we can hardly avoid the conclusion that the virtual assumption of the Moghul Empire at this time was due to his personal character and political projects.

As far back as February, 1801, the Governor-General had co-operated in European affairs by sending a contingent to Egypt under General Baird; though the force arrived too late to participate actively in a campaign by which the French were expelled from that country. A twelvemonth later the Marquis received official intimation of the virtual conclusion of the negotiations on which was based the Peace of Amiens. In the interval he had sent his brother, Mr. Henry Wellesley, to Lucknow, and had concluded through that agency the famous treaty of the 10th November, 1801, by which British rule was introduced into Gorakpur, the Eastern and Central Doáb, and a large part of Rohilkand. The immediate result of this will be seen ere long.

Having inaugurated these important changes in the position of British power in the East, Lord Wellesley now notified to the Court of Directors (by whom he had conceived himself thwarted), his intention to resign his office, and to return to Europe in the following December. At the same time he issued to General Lake, the Commander-in-Chief, instructions for a substantial reduction of the forces. He added however the following remarkable words: "It is indispensable to our safety in India that we should be prepared to meet any future crisis of war with unembarrassed resources;"[149] words whereby he showed that even reduction was undertaken with an eye to future exertions. In a similar spirit he rebuked the naval Commander Admiral Rainier, for refusing to employ against the Mauritius the forces that had been set free by the evacuation of Egypt; laying down in terms as decided as courtesy permitted the principle that, as responsible agent, he had a right to be implicitly obeyed by all His Majesty's servants.

And that bold assertion received the approbation of King George III., in a despatch of the 5th May; the further principle being communicated by the writer, Lord Hobart, in His Majesty's name, "that it should be explicitly understood that in the distant possessions of the British empire during the existence of war, the want of the regular authority should not preclude an attack upon the enemy in any case that may appear calculated to promote the public interest."

Thus fortified, the Governor-General was persuaded to reconsider his intention of at once quitting India, the more so since the terms in which the Court of Directors recorded their desire that he should do so, displayed an almost equal confidence, and amounted, if not to any apology for past obstruction, at least to a promise of support for the future. In his despatch of 24th December, 1802, Lord Wellesley plainly alluded to the opening for extending the British power in India which he considered to be offered by the then pending treaty of Bassein, though at the same time he records, apparently without apprehension, the intention of Sindhia to proceed from Ujan towards Punah to counteract the machinations of Holkar. On the 11th February, 1803, Lord Wellesley signified his willingness to remain at his post another year, though without referring to any military or political prospects.

But the direction in which his eye was constantly cast is soon betrayed by a despatch of the 27th March, to General Lake, conveying instructions for negotiating with General Perron, who, from motives we shall briefly notice lower down, was anxious to retire from the service of Sindhia. In this letter Lord Wellesley plainly says, "I am strongly disposed to accelerate Mr. Perron's departure, conceiving it to be an event which promises much advantage to our power in India."[150]

It appears, nevertheless, from the Marquis's address to the Secret Committee of the Court of Directors of 19th April, 1803, that, up to that time, he still entertained hopes that Sindhia would remain inactive, and would see his advantage in giving his adhesion to the treaty of Bassein, if not from friendship for England, from hostility to Holkar, against whom that settlement was primarily and ostensibly directed. Meanwhile, advices continued to arrive from Europe, showing the extremely precarious nature of the Peace of Amiens, and the imminent probability of a renewal of hostilities with France; thus keeping awake the Governor-General's jealousy of Sindhia's French officers, and delaying the restoration of French possessions in India, which had been promised by the treaty.

---

[149] Second Despatch of 8th February, para. 8.—"Wellesley Despatches," vol. ii. p. 625.

[150] "Wellesley Despatches," iii. p. 63.

In May the Marquis proceeded explicitly to forbid the crossing of the Narbadda by Sindhia, and to warn the Bhonsla Rájá of Berár or Nágpur against joining in the schemes of the former chief, to whom a long and forcible despatch was sent, through the Resident, Colonel Collins, in the early part of the following month (*vide W. Desp.*, p. 120). In this letter Colonel Collins—while vested with much discretionary power—was distinctly instructed to "apprise Scindiah (Sindhia) that his proceeding to Poonah, under any pretext whatever, will infallibly involve him in hostilities with the British power." The Resident was also to require from him "an explanation with regard to the object of any confederacy" with the Bhonsla chiefs of Berár and Nágpur, or with Holkar. Sindhia met all these approaches with the Oriental resources of equivocation and delay; apparently unable either to arrange with due rapidity any definite understanding with the other Mahratta leaders, or to make up his mind, or persuade his chief advisers to give a confident and unconditional reception to the friendship offered him by the British ruler. Whether the latter course would have saved him is a question that now can only be decided by each person's interpretation of the despatches above analysed.

Those who desire to study the subject further may refer to the first volume of Malcolm's *Political History*, to Mill's *History*, and to Grant Duff's concluding volume, but will hardly obtain much result from their labour. On the one hand, it may be presumed that, had the British Government really been ambitious of extending their North-Western frontier, they would have assisted Thomas in 1801; on the other hand, it is certain that they supplanted Sindhia at Punah soon afterwards, and that they had for some years been exceedingly jealous of French influence in India. In this connection should also be mentioned the invasion planned by the Czar Paul, in concert with the First Consul, in 1800, of which the details were first made public in English by Mr. Michell (Rawlinson's *England and Russia in the East*, p. 187). The general fact of Paul's submission to the ascendancy of Napoleon was, of course, well known to British statesmen at the time. There was also the fear of an Afghán invasion, which led to the mission of Malcolm to Persia, and which was, perhaps, not the mere bugbear which it now appears. A masterly statement of Lord Wellesley's political complications will be found in his brother's Memorandum, given as an Introduction to Professor Owen's *Selection*, published in 1880. It is quite clear, again, that Sindhia, for his part, was not unwilling to see the British espouse the Peshwa's cause as against Holkar; while it is highly probable that his mind was worked upon by Perron when the latter found himself under combined motives of self-interest and of national animosity.

The French General had been losing favour on account of his increasing unpopularity among the native chiefs of the army; and had been so contumeliously treated by Daulat Rao Sindhia at Ujain, in the beginning of the year 1803, that he had resigned the service.[151] But hardly was the treaty of Bassein communicated to Sindhia, when Perron consented to remain at his post, and even, it is believed, drew up a plan for hostilities against the British, although the latter had shown as yet no intention of declaring war, but, on the contrary, still maintained a minister in Sindhia's camp. These facts, together with the statistics that follow, are chiefly

[151] Skinner attests this; but see Colonel Collins's letter lower down, and also the Governor-General's despatch of 17th March, quoted above.

derived from the memoirs of an Anglo-Indian officer of Perron's, the late Colonel James Skinner, which have been edited by Mr. Baillie Fraser. "Sindhia and Rághoji together" (Rághoji was the name of the Bhonsla of Nágpur) "had about 100,000 men, of whom 50,000 were Mahratta horse, generally good; 30,000 regular infantry and artillery, commanded by Europeans; the rest half-disciplined troops. Sindhia is understood to have had more than 300 pieces of cannon. The army of Hindustan, under Perron, consisted of 16,000 to 17,000 regular infantry, and from 15,000 to 20,000 horse, with not less than twenty[152] pieces of artillery." It may be added, on the authority of Major Thorn,[153] that his army was commanded by about three hundred European officers, of whom all but forty were French. In this estimate must be included the forces of the Begam Sumroo.

The French plans, as far as they can now be learned, were as follows:—The blind and aged Sháh Alám was to be continued upon the Imperial throne, under the protection of the French Republic. "This great question being decided," proceeds the memorial from which I am extracting, "it remains to consider whether it is not possible that the branches of that unfortunate family may find protectors who shall assert their sacred rights and break their ignominious chains. It will then follow that mutual alliance and a judicious union of powers will secure the permanent sovereignty of the Emperor, to render his subjects happy in the enjoyment of personal security and of that wealth which springs from peace, agriculture, and free trade. The English Company, by its ignominious treatment of the great Moghul, has forfeited its rights as Deewan of the Empire." ("Memoir of Lieutenant Lefèbre," 6th August, 1803.)[154]

Lord Wellesley himself records this document, which was found in Pondicherry, it does not appear exactly how or when; he may have had an inkling of the policy previously, but the date is sufficient to show that he had not seen it before going to war with Sindhia. Lord Wellesley refers, about the same time, to the magnitude of the establishment sent out to take possession of the settlements which the French were to recover in India by the Peace of Amiens, an establishment obviously too large for the mere management of Pondicherry and Chandarnagar.

Perhaps the memoir in question (which was drawn up by an officer of the staff sent out on that occasion) may have expressed correctly the intentions which the First Consul held at the time; for nobody appears to have been very sincere or much in earnest on either side at the Peace of Amiens. And it is not impossible that the paper expresses intentions which might have been more thoroughly carried out had not the terrible explosion in St. Domingo subsequently diverted the attention of the French Government to another hemisphere.[155] At all events it is a thinly-veiled pretext of aggression; and the accusations against the English are scandalously false, as will be clear to those who may have perused

[152] This seems a misprint. One hundred and twenty is perhaps meant, which nearly corresponds to Thorn's statement.—"War in India," p. 78. Thorn's estimate of infantry is exactly the same as Skinner's.

[153] "War in India," p. 32.

[154] "Wellesley Despatches," vol. iv. App.

[155] The Marquis elsewhere says of this memoir that it "was presented to the First Consul, and is stated to have been considered at Pondicherry as a secret paper."

the preceding pages. Considering that it was Perron's own employer who kept the Imperial House in penury and durance, it was the extreme of impudence for one of Perron's compatriots to retort the charge upon the English, to whom Sháh Alám was indebted for such brief gleams of good fortune as he had ever enjoyed, and whose only offence against him had been a fruitless attempt to withhold him from that premature return to Dehli, which had been the beginning of his worst misfortunes. It was, moreover, a gross exaggeration to call the British the Diwáns of the empire now, whatever may have once been their titular position in Bengal. On the 6th of July Lord Wellesley received from the ministry in England a hint that war with France would be likely to be soon renewed; and on the 8th of the same month he addressed to his commander-in-chief a short private letter, of which the following extract shows the purport:—"I wish you to understand, my dear Sir, that I consider the reduction of Sindhia's power on the north-west frontier of Hindustan to be an important object in proportion to the probability of a war with France. M. de Boigne (Sindhia's late general) is now the chief confident of Bonaparte; he is constantly at St. Cloud. I leave you to judge why and wherefore."—(*Desp*. III. 182.)

The Governor-General here shows his own views, although his sagacity probably overleaped itself in the imputation against de Boigne, for which I have found no other authority.[156] Ten days later he sends Lake more detailed instructions, closing his covering letter with a sentence especially worthy of the reader's attention:—"I consider an active effort against Scindhia and Berár to be the best possible preparation for the renewal of the war with France." There is little doubt of this being the key-note of the policy that led the British to the conquest of Hindustan.—*Vide* App. E.

On the 31st July, General Wellesley wrote to the Resident at the court of Sindhia (Colonel Collins) stating that the reasons assigned by the confederates for not withdrawing their troops were illusory, and ordering Collins to leave their camp at once. On the 15th August Lord Wellesley received a packet, which the collector of Morádábád had transmitted nearly a month before, containing translation of a letter from the Nawáb of Najibábád, Bhanbu Khán, brother of the late Gholám Kádir, covering copy of a circular letter in which Sindhia was attempting to stir him and the other chiefs against the English as "that unprincipled race"; and begging them to co-operate with General Perron. War, however, had already been declared, and a letter addressed by the Governor-General to Sháh Alám.

The force with which General Lake was to meet the 35,000 Franco-Mahrattas in Hindustan, consisted of eight regiments of cavalry, of which three were European, one corps of European infantry, and eleven battalions of Sepoys, beside a proper complement of guns, with two hundred British artillerymen, making a total of 10,500, exclusive of the brigade at Anupshahar.

[156] The Address to the Municipality of Chambéry, 1st March, 1822, given in the Memoir of de Boigne, takes a very unfavourable view of the conduct and character of Napoleon. The language used by the General on that occasion does not look as if he could ever have been that statesman's intimate counsellor:—"During the reign of usurpation, the abuse of power being the system pursued, I was forced to wait until heaven, weary of so much injustice and iniquity, recalled to the thrones of Europe their lawful sovereigns."

The assembling of this force on the immediate frontier of the dominion occupied by Sindhia and the French, had been facilitated by the treaty of the 10th November, 1801, by which Säädat Ali Khán, whom the British had lately raised to the Viceroyship of Áudh, had ceded to them the frontier provinces above named. This cession was made in commutation for the subsidy which the Nawáb had been required to pay for the maintenance of the force by which he was supported against his own subjects. The Peshwa had previously ceded a portion of Bundelkand by the treaty of Bassein, and the red colour was thus surely, if slowly, creeping over the map of India. Perron resisted the cession of the new frontier under the treaty of Lucknow. The "*Old Resident*" makes the following note on the subject:—"When the British came to Sasnee, which was ceded by the Nawáb Wuzier of Lucknow by a treaty in 1802 to Government, the Pergunnahs of Sasnee, Akberabad, Jellalee, and Secundra came under British rule, but not without much bloodshed in the sieges of Sasnee, Bijey Gurh and Kuchoura fortresses; in all these places we buried the remains of British officers who first shed their blood for their King and country. At Sasnee the masonry graves in a decayed condition are still to be seen. At Bijey Gurh they are in the low 'Duhur' lands apart from the Fort, and at the Kuchoura in Locus Kanugla, lies the tomb of Major Naivve, Commanding the 2nd Cavalry, who was shot whilst leading his men to the assault. A surviving relation of the above officer had a monument built in 1853 at Bhudwas, on the Trunk Road, with the original tablet which was torn off from the tomb by the villagers, and by chance discovered by a European overseer of the roads after a lapse of fifty years."

In Sindhia's armies there were, as we have seen, a number of officers who were not Frenchmen. These were mostly half-castes, or (to use a term subsequently invented) Eurasians, Europeo-Asiatics, or persons of mixed blood; in other words, the offspring of connections which British officers in those days often formed with native females. Nearly all these officers, whether British or half-British, were upon this occasion discharged from the service by Perron,[157] who had probably very good reason to believe that they would not join in fighting against the army of their own sovereign. Carnegie, Stewart, Ferguson, Lucan, two Skinners, Scott, Birch, and Woodville, are the only names recorded, but there may have been others also who were dismissed from the army at Perron's disposal. The prospects of those who were absent on duty in the Deccan, and elsewhere, soon became far more serious. Though not at present dismissed, they were mostly reserved for a still harder fate. Holkar beheaded Colonel Vickers and seven others; Captain Mackenzie and several more were confined, and subsequently massacred, by orders of Sindhia; others perished "in wild Mahratta battle," fighting for money in causes not their own, nor of the smallest importance to the world. General Wellesley complained, after the battle of Assai, of "Sindhia's English officers." He says that his wounded men heard them give orders for their massacre as they lay upon the field, and promises to send up a list of their names after full inquiry (*Owen*, 311). No such list has ever been heard of; and it appears, from Lewis F. Smith's memoir, that the European officers there present were all French, or Italian, or German. It is barely

[157] The Governor-General, on 20th August, 1803, issued a proclamation warning them not to fight against the British. Most, if not all of them were provided for after the Conquest.

possible that they used English in conversing, certainly not probable; but the story was very likely prompted by the imagination of the wounded men who saw white faces among the enemy and concluded that they must be their own countrymen. The only European officers known to have been engaged on the Mahratta side are Pohlmann and Dupont (both named by Wellesley) and Saleur of the Begam's service who commanded the baggage-guard; with perhaps, J. B. da Fontaine.

Although the French officers were now without any Christian rivals, it does not appear that their position was a satisfactory one. The reader may refer to Law's remarks on this subject, during the Emperor's unsuccessful attempts to the eastward.[158] The isolation and impossibility of trusting native colleagues, of which that gallant adventurer complained, were still, and always must be, fatal to the free exercise of civilized minds serving an Asiatic ruler. All the accounts that we have of those times combine to show that, whoever was the native master, the condition of the European servant was precarious, and his influence for good weak. On the 24th of June, 1802, Colonel Collins, the British Resident at the Court of Sindhia, had written thus to his Government in regard to Perron whom he had lately visited at Aligarh:—"General Perron has been peremptorily directed by Sindhia to give up all the Maháls (estates) in his possession not appertaining to his own *jaidad* (fief); and I understand that the General is highly displeased with the conduct of Sindhia's ministers on this occasion, insomuch that he entertains serious intentions of relinquishing his present command."

This intention, as we have already seen, was at one time on the point of being carried out, and Perron was evidently at the time sincere in his complaints.

It is not however possible to use, as Mill does, these discontents—alleged by Perron in conversation with a British political officer—as a complete proof of his not having had, towards the British, hostile views of his own. The whole tenor of Colonel Skinner's Memoir, already frequently cited (the work, be it remembered, of a person in the service at the time), is to show an intense feeling of hostility on Perron's part towards the British, both as a community of individuals and as a power in India. It is more than probable that but for the Treaty of Bassein, which gave the British in India the command of the Indian Ocean and the Western Coast, and but for the contemporaneous successes of Abercromby and Hutchinson in Egypt, Perron, supported by the troops of the French Republic, might have proved to the British a most formidable assailant. Skinner gives a graphic account of his vainly attempting to get reinstated by Perron, who said:—"Go away, Monsieur Skinner! I no trust." He would not trust officers with British blood and sympathies.

But such was the fortune, and such were the deserts of those by whom England was at that time served, that they were able, without much expense of either time or labour, to conquer the half-hearted resistance of the French, and the divided councils of the Mahrattas. Holkar not only did not join Sindhia, but assisted the British cause by his known rivalry. Arthur Wellesley gave earnest of his future glory by the hard-fought battle of Assai, in which the Begam Sumroo's little contingent, under its French officers, gave Sindhia what support they could; and General Lake overthrew the resistance of M. Perron's army at Aligarh, and soon reduced

[158] *Vide* p. 40.

the Fort, in spite of the gallant defence offered by the garrison. Mention has been made of this Fort in the account of the overthrow of Najaf Khán's successors by Sindhia (*sup.* p. 81). Since those days it had been much improved. The following is the account of the *Dehli Gazette's "Old Resident."*—"The Fort of Allygurh was made by the Jauts while the place was under the Delhi Kings. Nawáb Nujjuff Khán, the Governor, improved the fortification, and de Boigne brought it into a regular defensive state according to the French system. Perron and Pédron subsequently added their skill in strengthening the fortress, which commanded a wide open plain, the most part being under water during the heavy rains on account of the lands being low." The gate was blown in and the place rapidly stormed by the 76th, piloted by a Mr. Lucan, who was made a captain in the British service for his treachery. He was afterwards taken prisoner during Monson's retreat and put to death by Holkar's orders. The enemy were commanded by natives, having withdrawn their confidence from Perron's French Lieutenant, Colonel Pédron, who was on that occasion made prisoner by the troops.[159] Perron himself, having first retreated upon Agra, and thence on Mathra, came over to the English with two subordinates, and was at once allowed a free passage to Chandarnagar with his family and his property. Bourquien, who commanded the army in Dehli, attempted to intrigue for the chief command, but was put under arrest by his native officers; and the Mahratta army, like sheep without a shepherd, came out to meet the advancing British on the Hindan, a few miles to the east of the capital, on the old road from the town of Sikandrabad, so often mentioned in this narrative. After they had killed six officers and about 160 men by a furious cannonade, their obstinacy was broken down by the undeniable and well-disciplined pertinacity of the 27th Dragoons and the 76th Foot; and they suffered a loss of 3,000 men and sixty-eight pieces of artillery, mounted in the best French style. This decisive victory was gained on the 11th September, 1803; when on the 14th the army crossed the Jamna, and General Bourquien, with four other French officers, threw themselves upon British protection. Their example was soon after followed by the Chevalier du Drenec and two other officers from the army of the Deccan; and shortly after by Hessing and other European officers in command of the garrison at Agra, which had at first confined them, but afterwards capitulated through their mediation.

No sooner did the ill-starred Emperor hear of the sudden overthrow of his custodians, than he opened formal negotiations with the British General, with whom he had been already treating secretly. The result was that on the 16th, the Heir-Apparent, Mirza Akbar, was despatched to wait upon General Lake in camp, and conduct him to the presence of the blind old man, who was the legitimate and undoubted fountain of all honour and power in Hindustan. The prince vindicated his dignity in a manner peculiar to Asiatics, by keeping the conqueror waiting for three hours. The cavalcade was at last formed, and, after a slow progress of five miles, reached the palace as the sun was setting. Rapid motion was rendered impossible by the dense collection of nearly 100,000 persons in the narrow ways; and even the courts of the Palace were on this occasion thronged with spectators, free at last. A tattered awning had been raised over the

[159] These events are detailed at full length in Mill and the standard histories of British India.

entrance to the famous Diwán-i-Khás, and underneath, on a mockery of a throne, was seated the descendant of Akbar and of Aurangzeb. It would be interesting to know what was the exact manner of General Lake's reception, and what were the speeches on either side; but the inflated enthusiasm of the "Court-Newsman," and the sonorous generalities of Major Thorn and the Marquess Wellesley, are all the evidence which survives. According to the latter, the people of Dehli were filled with admiring joy, and the Emperor with dignified thankfulness; according to the former, so great was the virtue of the joyful tears shed on this occasion by the Monarch, that they restored his eyesight—the eyesight destroyed fifteen years before by Gholám Kádir's dagger. Such is the nature of the stones offered by these writers to the seeker for historical nourishment.

What is certain is, that the British General received the title of Khan Daurán, which was considered the second in the Empire, and which implied perhaps a recognition of the claims of the Áudh Nawáb to be hereditary Vazir;[160] while the British Government "waived all question of the Imperial prerogative and authority"—in other words virtually reserved them to itself. The Emperor was only sovereign in the city and small surrounding district; and even that sovereignty was to be exercised under the control of a British Resident, who was to pay his Majesty the net proceeds, besides a monthly stipend of 90,000 rupees.

These conditions received the sanction of Government, and are recorded in despatches. No treaty is forthcoming; although native tradition asserts that one was executed, but afterwards suppressed; the copy recorded in the palace archives having been purloined at the instigation of the British. This suspicion is entirely unfounded; no treaty was ever concluded with Sháh Alám, though his Majesty formed the subject of a clause in the treaty with Sindhia.[161] This is of importance, as serving to show the position to which the Court of Directors was supposed to have succeeded; namely to that of *Vakil-mutlak* or Plenipotentiary Vicegerent of the Empire, in the room of the Mahratta Peshwa and his once all-powerful Deputy. They were subjects of George III., no doubt, but servants of Sháh Alám; money continued to be struck in the Emperor's name, and the laws then prevailing in Hindustan remained in force. The very disclaimer of all intention to usurp the royal prerogative or assert "on the part of His Majesty (Sháh Alám) any of the claims which, as Emperor of Hindustan he might be considered to possess upon the provinces composing the Moghul Empire," is full of significance.

On the 1st November Lake overthrew the brigade of du Drenec in the bloody battle of Laswári; and Arthur Wellesley having been equally victorious a second time in the Deccan, Sindhia consented to the Treaty of Sarji-Arjangaon. By that instrument Daulat. Rao Sindhia ceded, besides other territories, all his conquests in the Doáb.

Thus passed into the hands of British delegates the administration of the sceptre of Hindustan: a sceptre which had been swayed with success as long as it protected life, order, and property, leaving free scope to conduct, to commerce,

[160] General Lake, however, says, "He (Sháh 'Alám) would have conferred the first (title) had it not been previously bestowed on Scindhia."—To Duke of York, Oct. 20th, 1803.

[161] *Vide* Lord Wellesley to Secret Committee, 13th July, 1804.—Appendix E.

and to conscience; nor failed in discharging the former class of obligations until after it had ceased to recognize the latter.

CHAPTER IV.

CONCLUSION.

Effects of climate—Early immigrants—French and English—Mohammedan power not overthrown by British—Perron's administration—Changes since then—The Tálukdars—Lake's friendly intentions—Tálukdars' misconduct—Their power curbed—No protection for life, property, or traffic—Such things still dependent on foreign aid—Conclusion.

AFTER many blunderings and much labour, the judgment of history appears to have formed the final conclusion that the physical conditions of a given country will always be the chief determining agents in forming the national character of those who inhabit it; and that the people of one country, transplanted into another, where the soil and the sun act in a manner to which they have not been accustomed, will, in the course of a few generations, exhibit habits of mind and body very different to what characterized them in their original seats.[162]

It is therefore without legitimate cause for surprise that we hear from scholars that the feeble folk of Hindustan are the direct and often unmixed representatives of the dominant races of the world. To begin with the Hindus: the Brahmans and some of the other classes are believed to be descended from the brave and civilized peoples of ancient Asia, of whom sacred and profane writers make such frequent mention, of some of the founders of Nineveh and Babylon, and of the later empire of the Medes and Persians, which was on the eve of subjugating Europe when stopped by the Greeks at Marathon and Salamis. Nay, more, the ancient Greeks and Romans themselves, together with the modern inhabitants of Europe, are alike descended from the same grand stock.

The Mohamadans, again, are mainly of three noble tribes. The earlier Mohamadan invaders of India belonged to the victorious Arabian warriors of the Crescent, or to their early allies, the bold mountaineers of Ghazni and of Ghor; and their descendants are still to be found in India, chiefly under the names respectively of Shaikh and Páthan. A few Saiyids will also be found of this stock.

In later days came hordes of Turks and Mongols (Tartars as they are generically though inaccurately called by Europeans), the people of Janghiz and of Timur, terrible us the locusts of prophecy—the land before them like the garden of Eden, and behind them a desolate wilderness.

[162] It will be remembered how well Montesquieu has illustrated this view—which he was the first to develope—in his "Esprit des Lois."—See especially his Book xiv.

To these, again, succeeded many Persians, chiefly Saiyids, or so-called descendants of the Prophet; a later race of Afghâns, also called Páthans, and a fresh inroad of Tartars (converted to Islám) who finally founded the Moghul Empire.[163] Under the regime thus established the civilization of India assumed a Persian type; and the term "Moghul" in the present day, in India signifies rather a Persian than a Turkman or Tartar. They add the word "Beg" to their names, and are usually of the Shiah denomination; as also are the descendants of the Persian Saiyids. The Saiyids of Arab origin take the title of "Mir;" the Páthans are commonly known by the affix "Khan." All but the offspring of converted Hindus represent foreign invasions by races more warlike than the people of India.

All these mighty conquerors, one after another, succumbed to the enervating nature of the climate of Hindustan, with its fertile soil and scanty motives to an exertion which, in that heat, must always be peculiarly unwelcome.

It is not, however, the heat alone which causes this degeneracy. Arabia is one of the hottest countries in the world, but the Arabs have at one time or another overthrown both the Roman Empire of Byzantium and the Gothic monarchy of Spain. On the other hand, the lovely climate of Kashmir produces men more effeminate than the Hindustánis, some of whom indeed, notably the peasantry of the Upper Doáb, are often powerful men, innured to considerable outdoor labour; their country is far hotter. But the curse of Hindustan, as of Kashmir, and more or less of all countries where life is easy, lies in the absence of motives to sustained exertion; owing to which emulation languishes into envy, and the competitive instincts, missing their true vent, exhibit themselves chiefly in backbiting and malice. Whatever advantage may be derived by Kashmiris from their climate is shown in the superiority of their intellects.

Hence, after the battle of Pánipat, 1761, which exhausted the victors almost as much as it exhausted the vanquished, and left Hindustan so completely plundered as to afford no further incitements to invasion, little other immigration took place; and the effete and worn-out inhabitants were left to wrangle, in their own degenerate way, over the ruined greatness of their fathers. The anarchy and misery to the mass of the population that marked these times have been partly shown to the reader of these pages.

But there was fresh blood at hand from a most unexpected quarter. Bred in a climate which gives hardness to the frame (while it increases the number of human wants as much as it does the difficulty of satisfying them), the younger sons of the poorer gentry of England and France, then (at least) the two most active nations of Europe, began to seek in both hemispheres those means of sharing in the gifts of fortune which were denied to them by the laws and institutions of their own countries. Their struggles convulsed India and America at once. Still the empire of Hindustan did not fall by their contests there; nor were the valour and ambition of the new comers the only causes of its fall when at last the catastrophe arrived. But when, to predisposing causes, there was now added the grossest incompetence on the part of nearly all natives concerned in the administration, it became inevitable

[163] This subject will be found expandedly treated in the author's "History of Hindustan."

that one or other of the competing European nations should grasp the prize. Any one who wishes to study this subject in its romantic details should refer to Colonel Malleson's two works on the French in India.[164] Living under a better Home Government, and more regularly supported and supplied, the English prevailed.

In sketching a part of the process of substituting foreign rule for anarchy, it has been my task to exhibit the main events which caused, or accompanied the preparation of the *tabula rasa,* upon which was to be traced the British Empire of India. It has been shown that the occupation of the seaboard, and a few of the provinces thereto contiguous, long constituted the whole of the position; and that it was only in self-protection, and after long abstinence, that the "Company of Merchants" finally assumed the central power. Upper India, in the meanwhile, stood to their Calcutta Government in a very similar relation to that occupied, successively, by the Panjáb and by Afghánistan in later times towards its successors. This, though absolutely true, has been popularly ignored, owing to the accident of Calcutta continuing to be the chief seat of the Supreme Government after the empire had become British; but the events of 1857 are sufficient to show that, for the native imagination, Hindustan is the centre, and Dehli still the metropolis of the Empire. The idea, however, that the British have wrested the Empire from the Mohamadans is a mistake. The Mohamadans were beaten down—almost everywhere except in Bengal—before the British appeared upon the scene; Bengal they would not have been able to hold, and the name of the "Mahratta Ditch" of Calcutta shows how near even the British there were to extirpation by India's new masters. Had the British not won the battles of Plassey and Buxar, the whole Empire would ere now have become the fighting ground of Sikhs, Rájputs, and Mahrattas. Except the Nizám of the Deccan there was not a vigorous Musalman ruler in India after the firmán of Farokhsiar in 1716;[165] the Nizám owed his power to the British after the battle of Kurdla (*sup.* p. 127), and it was chiefly British support that maintained the feeble shadow of the Moghul Empire, from the death of Álamgir II. to the retirement of Mr. Hastings. Not only Haidarábád, but all the other existing Musalman principalities of modern India owe their existence, directly, or indirectly, to the British intervention.

It only now remains to notice, as well as the available materials will permit, what was the social condition of these capital territories of the empire when they passed into the hands of the ultimate conquerors.

Perhaps the best picture is that presented in a work published by order of the local Government, more than half a century later, upon the condition of that portion of the country which was under the personal management of the French general.[166]

This record informs us that, having obtained this territory for the maintenance of the army, Perron reigned over it in the plenitude of sovereignty. "He maintained all the state and dignity of an oriental despot, contracting alliances with the more

[164] *See* also Elphinstone's posthumous work quoted above; and Orme's "Indostan."

[165] *Sup.* p. 45.

[166] "Aleegurh Statistics, with a report on the general administration of that district, from A.D. 1803 to the present time." By J. R. Hutchinson and J. W. Sherer. Roorkee, 1856.

potent Rájahs and overawing by his military superiority, the petty chiefs. At Dehli, and within the circuit of the imperial dominions, his authority was paramount to that of the Emperor. His attention was chiefly directed to the prompt realization of revenue. Pargannahs were generally farmed; a few were allotted as *jaidad* to chiefs on condition of military service; [of the lands in the neighbourhood of Aligarh] the revenue was collected by the large bodies of troops always concentrated at head-quarters. A brigade was stationed at Sikandrabad for the express purpose of realizing collections. In the event of any resistance on the part of a land-holder, who might be in balance, a severe and immediate example was made by the plunder and destruction of his village; and life was not unfrequently shed in the harsh and hasty measures which were resorted to. The arrangements for the administration of justice were very defective; there was no fixed form of procedure, and neither Hindu nor Mohamadan law was regularly administered. The suppression of crime was regarded as a matter of secondary importance. There was an officer styled the Bakshi Adalat, whose business was to receive reports from the Amils [officials] in the interior, and communicate General Perron's orders respecting the disposal of any offenders apprehended by them. No trial was held; the proof rested on the Amil's report, and the punishment was left to General Perron's judgment.

"Such was the weakness of the administration that the Zamindars tyrannized over the people with impunity, levying imposts at their pleasure, and applying the revenues solely to their own use."[167] The *"Old Resident"* thus compares the past and present of Aligarh:—"Under the native rule no one attempted to build a showy masonry house for fear of being noticed as one possessing property, and thus become subject to heavy taxations. Even in de Boigne and Perron's time it was the same as before, people lived in a very low state both as regards their food and clothes, their marriages were not costly, and none of their females dared to put jewels on. In such a state of things, the well-to-do accumulated money and could not enjoy it, they buried it under ground, and often from death and other causes the wealth got into other hands by the sudden discovery of the place. What a mighty change in the space of seventy years the city of Coel bears now to what it did before? elegant houses now stand in the city everywhere, and the market is well stocked with articles of trade and consumption. Bankers and money changers have their shops open, free from any apprehension of danger, and the females go about with their trinkets and jewels, all enjoying the wholesome protection of law. The bazar street of the city of Coel was very narrow in Perron's time, and neither he nor de Boigne ever paid any attention to the improvement or welfare of the people. Their time was principally occupied in military tactics and preserving order in the country. They knew and were told by their own officers that their rule was only for the time being, and that a war with Scindhia would change the state of affairs, and with it eventually these provinces."

From a report written so near the time as 1808 confirmation of these statements is readily obtained. The Collector of Aligarh, in addressing the Board formed for constructing a system of administration in the conquered provinces, recommended cautious measures in regard to the assessment of the land tax or Government

[167] For a list of Perron's possessions, *vide* Note at end of this Chapter.

rental. He stated that, in consequence of former misrule, and owing to the ravages of famine in 1785,[168] and other past seasons, or to the habits induced by years of petty but chronic warfare, the land was fallen, in a great measure, into a state of nature. He anticipated an increase in cultivation and revenue of thirty-two per cent., if six years of peace should follow.

The great landholders, whether originally officials, or farmers who had succeeded in making good a position before the conquest, were numerous in this neighbourhood. The principal persons of importance were, to the westward, Játs, from Bhartpur; the eastward, Musalmans descended from converted Bargujar Rájputs. The long dissensions of the past had swept away the Moghul nobility, few or none of whom now held land on any large scale.

These Játs and these Musalmans were among the ancestors of the famous Tálukdars of the North-West Provinces; and as the limitation of their power has been the subject of much controversy, justice to the earlier British administrators requires that we should carefully note the position which they had held under the Franco-Mahratta rule, and the conditions under which they become members of British India.

We have already seen that the Tálukdars (to use by anticipation a term now generally understood, though not applied to the large landholders at the time) were in the habit of making unauthorized collections, which they applied to their own use. Every considerable village had its *Sáyar Chabutra* (customs-platform), where goods in transit paid such dues as seemed good to the rural potentates. Besides this, they derived a considerable income from shares in the booty acquired by highwaymen and banditti, of whom the number was constantly maintained by desertions from the army, and was still further swollen at the conquest by the general disbandment which ensued.

Both of these sources of emolument were summarily condemned by General Lake; though he issued a proclamation guaranteeing the landholders in the full possession of their legitimate rights. But the rights of fighting one another, and of plundering traders, were as dear to the Barons of Hindustan as ever they had been to their precursors in mediæval Europe; and, in the fancied security of their strong earthen ramparts, they very generally maintained these unsocial privileges.

So far back as the beginning of 1803, before war had been declared upon Sindhia, the whole force of the British in Upper India, headed by the Commander-in-Chief himself, had been employed in the reduction of some of the forts in that portion of the Doáb which had been ceded by the Nawáb of Áudh during the preceding year. The same course was pursued, after long forbearance, towards the Musalman chiefs of the conquered provinces. In December, 1804, they had rebelled in the neighbourhood of Aligarh, and occupied nearly the whole of the surrounding district. Captain Woods, commanding the fort of Aligarh, could only occasionally spare troops for the collector's support; and the rebellion was not finally suppressed until the following July, by a strong detachment sent from headquarters. They again broke out in October, 1806, after having in the interim

[168] *Vide sup.*, p. 81-82.

amassed large supplies by the plunder of their tenantry; the whole of the northern part of the Aligarh district, and the southern part of the adjoining district of Bolandshahar were overrun; the forts of Kamona and Ganora were armed and placed in a state of defence; and the former defended against the British army under Major-General Dickens, on the 19th November, 1807, with such effect that the loss of the assailants, in officers and men, exceeded that sustained in many pitched battles. The subjugation of the tribe shortly followed.

The Ját Tálukdars of the Aligarh district were not finally reduced to submission for nearly ten years more; and there is reason to believe that during this long interval they had continued to form the usual incubus upon the development of society, by impeding commerce and disturbing agriculture. At length the destruction of the fort of Hátras and the expulsion of Dáya Rám the contumacious Rájá, put the finishing stroke to this state of things in March, 1817.

It may be fairly assumed that the protection of life and property, and that amount of security under which merchants will distribute the productions of other countries, and husbandmen raise the means of subsistence from the soil, are among the primary duties of Government. But in the dark days of which our narrative has had to take note, such obligations had not been recognized.

"It is a matter of fact," say the authors of the "Statistics" before me, "that in those days the highways were unoccupied, and the travellers walked through by-ways. The facility of escape into the Begam Sumroo's territories, the protection afforded by the heavy jungles and numerous forts which then studded the country, and the ready sale for plundered property, combined to foster robbery."[169]

A special force was raised by the British conquerors, and placed under the command of Colonel Gardner, a distinguished Mahratta officer. His exertions were completely successful, as far as the actual gangs then in operation were concerned; but unfortunately they were soon encouraged to renewed attempts by the countenance which they received from Hira Sing, another Ját Tálukdar. This system also was finally concluded by the destruction of the Rájá of Hátras; nor will fourteen years appear a long time for the reorganization of order, which had been in abeyance for more than forty.

The following extract from Vol. I. of *Forbes's Oriental Memoirs*, is the result of observations made in a more southern part of the country between 1763 and 1783, and published, not with a purpose, or in controversy, but in the calm evening of retirement, and at least thirty years later. "Marre was the nearest Mahratta town of consequence to the hot wells; by crossing the river it was within a pleasant walk, and we made frequent excursions to an excavated mountain in its vicinity. Marre is fortified, large, and populous; the governor resided at Poona, inattentive to the misery of the people, whom his duan, or deputy, oppressed in a cruel manner; indeed the system of the Mahratta government is so uniformly oppressive that it appears extraordinary to hear of a mild and equitable administration; venality and corruption guide the helm of State and pervade the departments; if the sovereign requires money the men in office and governors of provinces must supply it; the

[169] *Vide* Appendix D for an account of the Begam's territories after the British conquest.

arbitrary monarch seldom inquires by what means it is procured; this affords them an opportunity of exacting a larger sum from their duans,[170] who fleece the manufacturers and farmers to a still greater amount than they had furnished; thus the country is subjected to a general system of tyranny. From the chieftains and nobles of the realm to the humblest peasant in a village, neither the property nor the life of a subject can be called his own. When Providence has blessed the land with the former and the latter rain, and the seed sown produces an hundredfold, the Indian ryot, conscious that the harvest may be reaped by other hands, cannot like an English farmer behold his ripening crop with joyful eyes; his cattle are in the same predicament; liable to be seized, without a compensation, for warlike service or any other despotic mandate; money he must not be known to possess; if by superior talent or persevering industry he should have accumulated a little more than his neighbours, he makes no improvements, lives no better than before, and through fear and distrust buries it in the earth, without informing his children of the concealment." And again at Vol. II. p. 339—"Of all Oriental despots the arbitrary power of the Mahrattas falls perhaps with the most oppressive weight; they extort money by every kind of vexatious cruelty, without supporting commerce, agriculture, and the usual sources of wealth and prosperity in well-governed States." We have further pictures of native rule, drawn in 1807, by the collectors of the newly-acquired districts of Etáwah and Koel, and to be found at pages 314 and 337 of the North-West Provinces *Selections from Revenue Records*, published in 1873. Says the Collector of Etáwah;—"The warlike tribes of this country, from disposition and habit, prefer plunder to peace, and court the exchange of the ploughshare for the sword. Foreign invasion and intestine tumults had materially checked population; whilst the poverty of the country, and the rapacity of its governors had almost annihilated commerce or had confined it, for the most part, to a few wealthy residents from the Lower Provinces" (to the Babu "Zemindar"). But he of Koel is even more bold:—"The consequences of the various revolutions which have taken place are sufficiently evident in an impoverished country and a declining population; the form of government which has existed has not operated to relieve the necessities of the subjects, or to improve the resources of this extensive empire, by the encouragement of husbandry and commerce; and military life has been embraced by a large body of the people. Habits of peace and industry have been neglected for the profession of arms, which was more suited to the disposition of the people and to the character of the times, and which has also tended to affect the revenue and to thin the population. The system of rent-oppression and extortion likewise, which has prevailed, has operated with the most injurious influence upon the country. The exertions of the landholders have been discouraged, and means of cultivation denied them by depriving them of the fair profits of their industry. They have found every attempt at improvement, instead of being beneficial to themselves, to have been subservient only to the rapacity of the Government, or of farmers; and without any inducement to stimulate their labours, agriculture as a natural consequence has languished and declined."

Aligarh (Koel) details are the more noticeable because they relate to the part of

[170] Diwáns = financial officers.

the country which had been first occupied by the conquering British, and still more because, having been under the immediate management of General Perron, that part may be supposed to have been a somewhat more favourable specimen than districts whose management had not had the advantage of European supervision. In districts administered exclusively by Asiatics, or which were more exposed to Sikh incursions, or where the natural advantages of soil, situation and climate were inferior, much greater misery, no doubt, prevailed; but what has been shown was perhaps bad enough. An administration without law, an aristocracy without conscience, roads without traffic, and fields overgrown by forest—such is the least discreditable picture that we have been able to exhibit of the results of self-government by the natives of Hindustan, immediately preceding British rule.

On the whole record of the past there emerge clearly a few indisputable truths. Setting apart the community of colour, and to a less degree of language, the British are no more foreigners to the people of India than the people of one part of India may be, and often are, to the people of another. Demoralized by the hereditary and traditional influence of many generations of misgovernment and of anarchy, none of these populations have as yet shown fitness for supreme rule over the entire peninsula, vast and thickly inhabited as it is. For example, the Brahmans and their system fell before the fury of the early Muslims, as these, again, were subdued by the Moghuls. When the Páthans and Moghuls in their turn became domesticated in Hindustan they formed nothing more than two new castes of Indians, having lost the pride and vigour of their hardy mountain ancestry. The alliance of a refugee, like M. Law, or of a runaway seaman, like George Thomas, became an object of as much importance as that of a Muslim noble with a horde of followers.

Nor is it to be overlooked that, in the best days of Muslim rule in Hindustan, however much the governing class had the chief attributes of sovereignty, the details of administration were, more or less, in the hands of the patient, painstaking natives of the land. And the immediate decay of the Muslim Empire was preceded by an attempt to centralize the administration in the Imperial Durbar, and to cashier and alienate the Hindu element. But the Hindus remained, as indeed we still see them, indispensable to the conduct of administrative details.

None the less is it certain that the real, if overbearing, superiority of the Muslim conquerors had emasculated the Hindu mind and paved the way for anarchy, which was reached as soon as immigration ceased and degeneration set in. Holding now the position once abused and lost by the Muslims, the British in India are bound alike by honour and by interest to mark the warning. Called and chosen by fortune and their own enterprise to rule so many tribes and nations in a stage of evolution so unlike their own, they have to be wary, gentle, and firm. Their office is to advance the natives and fit them for a true and noble political life.

It does not follow that the result will be to tempt the natives to demand Home Rule. Difficulty there will no doubt always be, and the end is hidden from our eyes. Moreover, that difficulty will be increased by the unavoidably secular character of State-education. When races lacking in material resources are also in a very submissive and very ignorant condition they may be kept on a dead level of immobility; and that has perhaps been the ideal of many not incompetent rulers. But it is not one which will satisfy the spirit of the day in England. Modern Englishmen have recognized that it is their bounden duty to impart knowledge in India. On the other hand, their relations towards the people forbid them to attempt religious instruction. Thus the students in British-Indian schools and colleges are in a fair way to lose their own spiritual traditions without gaining anything instead. It is likely enough that such a system may lead to discontent.

Men who lose their hopes of compensation in another state of being, will be the more anxious about securing the good things of that state in which they find themselves placed.

Nevertheless, of discontent there are, plainly, two sorts; and one sort tends to exclude the other. The multitude may hanker after the flesh-pots of Egypt, or they may long for the milk and honey of a Promised Land. In the one case they will be inclined to obey their leaders, in the other to murmur against them. It cannot be necessary to dwell upon the application. Let the rulers of India persuade the people that they are being conducted to light and to liberty. Let us hold up before those laborious and gentle millions the picture of a redeemed India moving in an orderly path among the members of a great Imperial system. That ideal may never be completely realized in the days of any of the existing generation. But it is one that may still be profitably maintained for the contemplation of all who aspire and work for the strength and welfare of Greater Britain.

NOTE.—The following list of Perron's possessions is taken from the schedule annexed to the treaty of Sarji Anjangaum (dated 30th December, 1803):—

Resumed Jaigirs, seven, yielding an annual income of	3,75,248
Talukas in the Doáb, four	84,047
To the west of the Jamna, three districts	65,000
Subah of Sahásránpur, eighteen	4,78,089
Formerly held by General de Boigne in the Doáb, twenty-seven	20,83,287
To the west of the Jamna, nine	10,31,852
Grand Total, Rs.	41,17,523

APPENDICES.

APPENDIX A.

In the foregoing pages I have endeavoured to steer a middle path between obliterating all trace of my materials and encumbering the margin with references that appeared superfluous. Wherever I have decided a disputed point, I have endeavoured to indicate the chief sources of information—at least throughout the portions which form the actual history—and to give my reasons for following one authority rather than another.

Besides the authorities—English and Persian—which have been thus cited, the following works have been occasionally consulted:—

1. *Amad us-Säádat.*—A history of the Viceroys of Lucknow from the death of Farokhsiar to the accession of Säádat Ali II., in 1797.

2. *Jám-i-Jum.*—Genealogical tables of the House of Timur.

3. *Tasallat-i-Sahibán Angriz.*—An account of the rise of British power in Hindustan and Bengal. By Munshi Dhonkal Singh; originally written for the information of Ranjit Singh, Thákur of Bhartpur, about the end of the last century.

4. *Hál-i-Begam Sáhiba.*—A little Persian memoir of Begam Sumroo, full of vagueness and error, written four years after her death, and from traditional sources.

Much information as to the views of the British chiefs of those days lies at present inaccessible at the Calcutta Foreign Office; and it is to be hoped that the Record Commission will ultimately make public many useful and interesting papers.

Other information perhaps exists, very difficult to be got at, in the private archives of old native families at Dehli. But the events of 1857 broke up many of these collections. A continuation of the *Tárikh-i-Mozafari,* down to the taking of Dehli by Sir A. Wilson, would be a most valuable work, if there be any native author possessed of the three requisites of leisure, knowledge, and a fearless love of truth.

Some account of the *Siar-ul-Mutákharin* has been already given (*vide* Note to Part II. Chap. i.). The author was a Saiyid of the noble stock of *Tabá-Tabá,* whose father had been employed by Safdar Jang, in Rohilkand, during that minister's temporary predominance. The family afterwards migrated to Patna. This celebrated history—which has been twice translated into English, and of which an edition in the original Persian has been likewise printed—is a work of suprising industry, and contains many just reflections on the position of the English and the feelings of the people towards them, which are almost as true now as they were when written. The translation of the *S. u. M.*, which has been mentioned in the text, was made by a French creole, styling himself Mustafa, but whose true name, it is believed, was Raymond. The notes are often interesting.

But my chief guide, where no other authority is cited, has been the *Tárikh-i-Mozafari,* the work of an *Ansári* of good family, some of whose descendants are still living at Pánipat. He was the grandson of Latfula Sádik, a nobleman who had held high office under the Emperor Mohammad Sháh. The historian himself was in civil employ in Bihár, under the Nawáb Mohammad Razá Khán, so famous in the history of Bengal during the last century. To him the work was dedicated, and its name is derived from his title of "Mozafar Jang." The work is laborious, free from party bias, and much thought of by the educated natives of Hindustan. For access to Persian MSS. I was indebted to the late Colonel Hamilton, formerly Commissioner of Dehli, and of his friendly assistance and encouragement I take this opportunity to make thankful acknowledgment.

APPENDIX B.

Reference has been made in the text, p. 74, to the tomb of Sumroo, in Padretola, or Padresanto, at Agra. This is one of the most ancient Christian cemeteries in Eastern Asia, consisting of a piece of land situated to the north of the Courts of Justice, and forming part of the original area attached to the neighbouring township of Lashkarpur. The estate was conferred upon the Roman Catholic Mission by the Emperor Akbar, or early in the reign of his son and successor. It contains many tombs, with Armenian and Portuguese inscriptions, more than two hundred years old, and promises, with ordinary care, long to continue in good preservation, owing to the great dryness of the air and soil. The mausoleum of the Sumroo family is a handsome octagon building, surmounted by a low dome rising out of a cornice, with a deep drip-stone, something in the style of a Constantinople fountain. The inscription is in Portuguese—a proof, most likely, that there were no French or English in Agra at the time of its being made. The following is its text:—AQVI IAZO WALTER REINHARD, MORREO AOS 4 DE MAYO, NO ANNO DE 1778. ("Here lies Walter Reinhard, died on the 4th May, in the year 1778.") There is also a Persian chronogram.

The tomb of John Hessing, hard by, is a still more splendid edifice, being a copy, in red sandstone, of the famous Táj Mahál, and on a pretty extensive scale too, though far smaller than the original. The tomb, which was completed in or about the year of the British conquest, bears an inscription in good English, setting forth that the deceased colonel was a Dutchman, who died Commandant of Agra, in his 63rd year, 21st of July, 1803, just before Lake's successful siege of the place.

APPENDIX C.

The following additional particulars regarding M. de Boigne are the last that the writer has been able to obtain from an eyewitness; they are from the enthusiastic pages of Colonel Tod, who knew the general at Chambéri, in 1826.

"Distinguished by his prince, beloved by a numerous and amiable family, and honoured by his native citizens, the years of the veteran now numbering more than four score, glide in agreeable tranquillity in his native city, which, with oriental magnificence, he is beautifying by an entire new street, and a handsome dwelling for himself."[171]

His occupation consisted chiefly in dictating the memoirs of his eventful life to his son, the Comte Charles de Boigne, by whom they were published in 1829. This statement is also made on the authority of Tod; but the memoir in my possession—though a second edition—lays claim to no such authority, but is a modest compilation, derived in great measure from Grant Duff, and originally, as appears from the "Advertissement sur cette edition," produced during the General's lifetime. The Royal Academic Society of Savoy—of which the veteran was honorary and perpetual President—gives the most extraordinary account of his munificence to his native city, which comprised the complete endowment of a college, a fund of over £4,000 sterling towards the relief of the poor, a hospital for contagious diseases, an entire new street leading from the Château to the Boulevard, and the restoration of the Hôtel de Ville; besides minor projects full of wise benevolence. He died on the 21st June, 1830, and his remains received a magnificent military funeral.

[171] Tod's "Rajasthan," vol. i. p. 765.

APPENDIX D.

LOVERS of detail may like the following view of Begam Sumroo's fief, as it appeared when it lapsed on her death. The facts and figures are from the report furnished to the Revenue Board in 1840, by the officer deputed to make the necessary fiscal settlement. This gentleman begins by saying that the assessments on the land were annual, but their average rates about one-third higher than those which prevailed on the neighbouring British district. In those days, the British took two-thirds of the net rental, so we see what was left to the Begam's tenants. The settlement officer at once reduced the total demand of land revenue from nearly seven lakhs (6,91,388) to little more than five. But, he did more than that, for he swept away the customs duties, which he thus describes:—"They were levied on all kinds of property, and equally on exports and imports; animals, wearing apparel, and clothes of every description; hides, cotton, sugar-cane, spices, and all other produce; all were subjected to a transit duty, in and out. Transfers of lands and houses, and sugar works, also paid duty; the latter very high."

The good side of this system has been already glanced at (Part III. Chap. ii.). It was strictly patriarchal. The staple crop (sugar) was grown on advances from the Begam: and, if a man's bullocks died, or he required the usual implements of husbandry, he received a loan from the Treasury, which he was strictly compelled to apply to its legitimate purpose. The revenue officers made an annual tour through their respective tracts in the ploughing season; sometimes encouraging, and oftener compelling the inhabitants to cultivate. A writer in the *Meerut Universal Magazine* stated about the same time, that the actual presence in the fields of soldiers with fixed bayonets was sometimes required for this purpose.

The settlement officer adds that the advances to agriculturists were always recovered at the close of the year, together with interest at 24 per cent. The cultivators were, in fact, rack-rented up to the minimum of subsistence, but this much was insured to them; in other words, they were predial serfs. "To maintain such system," he proceeds, "required much tact; and, with the energy of the Begam's administration, this was not wanting; but when her increasing age and infirmities devolved the uncontrolled management on her heir, the factitious nature of her system was clearly demonstrated." The result of these last few years was, that one-third of the estate of which the fief consisted fell under "direct management;" the plain meaning of which is that they were, more or less, abandoned by their owners, and by the better class of the peasantry, and tilled by a sort of serfs.

"Nothing, in fact," concludes this portion of the Report, "could more satisfactorily have shown the estimation in which the British rule is held by those who do not enjoy its blessings, than the rapid return of the population to their homes, which followed immediately on the lapse." (Trevor Plowden, Esq., to Board of Revenue, *Reports of Revenue Settlement, N.W.P.*, vol. i.)

This, be it remembered, is the picture of a fief in the heart of our own provinces, as swayed in quite recent times, by a ruler of Christian creed desirous of British friendship.

APPENDIX E.

No. CXV.

The Governor-General in Council *to the* Secret Committee of the Honourable the Court of Directors. (*Extract.*)

Fort William. *June 2nd,* 1805.

Honourable Sirs,—The Governor-General in Council now submits to your honourable Committee the arrangement which has been adopted by this Government for the purpose of providing for the future maintenance of his Majesty Sháh Allum, and the royal family, and for the general settlement of his Majesty's affairs, and the principles upon which that arrangement is formed.

It has never been in the contemplation of this Government to derive from the charge of supporting and protecting his Majesty, the privilege of employing the royal prerogative, as an instrument of establishing any control or ascendancy over the states and chieftains of India, or of asserting on the part of his Majesty any of the claims which, in his capacity of Emperor of Hindustan, his Majesty may be considered to possess upon the provinces originally composing the Moghul Empire. The benefits which the Governor-General in Council expected to derive from placing the King of Dehli and the royal family under the protection of the British Government are to be traced in the statements contained in our despatch to your honourable Committee of the 13th of July, 1804, relative to the evils and embarrassments to which the British power might have been exposed by the prosecution of claims and pretentions on the part of the Mahrattas, or of the French, in the name and under the authority of his Majesty Sháh Allum, if the person and family of that unhappy monarch had continued under the custody and control of those powers, and especially of the French. With reference to this subject, the Governor-General in Council has the honour to refer your honourable Committee to the contents of the inclosure of our despatch of the 13th of July, 1804, marked A, and to the seventy-third paragraph of that despatch, in proof of the actual existence of a project for the subversion of the British Empire in India, founded principally upon the restoration of the authority of the Emperor Sháh Allum under the control and direction of the agents of France. The difficulty of every project of that nature has been considerably increased by the events which have placed the throne of Dehli under the protection of the Honourable Company. The Governor-General in Council further contemplated the advantages of the reputation which the British Government might be expected to derive from the substitution of a system of lenient protection, accompanied by a liberal provision for the ease, dignity, and comfort of the aged monarch and his distressed family, in the room of that oppressive control and the degraded condition of poverty, distress, and insult, under which the unhappy representative of the house of Timur and his numerous family had so long laboured.

Regulated by these principles and views, the attention of the British Government has been directed exclusively to the object of forming such an arrangement for the future support of the King and the royal family, as might secure to them the enjoyment of every reasonable comfort and convenience, and every practicable degree of external state and dignity compatible with the extent of our resources, and with the condition of dependence in which his Majesty and the Royal Family must necessarily be placed with relation to the British power. In extending to the Royal Family the benefits of the British protection, no obligation was imposed upon us to consider the rights and claims of his Majesty Sháh Allum as Emperor of Hindustan, and the Governor-General has deemed it equally unnecessary and inexpedient to combine with the intended provision for his Majesty, and his household, the consideration of any question connected with the future exercise of the Imperial prerogative and authority.

The Governor-General in Council has determined to adopt an arrangement upon the basis of the following provisions:—

That a specified portion of the territories in the vicinity of Dehli situated on the right bank of the Jamna should be assigned in part of the provision for the maintenance of the Royal Family. That those lands should remain under charge of the Resident at Dehli, and that the revenue should be collected, and justice should be administered in the name of his Majesty Sháh Allum, under regulations to be fixed by the British Government. That his Majesty should be permitted to appoint a Deewan, and other inferior officers to attend at the office of collector, for the purpose of ascertaining and reporting to his Majesty the amount of the revenues which should be received, and the charges of collection, and of satisfying his Majesty's mind that no part of the produce of the assigned territory was misappropriated. That two courts of justice should be established for the administration of civil and criminal justice, according to the Mahomedan law, to the inhabitants of the city of Dehli, and of the assigned territory. That no sentences of the criminal courts extending to death should be carried into execution without the express sanction of his Majesty, to whom the proceedings in all trials of this description should be reported, and that sentences of mutilation should be commuted.

That to provide for the immediate wants of his Majesty and the Royal household, the following sums should be paid monthly, in money from the treasury of the Resident at Dehli, to his Majesty for his private expenses, Sa. Rs. 60,000; to the heir-apparent, exclusive of certain Jagheers, Sa. Rs. 10,000; to a favourite son of his Majesty named Mirza Izzut Buksh, Sa. Rs. 5,000; to two other sons of his Majesty, Sa. Rs. 1,500; to his Majesty's fifty younger sons and daughters, Sa. Rs. 10,000; to Sháh Newanze Khán, his Majesty's treasurer, 2,50O; to Syud Razzee Khán, British agent at his Majesty's Court, and related to his Majesty by marriage, Sa. Rs. 1,000; total *per mensem*, Sa. Rs. 90,000.

That if the produce of the revenue of the assigned territory should hereafter admit of it, the monthly sum to be advanced to his Majesty for his private expenses might be increased to one lakh of rupees.

That in addition to the sums specified, the sum of Sa. Rs. 10,000 should be annually be paid to his Majesty on certain festivals agreeably to ancient usage.

The Governor-General in Council deemed the arrangement proposed by the Resident at Dehli for the establishment of a military force for the protection of the assigned territory and of the North-Western frontier of our possessions in Hindustan, to be judicious, and accordingly resolved to confirm those arrangements, with certain modifications calculated to afford a provision for part of the irregular force in the service of the British Government, from the expense of which it was an object of the British Government to be relieved, and also for a proportion of the European officers heretofore in the service of Dowlut Rao Scindiah, who quitted that service under the proclamation of the Governor-General in Council of the 29th August, 1803.

On the basis of this plan of arrangement detailed instructions were issued to the Resident at Dehli, under the date the 23rd May, with orders to carry it into effect with the least practicable delay.

The Governor-General in Council entertains a confident expectation that the proposed arrangement and provision will be satisfactory to his Majesty, and will be considered throughout all the states of India to be consistent with the acknowledged justice, liberality, and benevolence of the British Government.

The Governor-General in Council also confidently trusts that the proposed arrangement will be sanctioned by the approbation of your honourable Committee, and of the honourable the Court of Directors.

We have the honour to be,

Honourable Sirs,

Your most faithful, humble servants,

(Signed) Wellesley,

G. H. Barlow,

G. Udny.

["Wellesley Despatches," vol. iv. p. 553.]

APPENDIX F.

Note to page 117.

SINCE printing the following indication has been found of the possible original of name printed "Du Drenec." In the "Familles Françaises" of Count Régis de l'Estourbeillon (Names, 1886) is a list of extinct Breton families. One of these is given as "Du Drenec-Keroulas, fondue dans Keroulas." This was, most likely, the true orthography of the Indian adventurer's name.

INDEX.

A

B

C

D

Printed by Libri Plureos GmbH in Hamburg,
Germany